SIMON OLIVER WRITER

THE EXTERMINATORS
BUG BROTHERS FOREVER

BUFFET OF DARKNESS
ALL REDNECKS GO TO HEAVEN
BUG BROTHERS FOREVER

TONY MOORE PENCILLER

JOHN LUCAS INKER

LAURA GOES DOWN

TY TEMPLETON ARTIST

RAISING CHÉ

JOHN LUCAS ARTIST

BRIAN BUCCELLATO COLORIST
PAT BROSSEAU LETTERER
INTRODUCTION BY SIMON OLIVER

THE EXTERMINATORS CREATED BY
SIMON OLIVER & TONY MOORE

I N T R O D U C T I O N

I'd like to start by making a confession to you.

There have been a lot of mornings lately, after I've kissed my wife and young sons goodbye, taken my four-mile commute, stepped over the crackheads in my office building's doorway and taken a seat at my desk (in a office that's all in all probably a little too reminiscent of *Barton Fink*)—and that's when it hits me.

I'm gripped with this overwhelming fear, a deep sense of professional doom, that I'll never enjoy writing anything as much as I've enjoyed writing THE EXTERMINATORS.

You see, this whole thing has truly been a great ride for me. As my first piece of writing work, it's where I got to cut, and break, some of my storytelling teeth. I had the opportunity to create this seedy, nasty world of my imagination, a world where even the good guys got to have some very human failings, and bring to life a cast of strange and unsavory characters. Then I got to throw them around, and, well...

Before this, I never thought of myself as having a God complex. But I think maybe I just discovered that I do.

But that's one of the great things I discovered about writing a monthly comic, and don't ever let a jaded comic book writer tell you otherwise, it's fuck-ing fun playing with a world you create. Also you get to do something that, I think, no other medium except maybe the literary novel lets you do. You have

the luxury of spinning off on bizarre tangents and side stories that focus on supporting characters that movies and most TV shows would just pass by.

Some of my favorite EXTERMINATORS issues are the ones about supporting characters: Saloth's two-part flashback arc (see Vol. 3, *Lies of Our Fathers*), AJ in the Afterlife (in this volume), and the only truly standalone issue, a story on a tangent all its own, "Buffet of Darkness".

That's just one of the things I've learned during my time on THE EXTERMINATORS. And obviously there's a lot of other writing/story/comic book stuff that I'm not going to bore you with here. But there are other, way more unexpected things that I've learned that have to do with how people react to a comic book about bugs.

First off, when I started this I had no idea what a visceral, deep-rooted horror of bugs some people have. I knew most people may not be fans as such, and personally, I'm not too excited about physical contact with cockroaches.

But a lot of people—and I'm talking about people who watch blood and guts slasher movies, people who obviously get some pleasure in having their fear buttons pushed—told me they just couldn't bring themselves to even consider reading a comic book about pests.

Seriously, as you can imagine, it came as a big shock to me when I realized I'd picked a subject that immediately eliminated probably 25 percent of potential readers.

But that contrasts nicely with my next point, and as points go, this is a big one. For the entire history of mankind we've searched for some common thread, some element that connects us all, as a species. And outside of the obvious — sex, death and pooping — it's kind of been a bust.

Religion? Never really panned out. The United Nations — better but no cigar. And Coca Cola? Well, rotting out kids' teeth the world over...

But I think that in writing my humble piece of low-grade smut about pests and the men who hunt them, I may have stumbled on something that ties us all together regardless of any race, color, age, or sexual preference,

Everyone (and here I'm including the 25 percent with the visceral fear of bugs) has their own bug/rat/vermin/pest story to tell. And I do mean fucking *everyone*.

How do I know this? Personal experience. Any time, any place, any situation when it happened to come up in casual conversation that I was writing a book about bug exterminators, after a brief pause while that sunk in, I could literally

set my watch to the time it took for the first person to share his or her pest story. Then everyone else would follow.

It's freakish, and I'll leave you with that thought. Feel free to use it in the future. You find yourself in a social situation where there's a painful lull in the conversation, or you're stuck at your sister's husband's brother's wedding and you're wondering how the fuck you're going to talk with these people you have less than zero in common with. I'm telling you, just subtly steer the conversation into the topic of pest experiences, and then silently thank me.

Of course, don't ever do it in food-related situations. And no, guys, it's probably never going to get you laid.

Simon Oliver AUGUST 2008

BUFFET OF DARKNESS

COVER ART BY PHILIP BOND

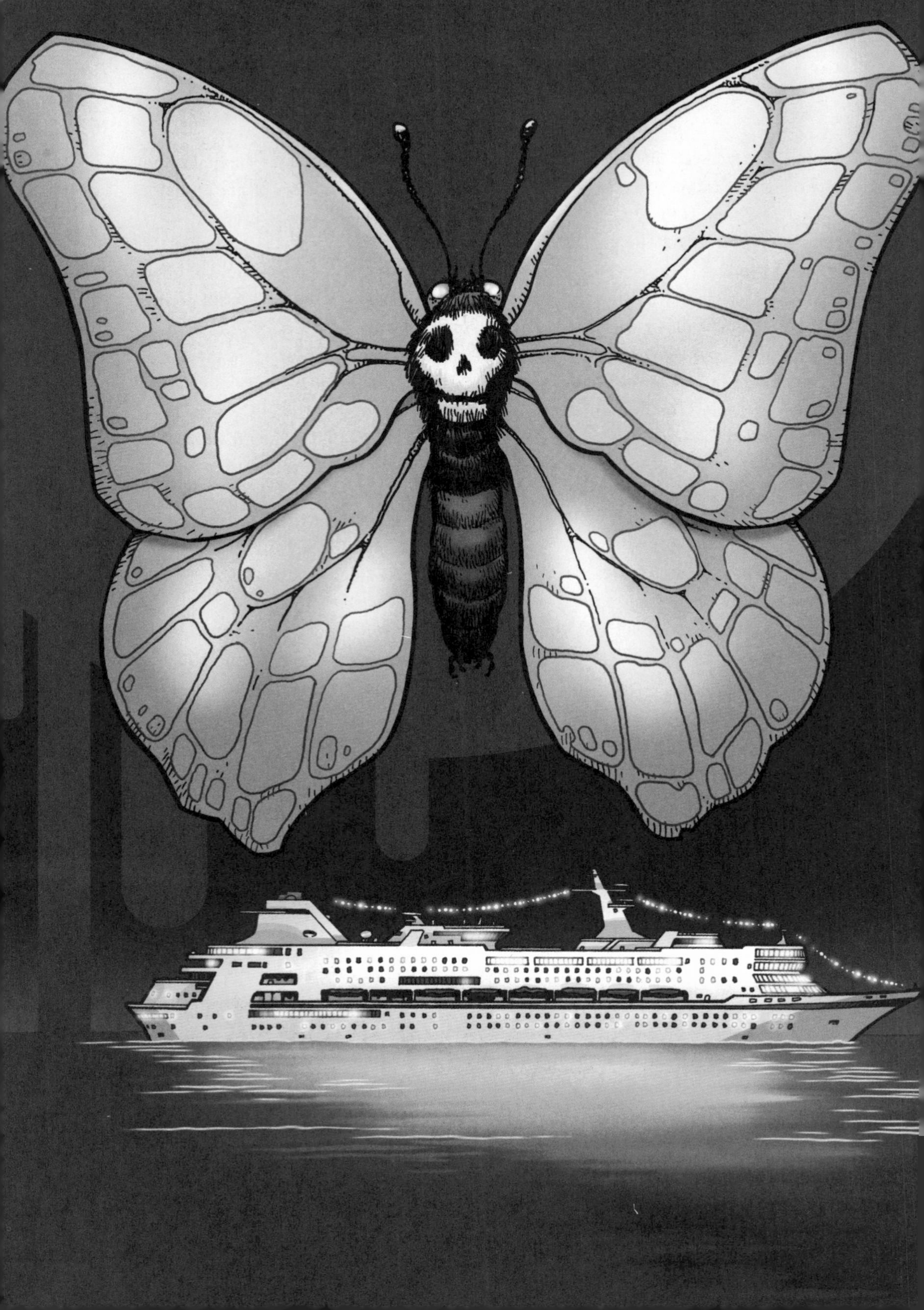

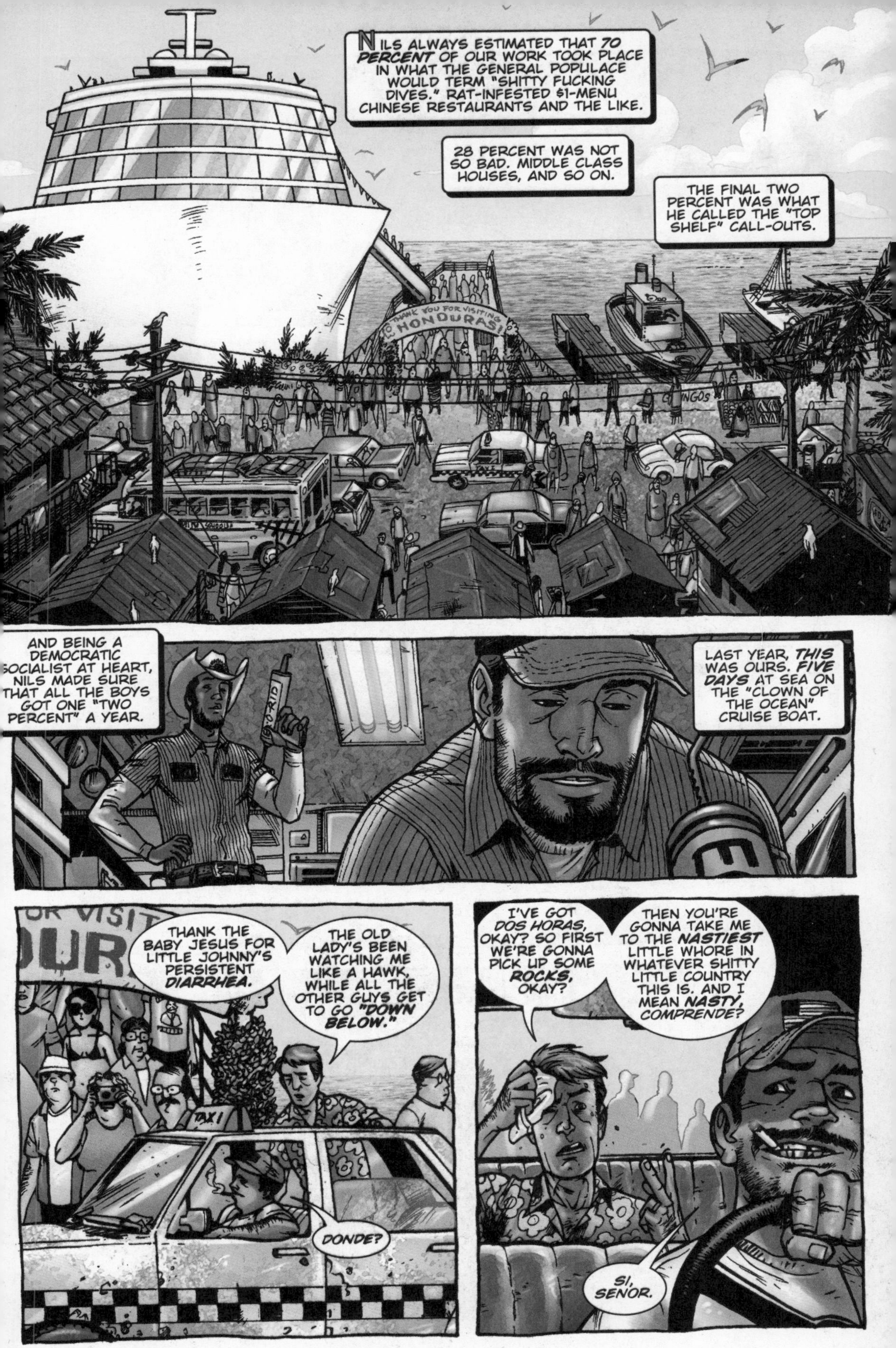
NILS ALWAYS ESTIMATED THAT *70 PERCENT* OF OUR WORK TOOK PLACE IN WHAT THE GENERAL POPULACE WOULD TERM "SHITTY FUCKING DIVES." RAT-INFESTED $1-MENU CHINESE RESTAURANTS AND THE LIKE.
28 PERCENT WAS NOT SO BAD. MIDDLE CLASS HOUSES, AND SO ON.
THE FINAL TWO PERCENT WAS WHAT HE CALLED THE "TOP SHELF" CALL-OUTS.
THANK YOU FOR VISITING
HONDURAS!
AND BEING A DEMOCRATIC SOCIALIST AT HEART, NILS MADE SURE THAT ALL THE BOYS GOT ONE "TWO PERCENT" A YEAR.
LAST YEAR, *THIS* WAS OURS. *FIVE DAYS* AT SEA ON THE "CLOWN OF THE OCEAN" CRUISE BOAT.
THANK THE BABY JESUS FOR LITTLE JOHNNY'S PERSISTENT *DIARRHEA.*
THE OLD LADY'S BEEN WATCHING ME LIKE A HAWK, WHILE ALL THE OTHER GUYS GET TO GO *"DOWN BELOW."*
TAXI
DONDE?
I'VE GOT *DOS HORAS,* OKAY? SO FIRST WE'RE GONNA PICK UP SOME *ROCKS,* OKAY?
THEN YOU'RE GONNA TAKE ME TO THE *NASTIEST* LITTLE WHORE IN WHATEVER SHITTY LITTLE COUNTRY THIS IS. AND I MEAN *NASTY,* *COMPRENDE?*
SI, SENOR.

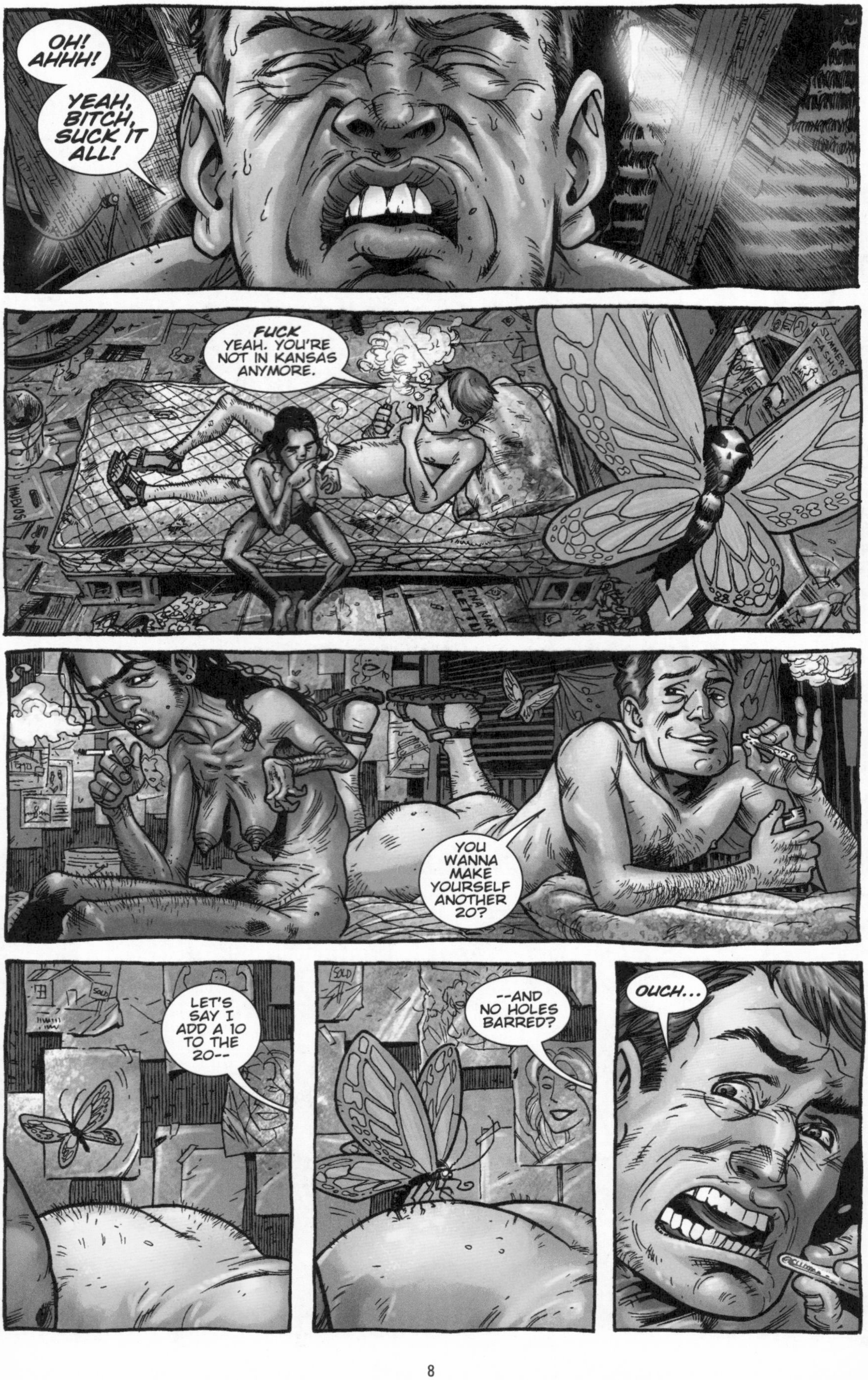
OH! AHHH!
YEAH, BITCH, SUCK IT ALL!
FUCK YEAH. YOU'RE NOT IN KANSAS ANYMORE.
YOU WANNA MAKE YOURSELF ANOTHER 20?
LET'S SAY I ADD A 10 TO THE 20--
--AND NO HOLES BARRED?
OUCH...

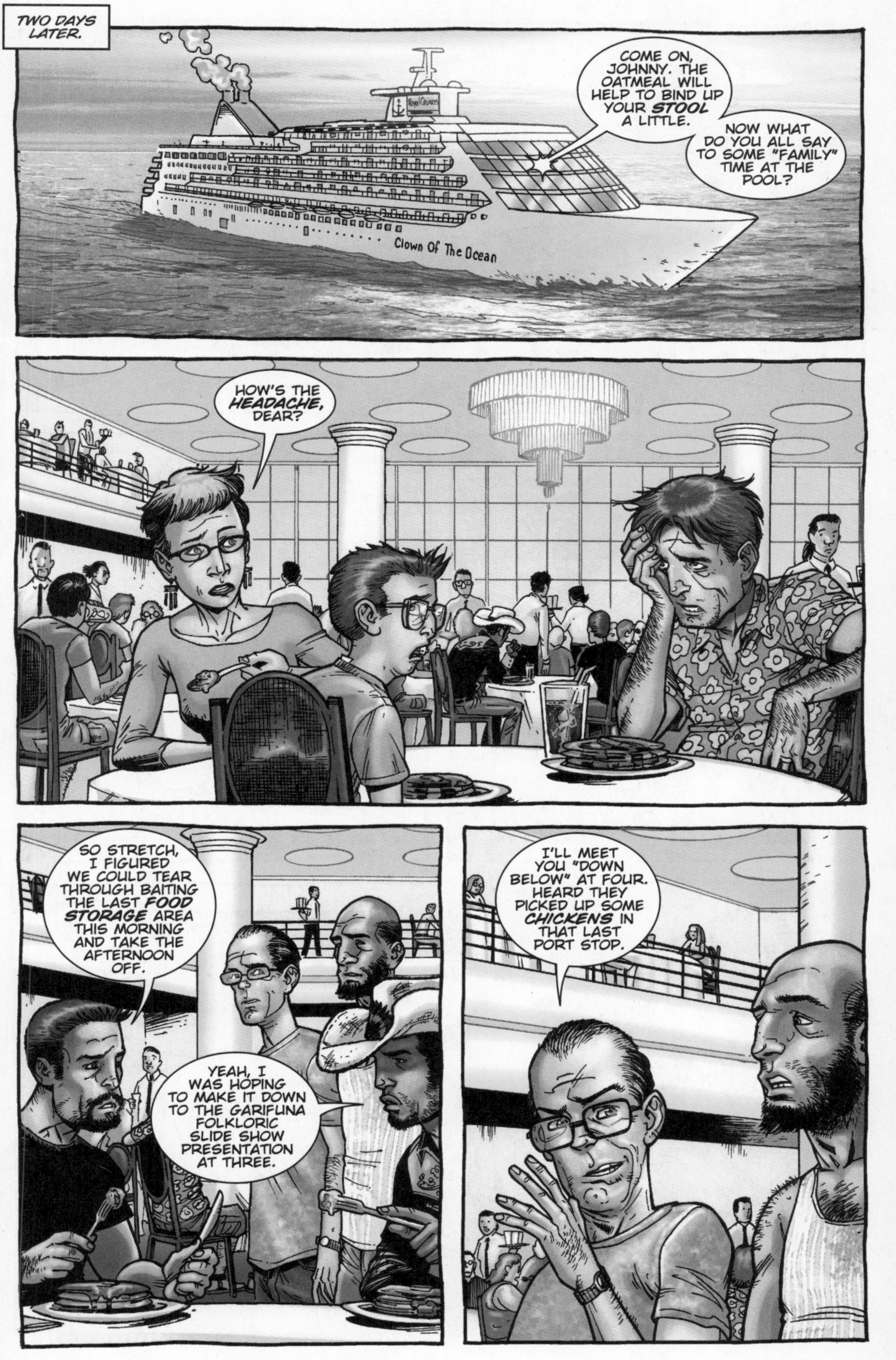
TWO DAYS LATER.
Clown Of The Ocean
COME ON, JOHNNY. THE OATMEAL WILL HELP TO BIND UP YOUR *STOOL* A LITTLE.
NOW WHAT DO YOU ALL SAY TO SOME "FAMILY" TIME AT THE POOL?
HOW'S THE *HEADACHE,* DEAR?
SO STRETCH, I FIGURED WE COULD TEAR THROUGH BAITING THE LAST *FOOD STORAGE* AREA THIS MORNING AND TAKE THE AFTERNOON OFF.
YEAH, I WAS HOPING TO MAKE IT DOWN TO THE GARIFUNA FOLKLORIC SLIDE SHOW PRESENTATION AT THREE.
I'LL MEET YOU "DOWN BELOW" AT FOUR. HEARD THEY PICKED UP SOME *CHICKENS* IN THAT LAST PORT STOP.

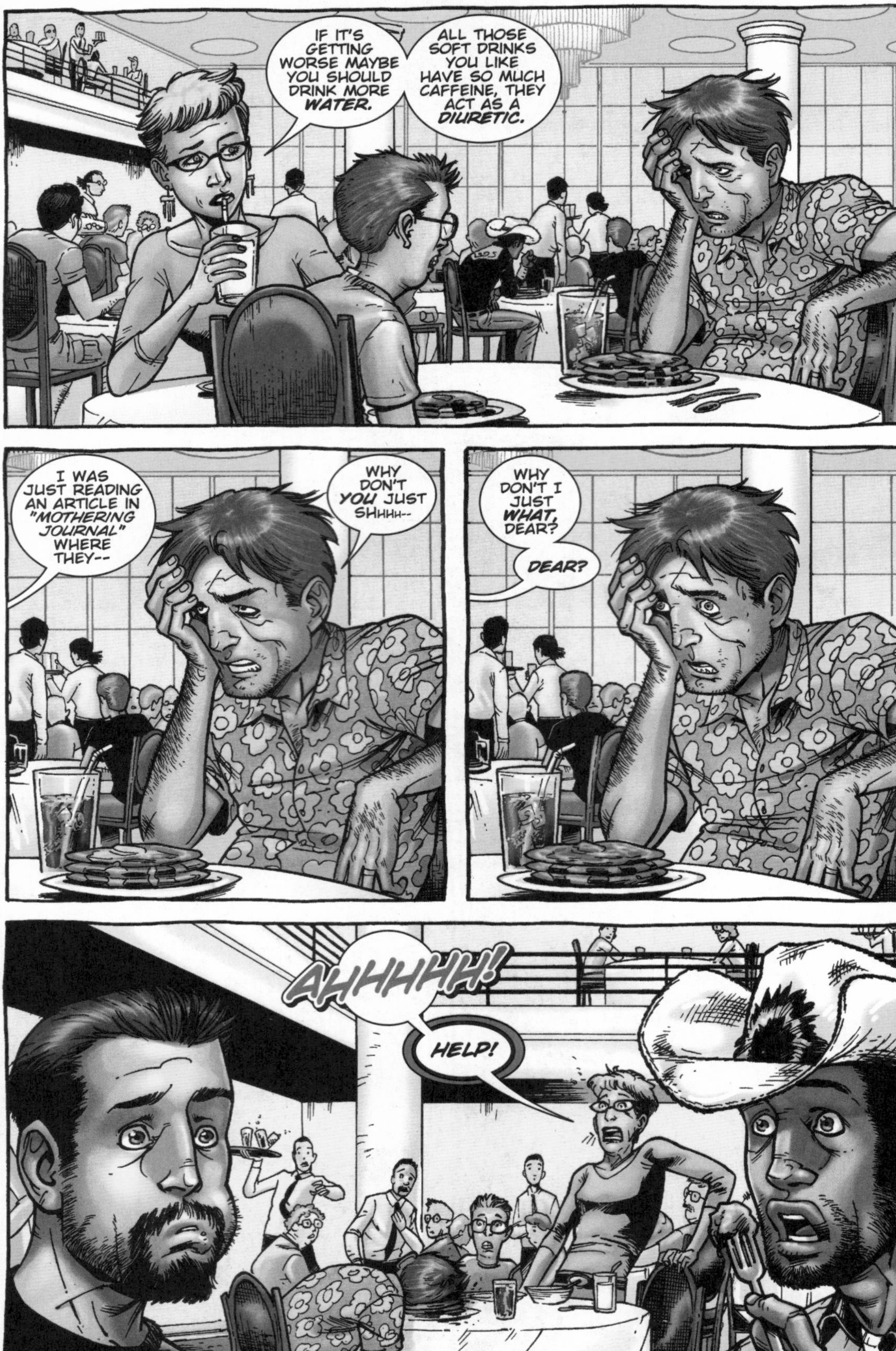
IF IT'S GETTING WORSE MAYBE YOU SHOULD DRINK MORE WATER.
ALL THOSE SOFT DRINKS YOU LIKE HAVE SO MUCH CAFFEINE, THEY ACT AS A DIURETIC.
I WAS JUST READING AN ARTICLE IN "MOTHERING JOURNAL" WHERE THEY--
WHY DON'T YOU JUST SHHHH--
WHY DON'T I JUST WHAT, DEAR?
DEAR?
AHHHHH!
HELP!

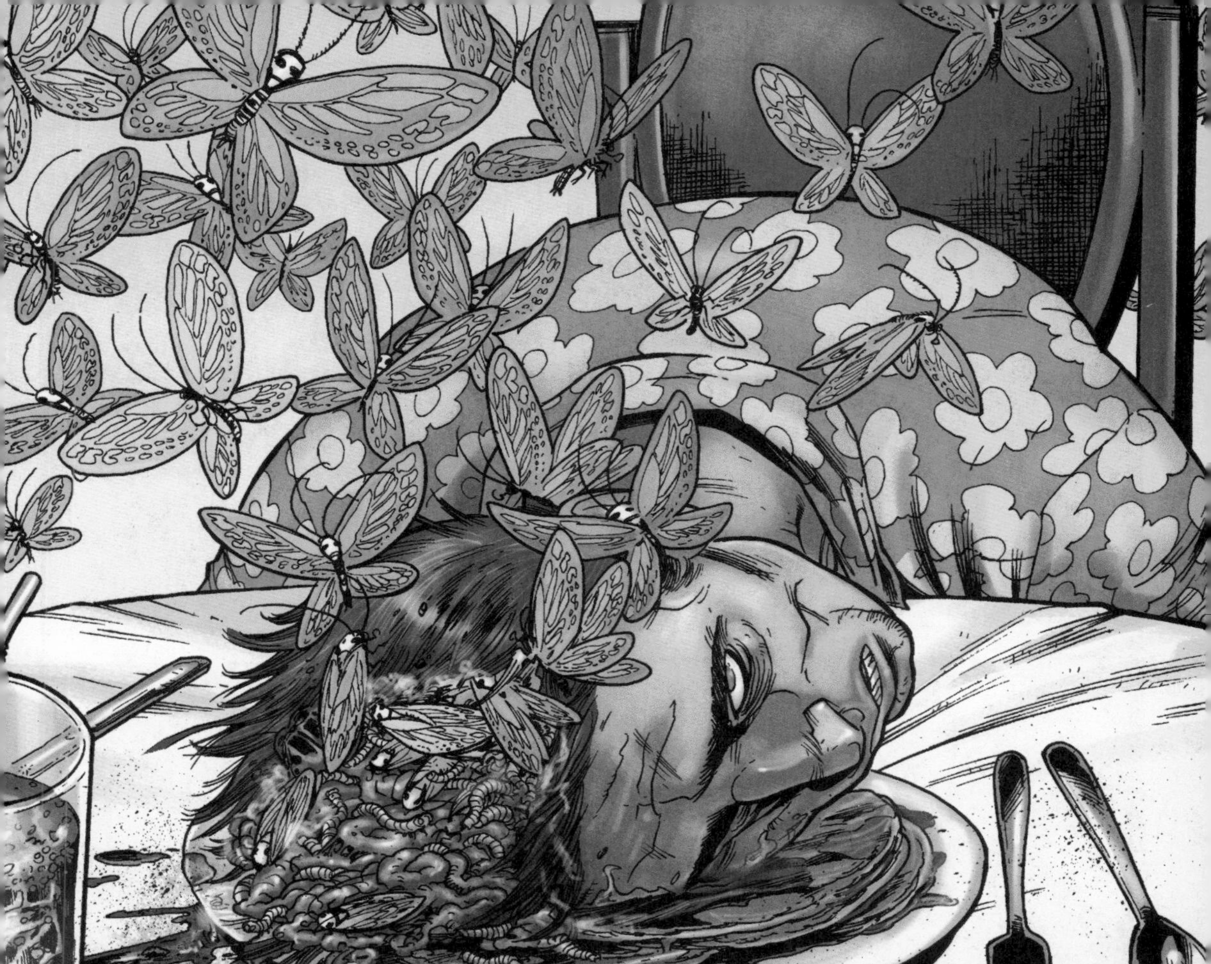

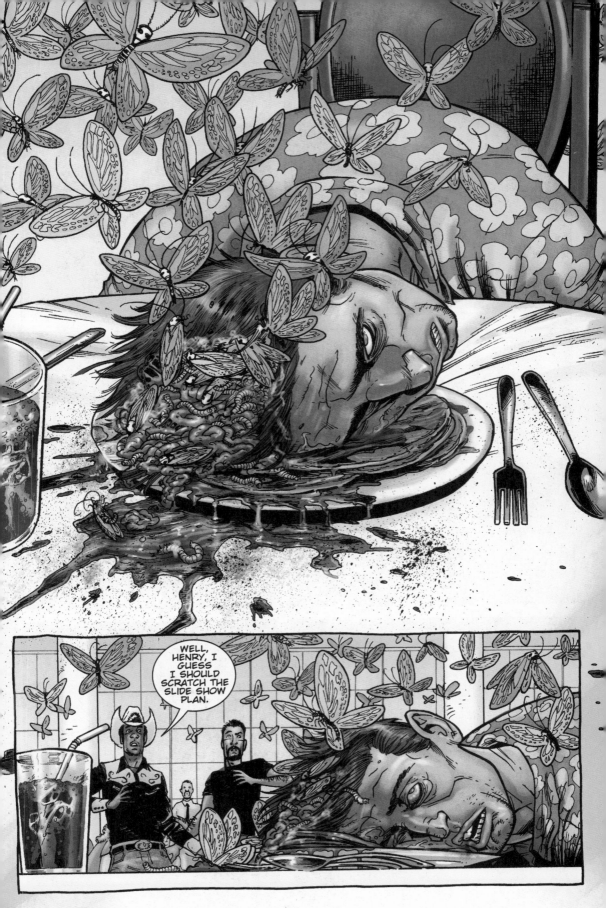

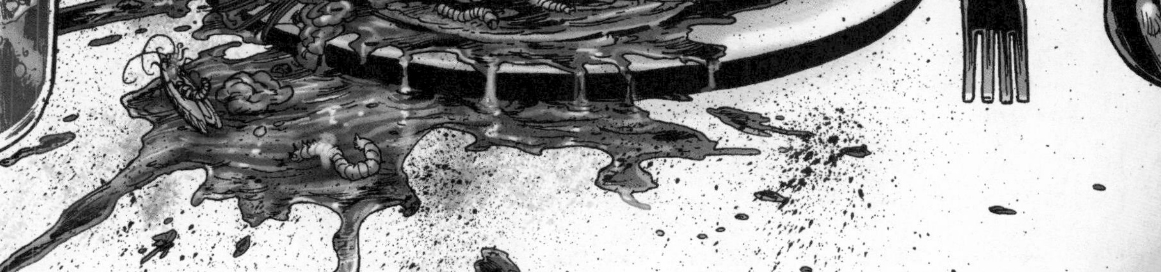
WELL, HENRY, I GUESS I SHOULD SCRATCH THE SLIDE SHOW PLAN.

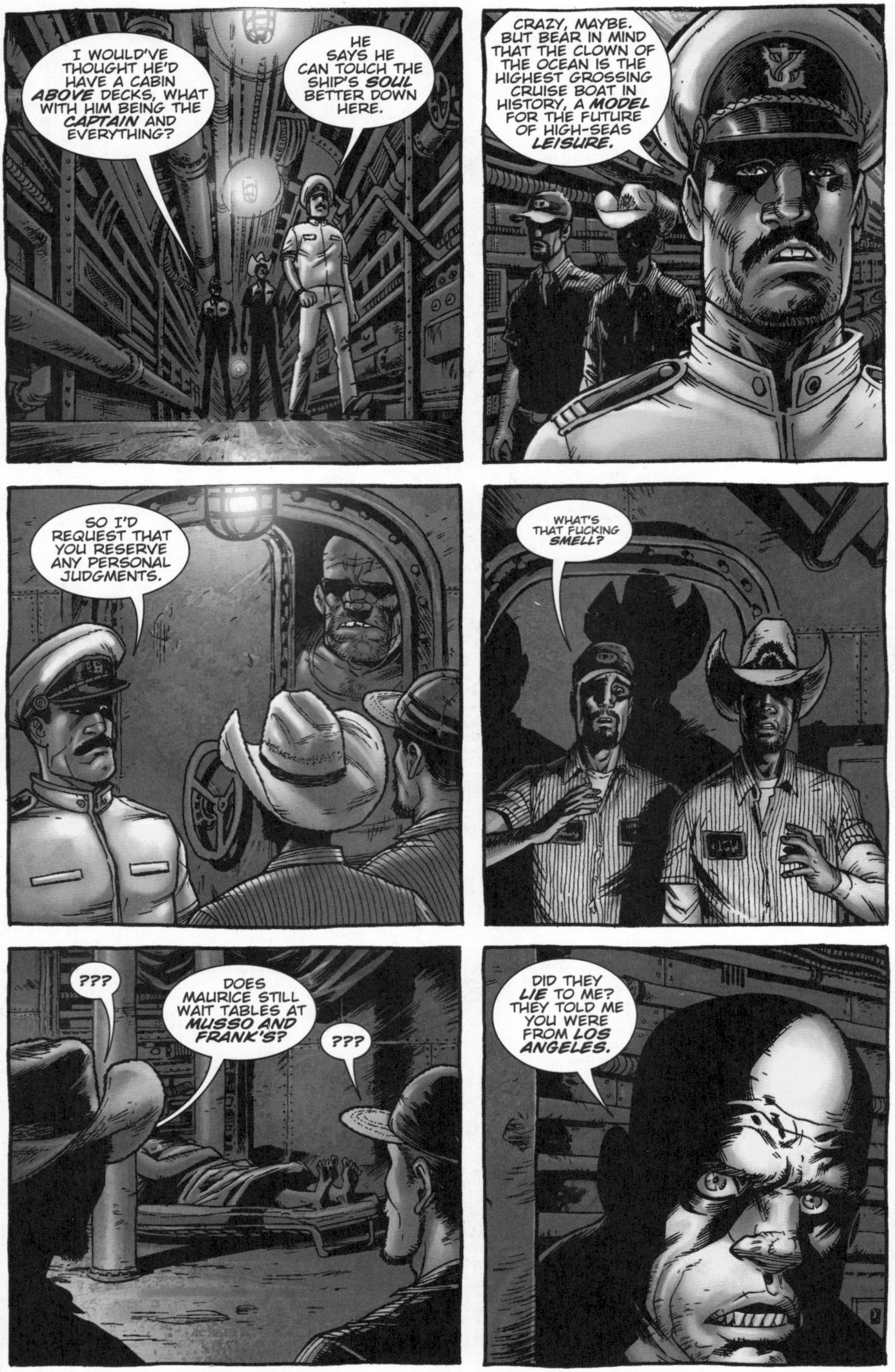
I WOULD'VE THOUGHT HE'D HAVE A CABIN ABOVE DECKS, WHAT WITH HIM BEING THE CAPTAIN AND EVERYTHING?
HE SAYS HE CAN TOUCH THE SHIP'S SOUL BETTER DOWN HERE.
CRAZY, MAYBE. BUT BEAR IN MIND THAT THE CLOWN OF THE OCEAN IS THE HIGHEST GROSSING CRUISE BOAT IN HISTORY, A MODEL FOR THE FUTURE OF HIGH-SEAS LEISURE.
SO I'D REQUEST THAT YOU RESERVE ANY PERSONAL JUDGMENTS.
WHAT'S THAT FUCKING SMELL?
???
DOES MAURICE STILL WAIT TABLES AT MUSSO AND FRANK'S?
???
DID THEY LIE TO ME? THEY TOLD ME YOU WERE FROM LOS ANGELES.

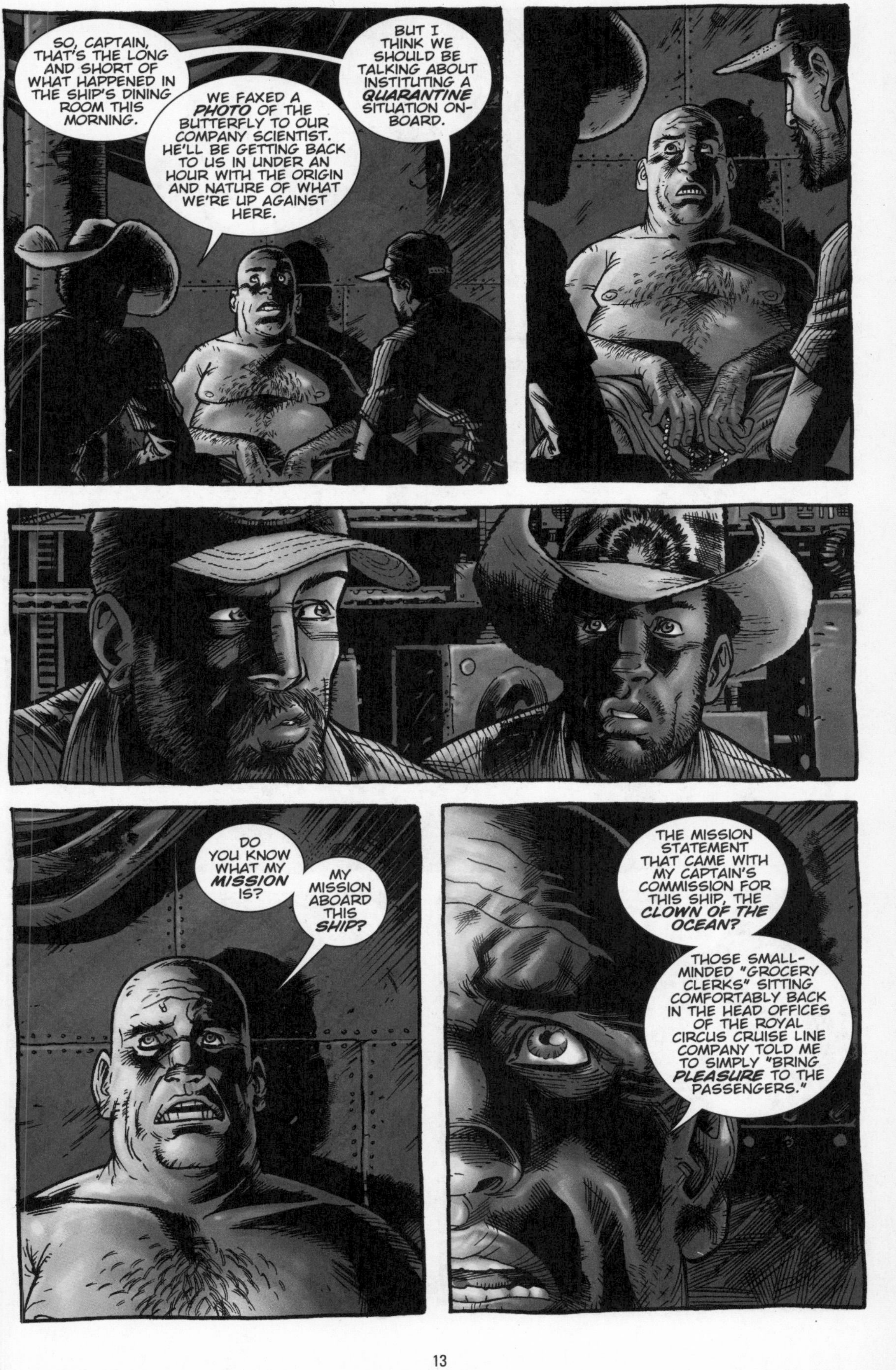
SO, CAPTAIN, THAT'S THE LONG AND SHORT OF WHAT HAPPENED IN THE SHIP'S DINING ROOM THIS MORNING.
WE FAXED A PHOTO OF THE BUTTERFLY TO OUR COMPANY SCIENTIST. HE'LL BE GETTING BACK TO US IN UNDER AN HOUR WITH THE ORIGIN AND NATURE OF WHAT WE'RE UP AGAINST HERE.
BUT I THINK WE SHOULD BE TALKING ABOUT INSTITUTING A QUARANTINE SITUATION ON-BOARD.
DO YOU KNOW WHAT MY MISSION IS?
MY MISSION ABOARD THIS SHIP?
THE MISSION STATEMENT THAT CAME WITH MY CAPTAIN'S COMMISSION FOR THIS SHIP, THE CLOWN OF THE OCEAN?
THOSE SMALL-MINDED "GROCERY CLERKS" SITTING COMFORTABLY BACK IN THE HEAD OFFICES OF THE ROYAL CIRCUS CRUISE LINE COMPANY TOLD ME TO SIMPLY "BRING PLEASURE TO THE PASSENGERS."

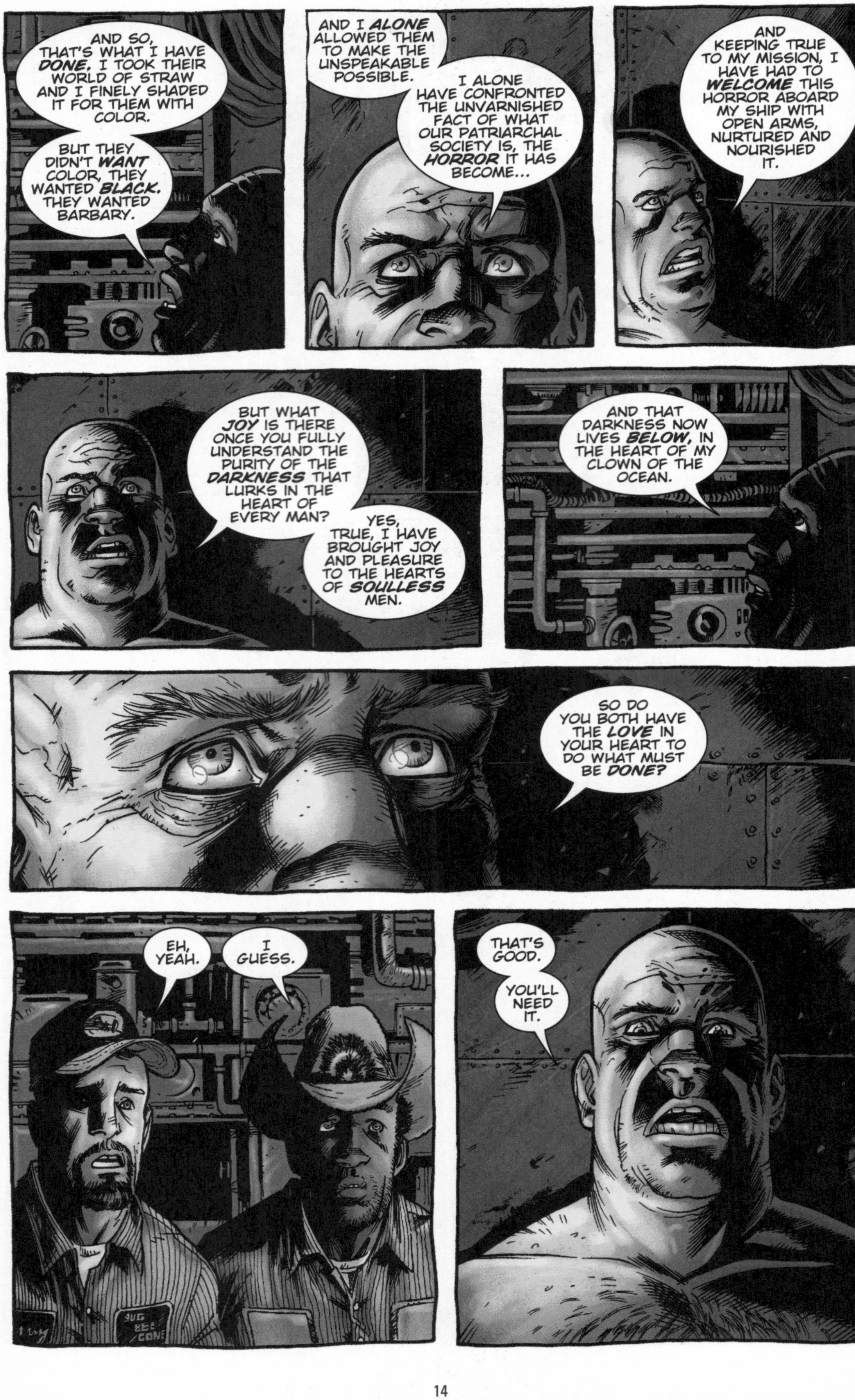
AND SO, THAT'S WHAT I HAVE DONE. I TOOK THEIR WORLD OF STRAW AND I FINELY SHADED IT FOR THEM WITH COLOR.
BUT THEY DIDN'T WANT COLOR, THEY WANTED BLACK. THEY WANTED BARBARY.
AND I ALONE ALLOWED THEM TO MAKE THE UNSPEAKABLE POSSIBLE.
I ALONE HAVE CONFRONTED THE UNVARNISHED FACT OF WHAT OUR PATRIARCHAL SOCIETY IS, THE HORROR IT HAS BECOME...
AND KEEPING TRUE TO MY MISSION, I HAVE HAD TO WELCOME THIS HORROR ABOARD MY SHIP WITH OPEN ARMS, NURTURED AND NOURISHED IT.
BUT WHAT JOY IS THERE ONCE YOU FULLY UNDERSTAND THE PURITY OF THE DARKNESS THAT LURKS IN THE HEART OF EVERY MAN?
YES, TRUE, I HAVE BROUGHT JOY AND PLEASURE TO THE HEARTS OF SOULLESS MEN.
AND THAT DARKNESS NOW LIVES BELOW, IN THE HEART OF MY CLOWN OF THE OCEAN.
SO DO YOU BOTH HAVE THE LOVE IN YOUR HEART TO DO WHAT MUST BE DONE?
EH, YEAH.
I GUESS.
THAT'S GOOD.
YOU'LL NEED IT.

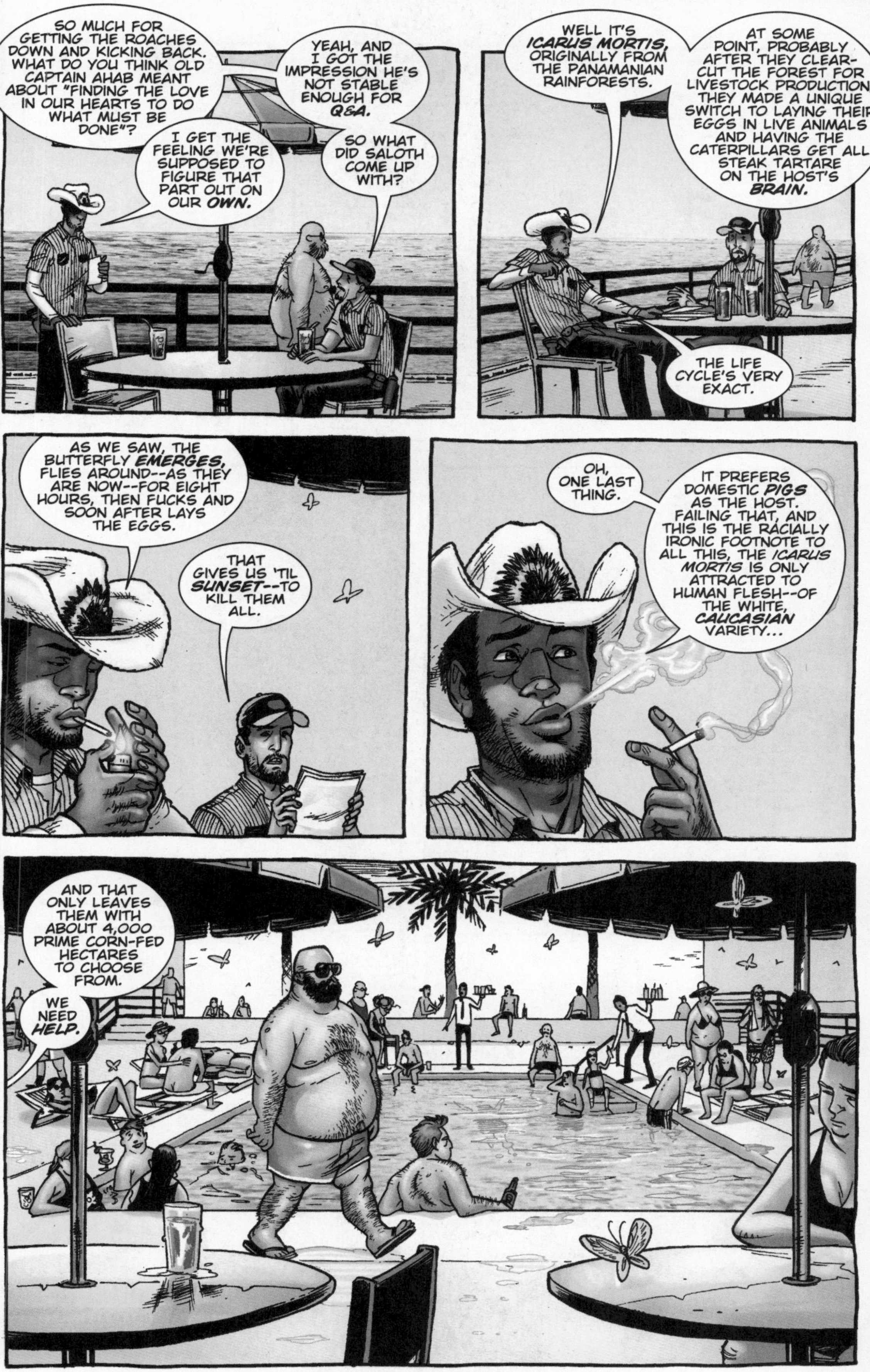

SO MUCH FOR GETTING THE ROACHES DOWN AND KICKING BACK. WHAT DO YOU THINK OLD CAPTAIN AHAB MEANT ABOUT "FINDING THE LOVE IN OUR HEARTS TO DO WHAT MUST BE DONE"?
YEAH, AND I GOT THE IMPRESSION HE'S NOT STABLE ENOUGH FOR Q&A.
I GET THE FEELING WE'RE SUPPOSED TO FIGURE THAT PART OUT ON OUR OWN.
SO WHAT DID SALOTH COME UP WITH?
WELL IT'S ICARUS MORTIS, ORIGINALLY FROM THE PANAMANIAN RAINFORESTS.
AT SOME POINT, PROBABLY AFTER THEY CLEAR-CUT THE FOREST FOR LIVESTOCK PRODUCTION, THEY MADE A UNIQUE SWITCH TO LAYING THEIR EGGS IN LIVE ANIMALS AND HAVING THE CATERPILLARS GET ALL STEAK TARTARE ON THE HOST'S BRAIN.
THE LIFE CYCLE'S VERY EXACT.
AS WE SAW, THE BUTTERFLY EMERGES, FLIES AROUND--AS THEY ARE NOW--FOR EIGHT HOURS, THEN FUCKS AND SOON AFTER LAYS THE EGGS.
THAT GIVES US 'TIL SUNSET--TO KILL THEM ALL.
OH, ONE LAST THING.
IT PREFERS DOMESTIC PIGS AS THE HOST. FAILING THAT, AND THIS IS THE RACIALLY IRONIC FOOTNOTE TO ALL THIS, THE ICARUS MORTIS IS ONLY ATTRACTED TO HUMAN FLESH--OF THE WHITE, CAUCASIAN VARIETY...
AND THAT ONLY LEAVES THEM WITH ABOUT 4,000 PRIME CORN-FED HECTARES TO CHOOSE FROM.
WE NEED HELP.

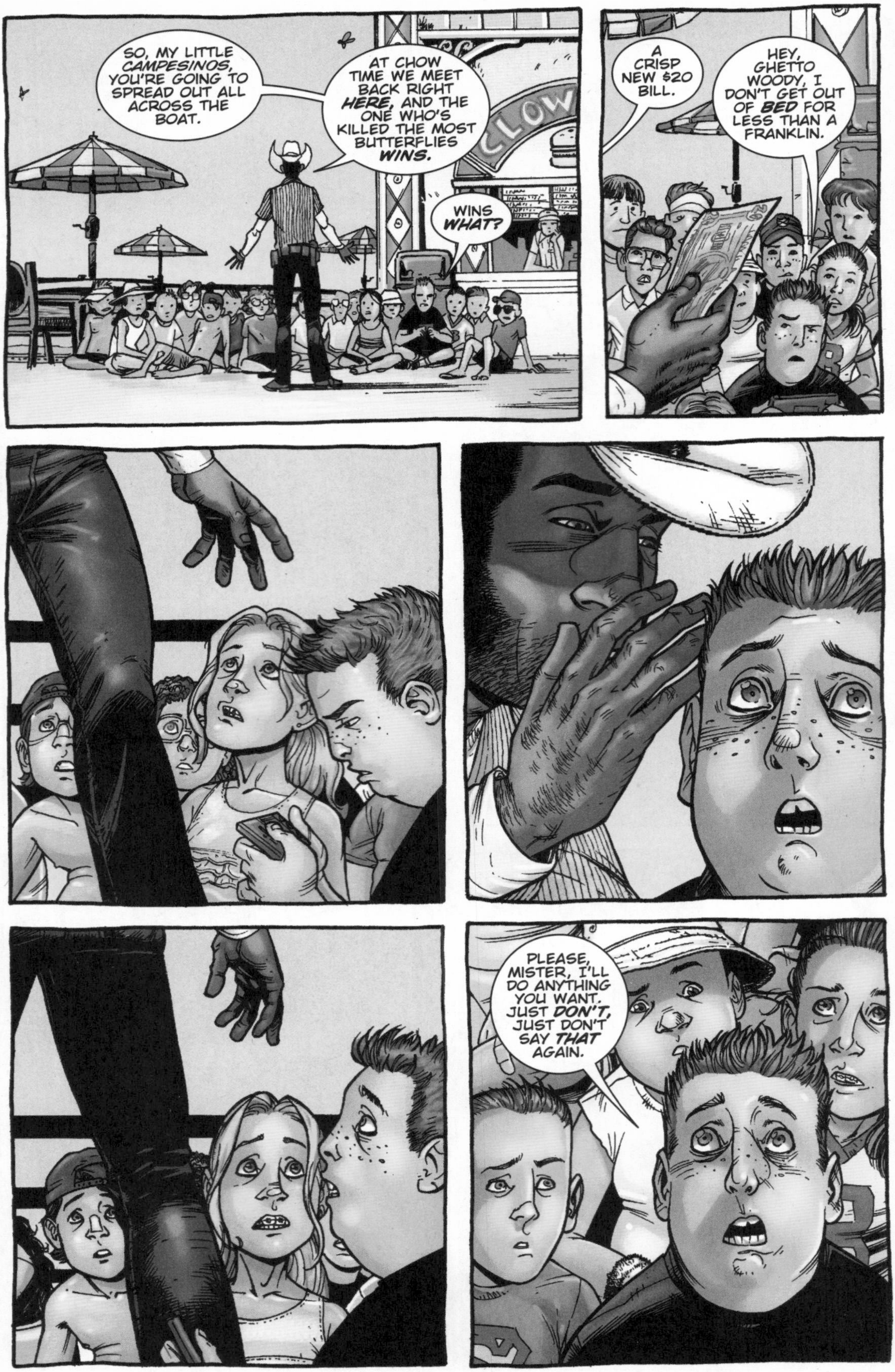
SO, MY LITTLE *CAMPESINOS*, YOU'RE GOING TO SPREAD OUT ALL ACROSS THE BOAT.
AT CHOW TIME WE MEET BACK RIGHT ***HERE,*** AND THE ONE WHO'S KILLED THE MOST BUTTERFLIES ***WINS.***
WINS ***WHAT?***
CLOW
A CRISP NEW $20 BILL.
HEY, GHETTO WOODY, I DON'T GET OUT OF ***BED*** FOR LESS THAN A FRANKLIN.
PLEASE, MISTER, I'LL DO ANYTHING YOU WANT. JUST ***DON'T,*** JUST DON'T SAY ***THAT*** AGAIN.

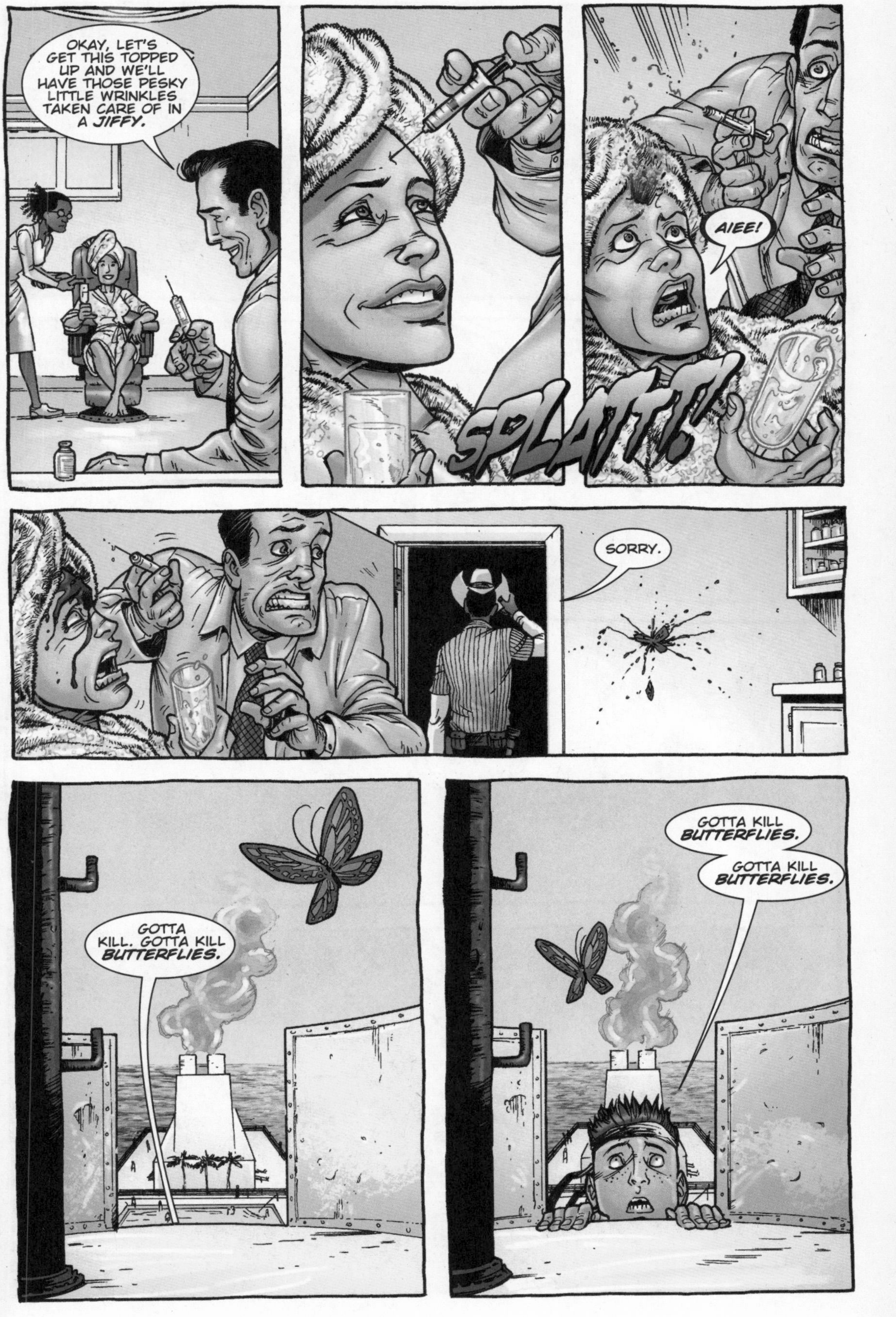
OKAY, LET'S GET THIS TOPPED UP AND WE'LL HAVE THOSE PESKY LITTLE WRINKLES TAKEN CARE OF IN A *JIFFY.*
AIEE!
SPLATT!
SORRY.
GOTTA KILL. GOTTA KILL *BUTTERFLIES.*
GOTTA KILL *BUTTERFLIES.*
GOTTA KILL *BUTTERFLIES.*

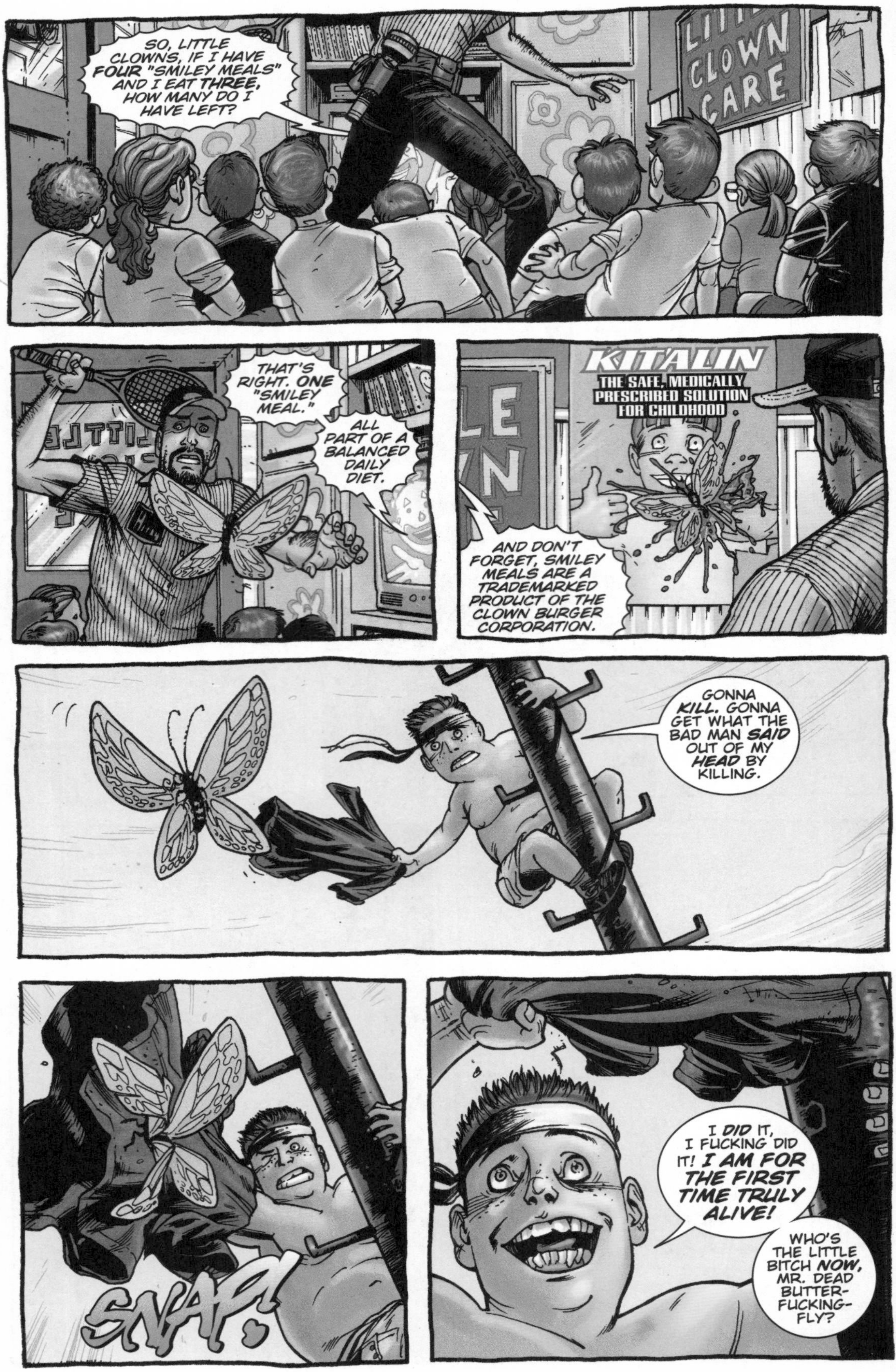

SO, LITTLE CLOWNS, IF I HAVE FOUR "SMILEY MEALS" AND I EAT THREE, HOW MANY DO I HAVE LEFT?
LITTLE CLOWN CARE
THAT'S RIGHT. ONE "SMILEY MEAL."
ALL PART OF A BALANCED DAILY DIET.
KIT'ALIN
THE SAFE, MEDICALLY PRESCRIBED SOLUTION FOR CHILDHOOD
AND DON'T FORGET, SMILEY MEALS ARE A TRADEMARKED PRODUCT OF THE CLOWN BURGER CORPORATION.
GONNA KILL. GONNA GET WHAT THE BAD MAN SAID OUT OF MY HEAD BY KILLING.
SNAP!
I DID IT, I FUCKING DID IT! I AM FOR THE FIRST TIME TRULY ALIVE!
WHO'S THE LITTLE BITCH NOW, MR. DEAD BUTTER-FUCKING-FLY?

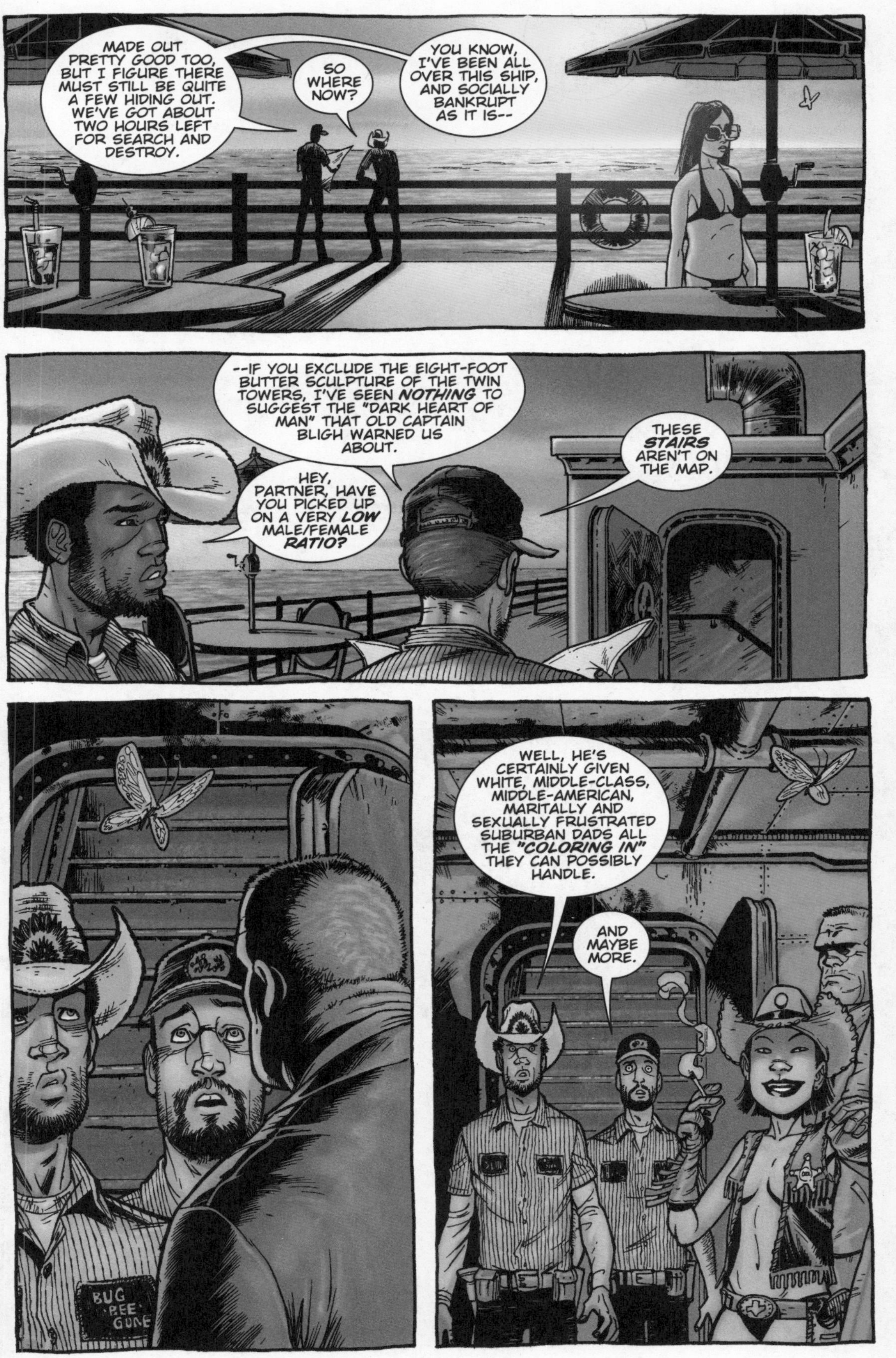
MADE OUT PRETTY GOOD TOO, BUT I FIGURE THERE MUST STILL BE QUITE A FEW HIDING OUT. WE'VE GOT ABOUT TWO HOURS LEFT FOR SEARCH AND DESTROY.
SO WHERE NOW?
YOU KNOW, I'VE BEEN ALL OVER THIS SHIP, AND SOCIALLY BANKRUPT AS IT IS--
--IF YOU EXCLUDE THE EIGHT-FOOT BUTTER SCULPTURE OF THE TWIN TOWERS, I'VE SEEN ***NOTHING*** TO SUGGEST THE "DARK HEART OF MAN" THAT OLD CAPTAIN BLIGH WARNED US ABOUT.
HEY, PARTNER, HAVE YOU PICKED UP ON A VERY ***LOW*** MALE/FEMALE ***RATIO?***
THESE ***STAIRS*** AREN'T ON THE MAP.
WELL, HE'S CERTAINLY GIVEN WHITE, MIDDLE-CLASS, MIDDLE-AMERICAN, MARITALLY AND SEXUALLY FRUSTRATED SUBURBAN DADS ALL THE ***"COLORING IN"*** THEY CAN POSSIBLY HANDLE.
AND MAYBE MORE.

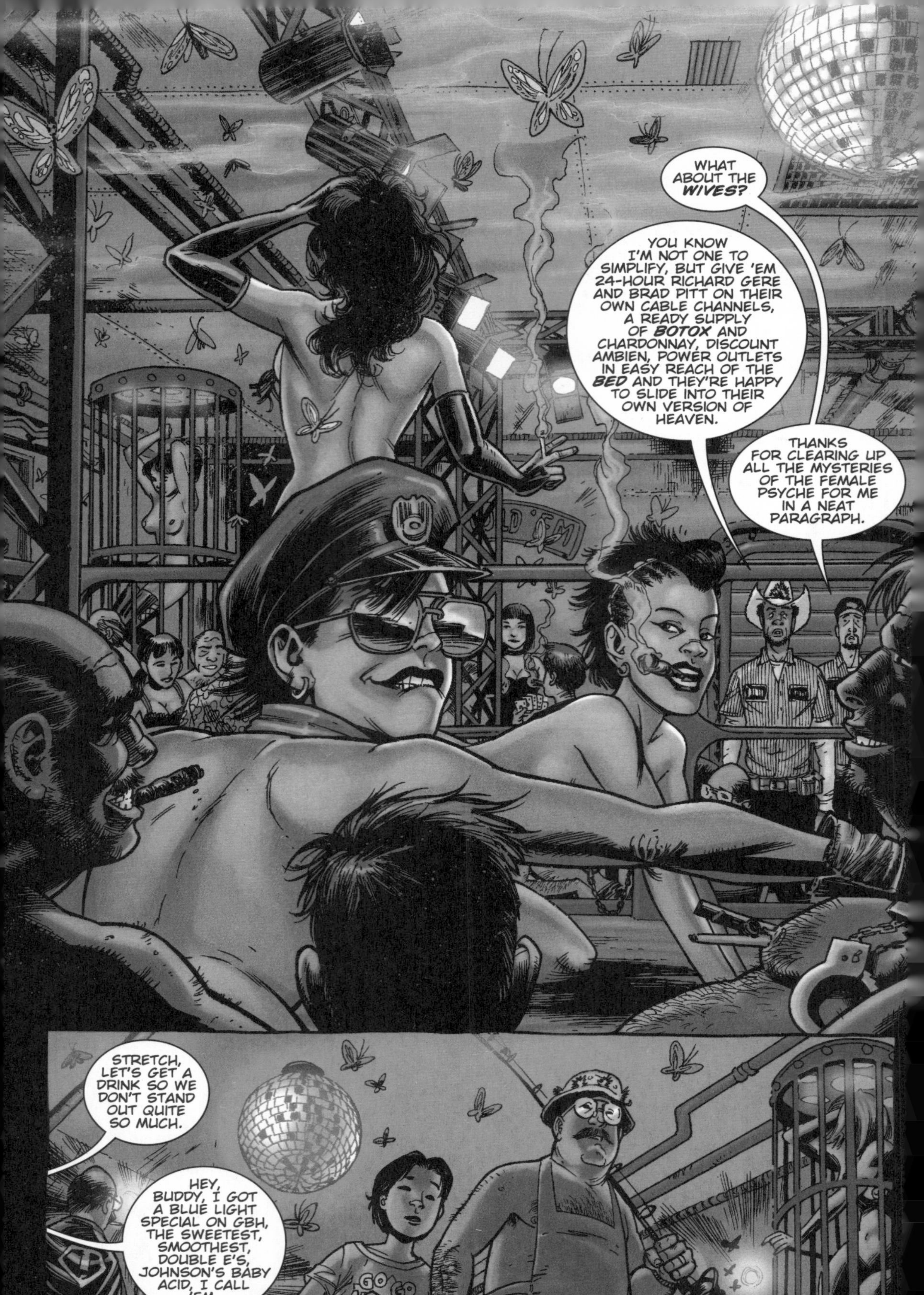
WHAT ABOUT THE *WIVES?*
YOU KNOW I'M NOT ONE TO SIMPLIFY, BUT GIVE 'EM 24-HOUR RICHARD GERE AND BRAD PITT ON THEIR OWN CABLE CHANNELS, A READY SUPPLY OF *BOTOX* AND CHARDONNAY, DISCOUNT AMBIEN, POWER OUTLETS IN EASY REACH OF THE *BED* AND THEY'RE HAPPY TO SLIDE INTO THEIR OWN VERSION OF HEAVEN.
THANKS FOR CLEARING UP ALL THE MYSTERIES OF THE FEMALE PSYCHE FOR ME IN A NEAT PARAGRAPH.
STRETCH, LET'S GET A DRINK SO WE DON'T STAND OUT QUITE SO MUCH.
HEY, BUDDY, I GOT A BLUE LIGHT SPECIAL ON GBH, THE SWEETEST, SMOOTHEST, DOUBLE E'S, JOHNSON'S BABY ACID, I CALL 'EM.

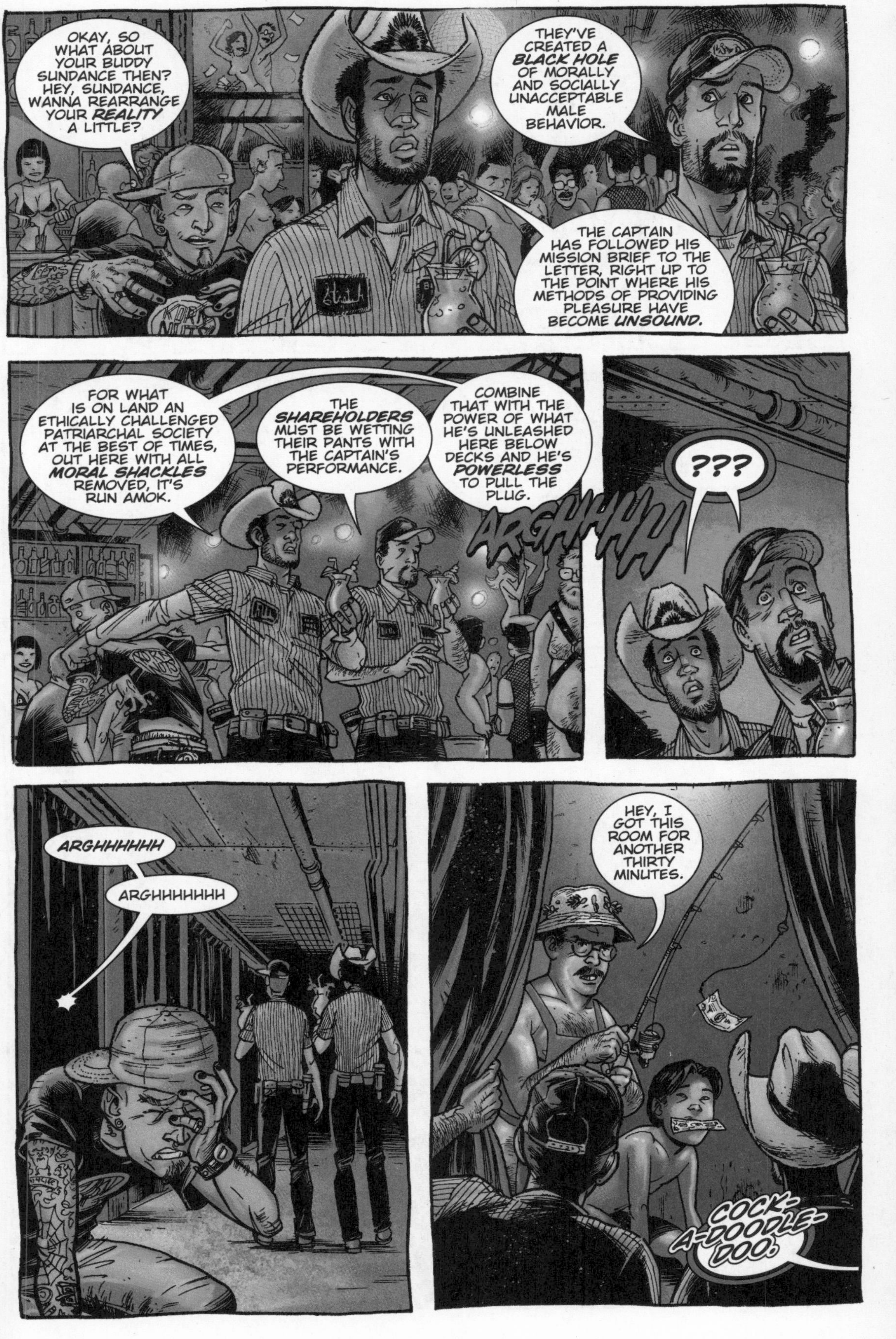
OKAY, SO WHAT ABOUT YOUR BUDDY SUNDANCE THEN? HEY, SUNDANCE, WANNA REARRANGE YOUR REALITY A LITTLE?
THEY'VE CREATED A BLACK HOLE OF MORALLY AND SOCIALLY UNACCEPTABLE MALE BEHAVIOR.
THE CAPTAIN HAS FOLLOWED HIS MISSION BRIEF TO THE LETTER, RIGHT UP TO THE POINT WHERE HIS METHODS OF PROVIDING PLEASURE HAVE BECOME UNSOUND.
FOR WHAT IS ON LAND AN ETHICALLY CHALLENGED PATRIARCHAL SOCIETY AT THE BEST OF TIMES, OUT HERE WITH ALL MORAL SHACKLES REMOVED, IT'S RUN AMOK.
THE SHAREHOLDERS MUST BE WETTING THEIR PANTS WITH THE CAPTAIN'S PERFORMANCE.
COMBINE THAT WITH THE POWER OF WHAT HE'S UNLEASHED HERE BELOW DECKS AND HE'S POWERLESS TO PULL THE PLUG.
ARGHHHH
???
ARGHHHHHHH
ARGHHHHHHHH
HEY, I GOT THIS ROOM FOR ANOTHER THIRTY MINUTES.
COCK-A-DOODLE-DOO.

THESE TWO--

SUN'S GOING DOWN.

WHAT'S WITH ALL THESE BUTTERFLIES DOING THIS, LIKE, *PIGGY-BACK* THING?

WHATEVER! LIKE, INSECTS ARE *SOOOO* INTERESTING.

I WAS THINKING WE SHOULD HIT THE STARZ LOUNGE AT SEVEN, 3-FOR-2 PITCHERS OF MOJITOS, THEN MAYBE *HOOK UP* WITH THAT WAITER AGAIN.

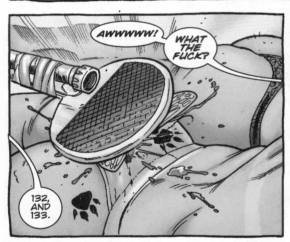

AWWWWW!

WHAT THE FUCK?

132, AND 133.

I HAVE TO *DO* THIS. I HAVE TO KILL *BUTTERFLIES.*

YOU LITTLE SHIT, DO YOU HAVE ANY FUCKING IDEA HOW *TACKY* ASS-BRUISES LOOK ON NIGHT-VISION VIDEO?

I DON'T GIVE A *SHIT* WHAT YOU CONSIDER RIGHT AND WRONG.

AND I DON'T GIVE A SHIT ABOUT *DISCUSSING* IT IN THE FORM OF AN INTELLIGENT AND CIVILIZED DEBATE.

FUCK TALKING WITH THESE TWO PINKO, FAGGOT LIBERALS. THIS IS 21ST-CENTURY *AMERICA* GODDAM IT! THEY'RE EITHER WITH US OR *AGAINST* US.

THEY'RE *AGAINST* US!

OKAY, LET'S DUMP 'EM OVER THE *SIDE* AND LET 'EM DO THE *AL QAEDA CRAWL* ALL THE WAY TO FUCKING CUBA.

AND JUST WHAT DO YOU THINK YOU'RE DOING TO MY *SON?*

DROP THE *COMMIES!* LET'S GET THE *HO'S.*

I CAN'T BELIEVE IT, DAD. YOU ACTUALLY *SAVED* ME.

WOW, IT'S ACTUALLY QUITE A TOUCHING MOMENT.

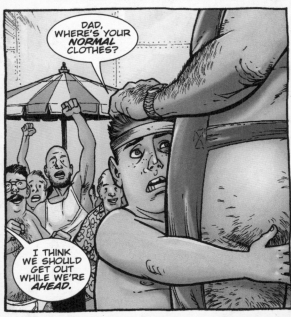

DAD, WHERE'S YOUR *NORMAL* CLOTHES?

I THINK WE SHOULD GET OUT WHILE WE'RE *AHEAD.*

THEY'RE ENTERING INTO REPRODUCTIVE PHASE.

BROTHER, THE BIG HAND'S ON THE LITTLE HAND IN THIS MISSION.

TO THE *BRIDGE.*

25

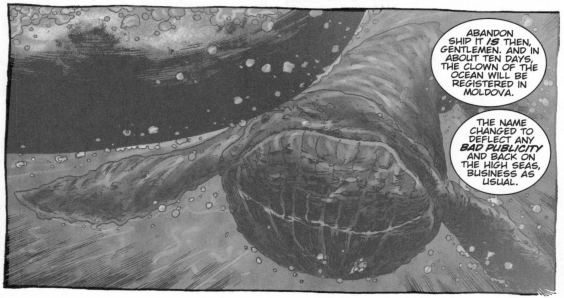

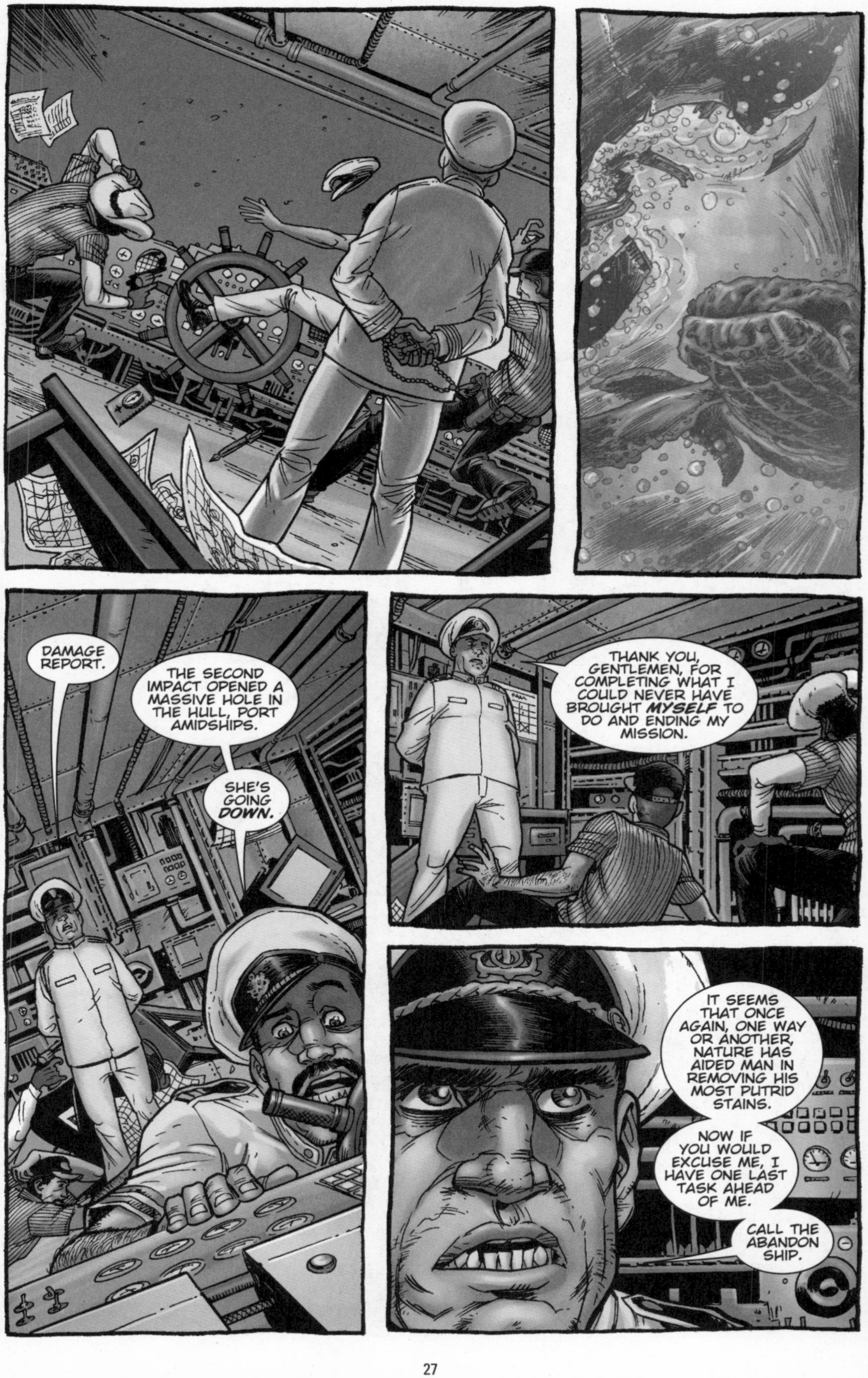

DAMAGE REPORT.
THE SECOND IMPACT OPENED A MASSIVE HOLE IN THE HULL, PORT AMIDSHIPS.
SHE'S GOING **DOWN.**
THANK YOU, GENTLEMEN, FOR COMPLETING WHAT I COULD NEVER HAVE BROUGHT **MYSELF** TO DO AND ENDING MY MISSION.
IT SEEMS THAT ONCE AGAIN, ONE WAY OR ANOTHER, NATURE HAS AIDED MAN IN REMOVING HIS MOST PUTRID STAINS.
NOW IF YOU WOULD EXCUSE ME, I HAVE ONE LAST TASK AHEAD OF ME.
CALL THE ABANDON SHIP.

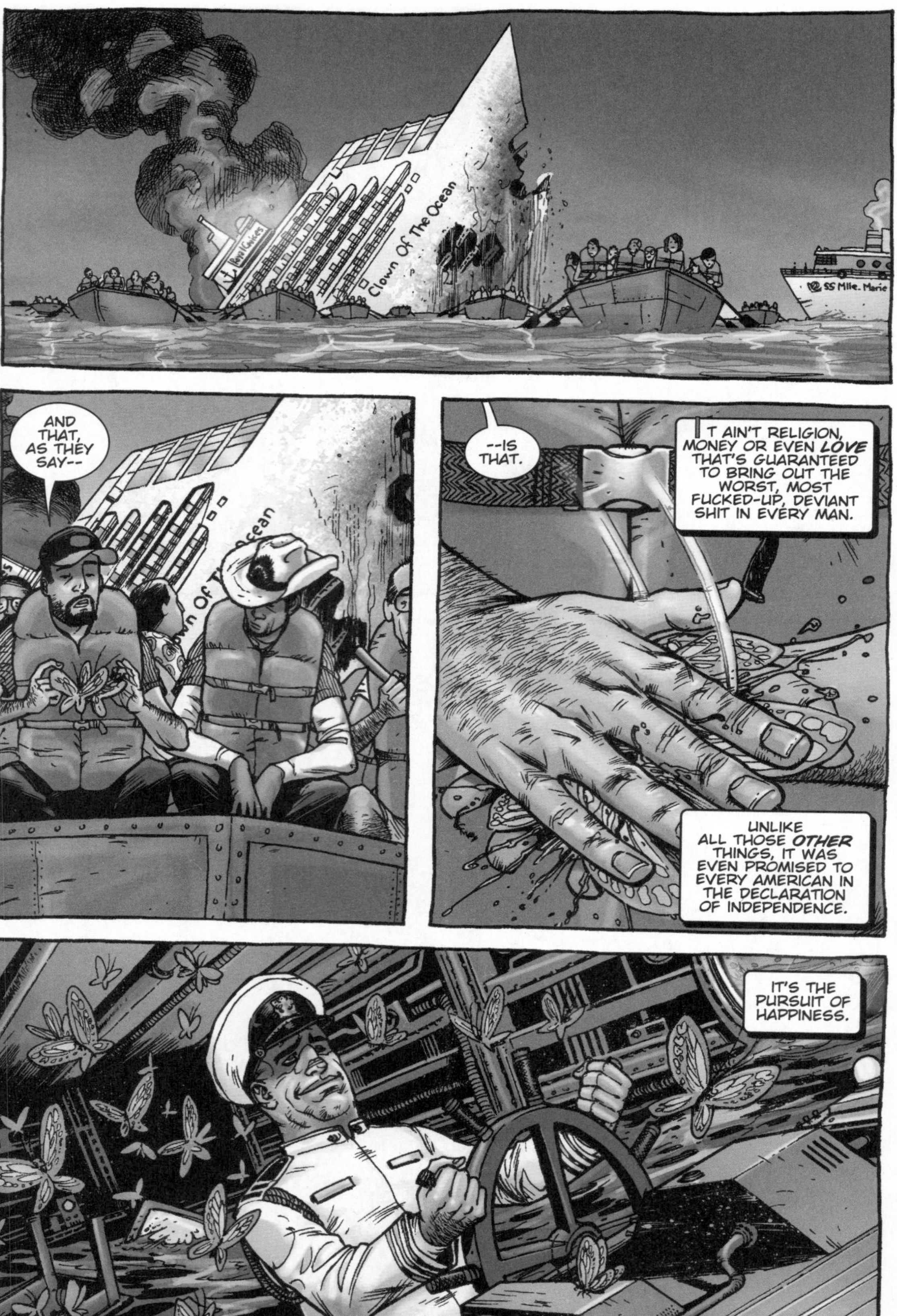
Clown Of The Ocean
SS Mlle. Marie
AND THAT, AS THEY SAY--
--IS THAT.
T AIN'T RELIGION, MONEY OR EVEN LOVE THAT'S GUARANTEED TO BRING OUT THE WORST, MOST FUCKED-UP, DEVIANT SHIT IN EVERY MAN.
UNLIKE ALL THOSE OTHER THINGS, IT WAS EVEN PROMISED TO EVERY AMERICAN IN THE DECLARATION OF INDEPENDENCE.
IT'S THE PURSUIT OF HAPPINESS.

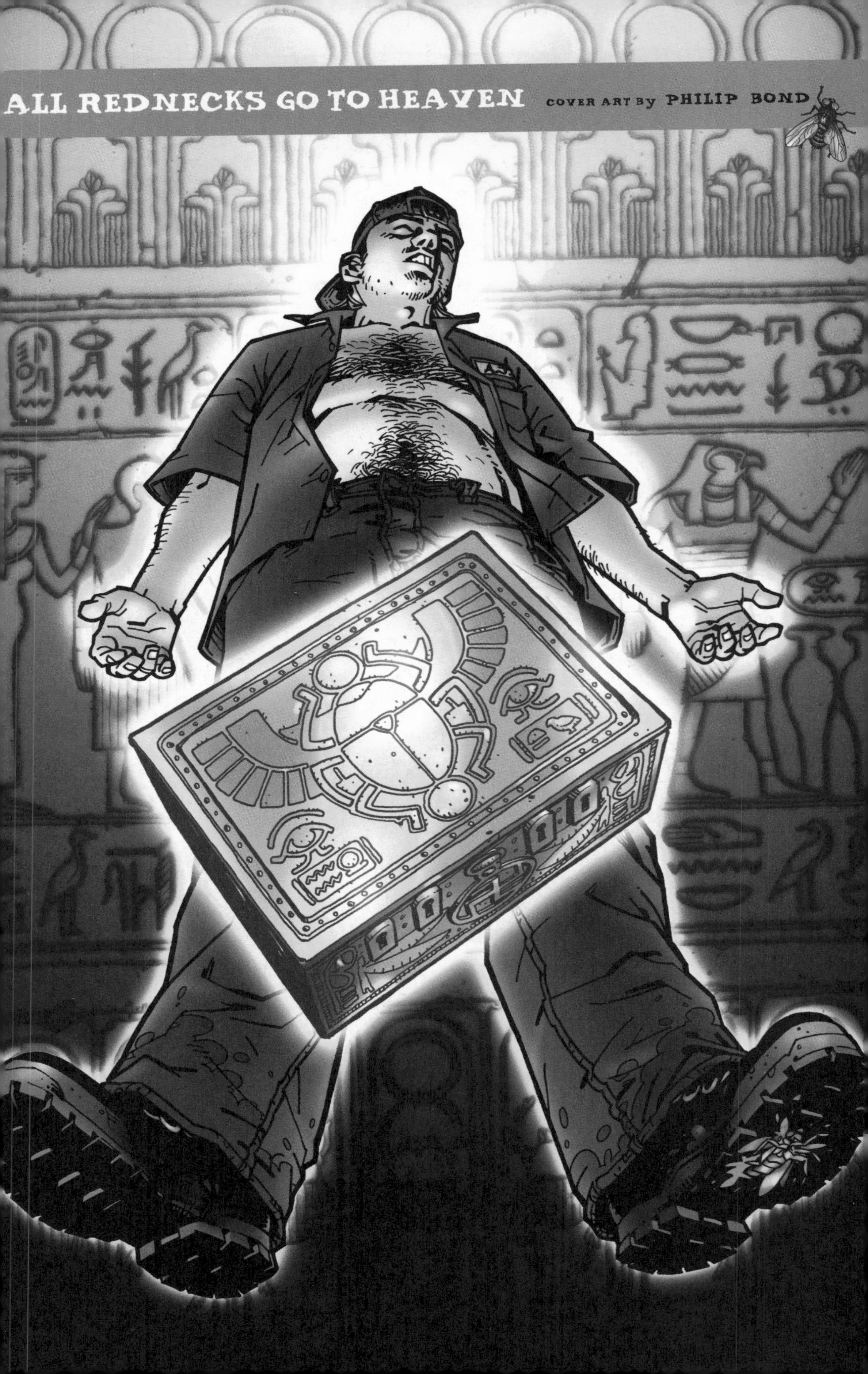
ALL REDNECKS GO TO HEAVEN
COVER ART BY PHILIP BOND
A.J.

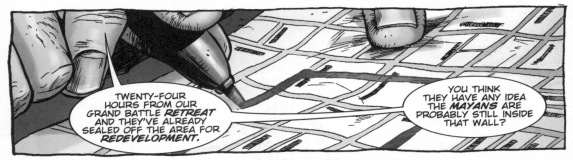

TWENTY-FOUR HOURS FROM OUR GRAND BATTLE *RETREAT* AND THEY'VE ALREADY SEALED OFF THE AREA FOR *REDEVELOPMENT.*

YOU THINK THEY HAVE ANY IDEA THE *MAYANS* ARE PROBABLY STILL INSIDE THAT WALL?

OCRAN TOWERS DEVELOPMENT? WELL, HENRY, I'M GUESSING IT'S PROBABLY HARD FOR LAURA TO JUSTIFY A MAYAN *BREEDING SANCTUARY* AS A LEGITIMATE TAX WRITE-OFF.

SO WHAT'S LAURA'S AND OCRAN'S CONNECTION TO THE MAYAN HISSERS, THEN?

I DON'T KNOW. BUT I KNOW I'M NOT BUYING INTO *COINCIDENCE* ON THIS, NOT ON THIS SCALE.

ABSOLUTELY —NO— TRESPASSING

FUTURE SITE OF THE OCRAN TOWERS DEVELOPMENT

BEE-GONE
BUG GONE

IF OCRAN'S TEAMED UP WITH AJ MARK II, HIS MAYAN HISSER ARMY AND A TEAM OF SOUTH SEAS KUNG FU DUDES TO DESTROY MANKIND--WHERE'S THE *PROFIT* ANGLE?

MAYBE IT'S *NOT* MONEY THIS TIME, BUT THERE'S A CONNECTION SOMEWHERE. AND SOMEONE WITHIN OCRAN HAS A REASON OTHER THAN REAL ESTATE DEVELOPMENT FOR THIS *WALL.*

WELL, IF THE MAYANS HAVE A HUMAN FIFTH COLUMN WITH THIS MUCH *POWER,* WE'RE GOING TO NEED TO CUT THEM OFF FAST.

I'M GONNA HAVE TO ASK YOU GOOD FOLKS TO *MOVE ON* NOW.

IT'S A *PUBLIC* STREET, ISN'T IT?

SECURITY

AS A GOVERNMENT-CONTRACTED CORPORATION, OCRAN HAS CERTAIN SECURITY RIGHTS GRANTED THEM UNDER THE PATRIOT ACT.

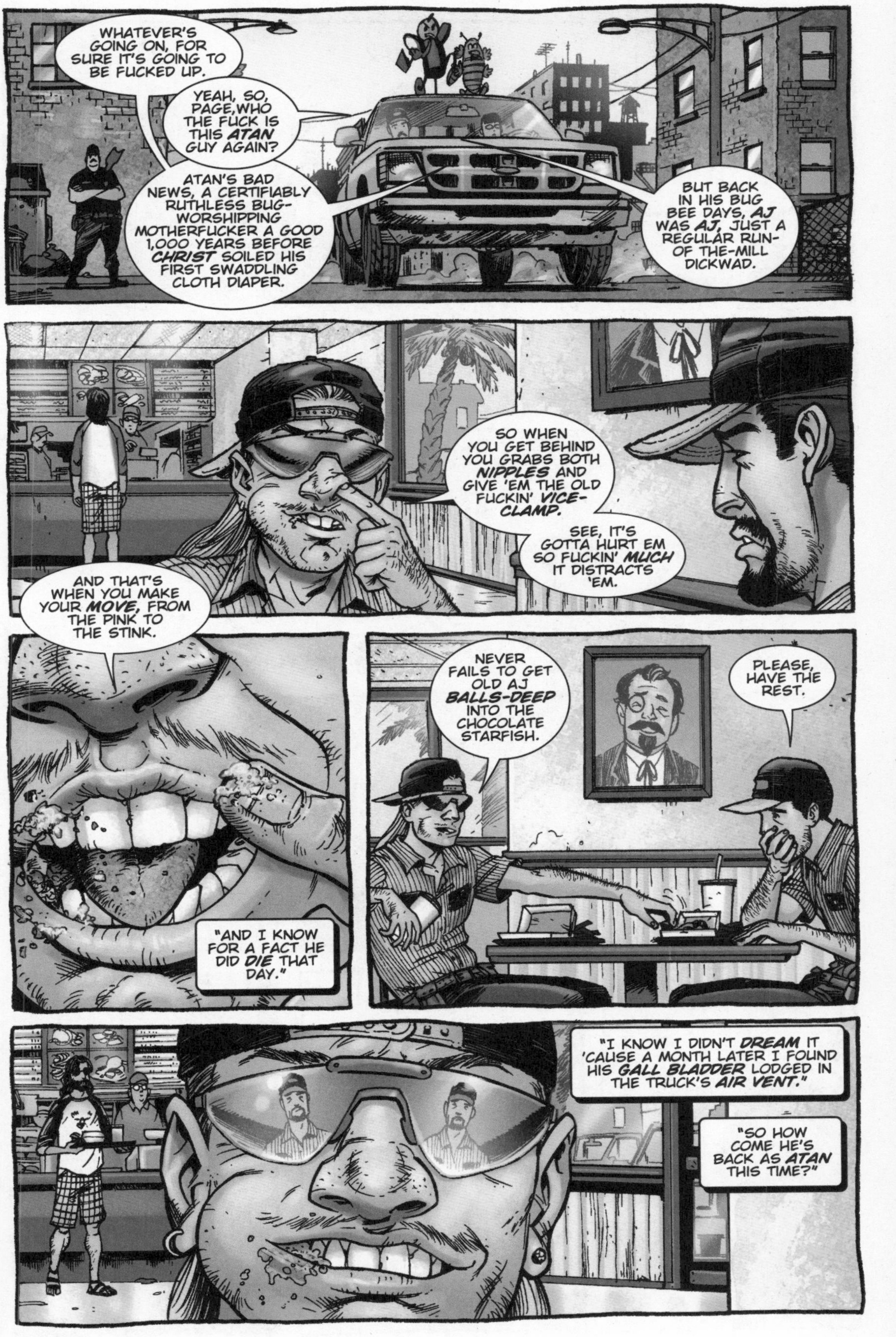
WHATEVER'S GOING ON, FOR SURE IT'S GOING TO BE FUCKED UP.
YEAH, SO, PAGE, WHO THE FUCK IS THIS ATAN GUY AGAIN?
ATAN'S BAD NEWS, A CERTIFIABLY RUTHLESS BUG-WORSHIPPING MOTHERFUCKER A GOOD 1,000 YEARS BEFORE CHRIST SOILED HIS FIRST SWADDLING CLOTH DIAPER.
BUT BACK IN HIS BUG BEE DAYS, AJ WAS AJ, JUST A REGULAR RUN-OF THE-MILL DICKWAD.
SO WHEN YOU GET BEHIND YOU GRABS BOTH NIPPLES AND GIVE 'EM THE OLD FUCKIN' VICE-CLAMP.
SEE, IT'S GOTTA HURT EM SO FUCKIN' MUCH IT DISTRACTS 'EM.
AND THAT'S WHEN YOU MAKE YOUR MOVE, FROM THE PINK TO THE STINK.
"AND I KNOW FOR A FACT HE DID DIE THAT DAY."
NEVER FAILS TO GET OLD AJ BALLS-DEEP INTO THE CHOCOLATE STARFISH.
PLEASE, HAVE THE REST.
"I KNOW I DIDN'T DREAM IT 'CAUSE A MONTH LATER I FOUND HIS GALL BLADDER LODGED IN THE TRUCK'S AIR VENT."
"SO HOW COME HE'S BACK AS ATAN THIS TIME?"

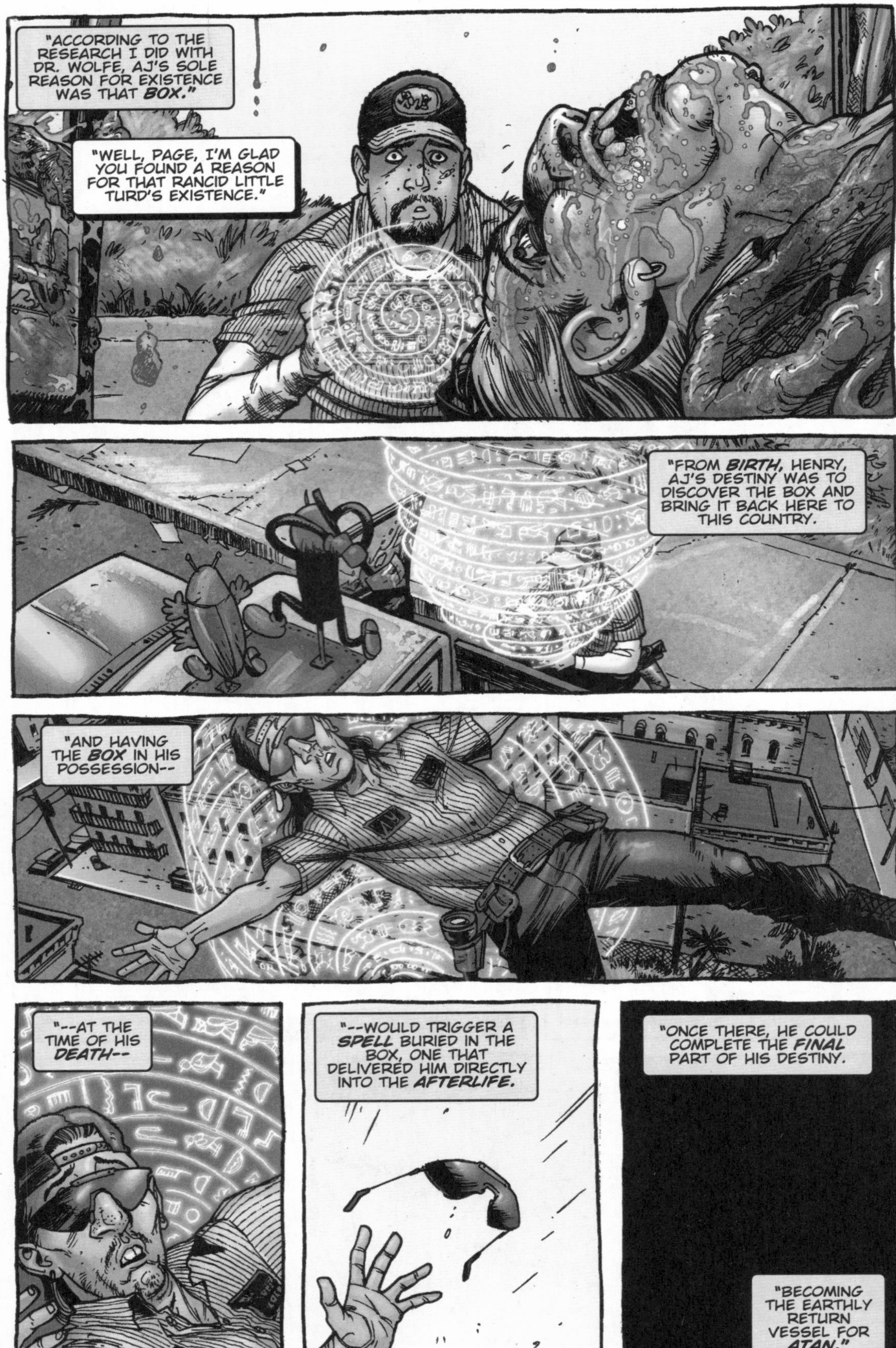
"ACCORDING TO THE RESEARCH I DID WITH DR. WOLFE, AJ'S SOLE REASON FOR EXISTENCE WAS THAT BOX."
"WELL, PAGE, I'M GLAD YOU FOUND A REASON FOR THAT RANCID LITTLE TURD'S EXISTENCE."
"FROM BIRTH, HENRY, AJ'S DESTINY WAS TO DISCOVER THE BOX AND BRING IT BACK HERE TO THIS COUNTRY.
"AND HAVING THE BOX IN HIS POSSESSION--
"--AT THE TIME OF HIS DEATH--
"--WOULD TRIGGER A SPELL BURIED IN THE BOX, ONE THAT DELIVERED HIM DIRECTLY INTO THE AFTERLIFE.
"ONCE THERE, HE COULD COMPLETE THE FINAL PART OF HIS DESTINY.
"BECOMING THE EARTHLY RETURN VESSEL FOR ATAN."

33

"HALL OF JUDGMENT" IS A BIT *MISLEADING*, REALLY. MORE OF A CLEARING HOUSE. THE REAL *JUDGING* BUSINESS IS ALL DONE OUT HERE.

QUITE A CROWD. BEEN A LONG TIME SINCE THEY HAD ANY "NEW BLOOD" COME IN.

WHAT THE FUCK IS ALL *THIS*?

SMALL *FORMALITY*, REALLY.

JUST WEIGHING YOUR *HEART* AGAINST THE SACRED *FEATHER OF PURITY*.

HEY, WHERE THE FUCK YOU GET *THAT???*

BOOK OF THE DEAD, PARAGRAPH 4, CLAUSE 6: "PREREQUISITE, BEFORE ALLOWING ENTRY TO THE AFTERLIFE, WE HAVE TO ASCERTAIN THE PURITY OF THE APPLICANT'S HEART."

IS THAT *BAD*?

QUITE *EXTRAORDINARY*, ACTUALLY. WHAT DID YOU GET *UP TO* ON EARTH?

EVEN *TOTH THE INFANT DEFILER* COULDN'T TIP THE SCALES DOWN THIS FAR, LET ALONE BREAK THEM.

SO I LIKE TO PARTY SOME. AND SINCE WHEN'S THAT A FUCKING *CRIME* IN VEGAS?

DID THAT SKANKY BITCH IN BAKERSFIELD SET ME UP TO THIS? 'CAUSE SHE GAVE ME CRABS.

SORRY, THIS IS A SECTION 5 ISSUE, IT'S REALLY *OUT* OF MY HANDS.

SUMMON *AMMIT*.

THIS ISN'T FUCKING *VEGAS*, IS IT?

NO, AJ.

YOU'RE ACTUALLY *DEAD*.

DEAD?

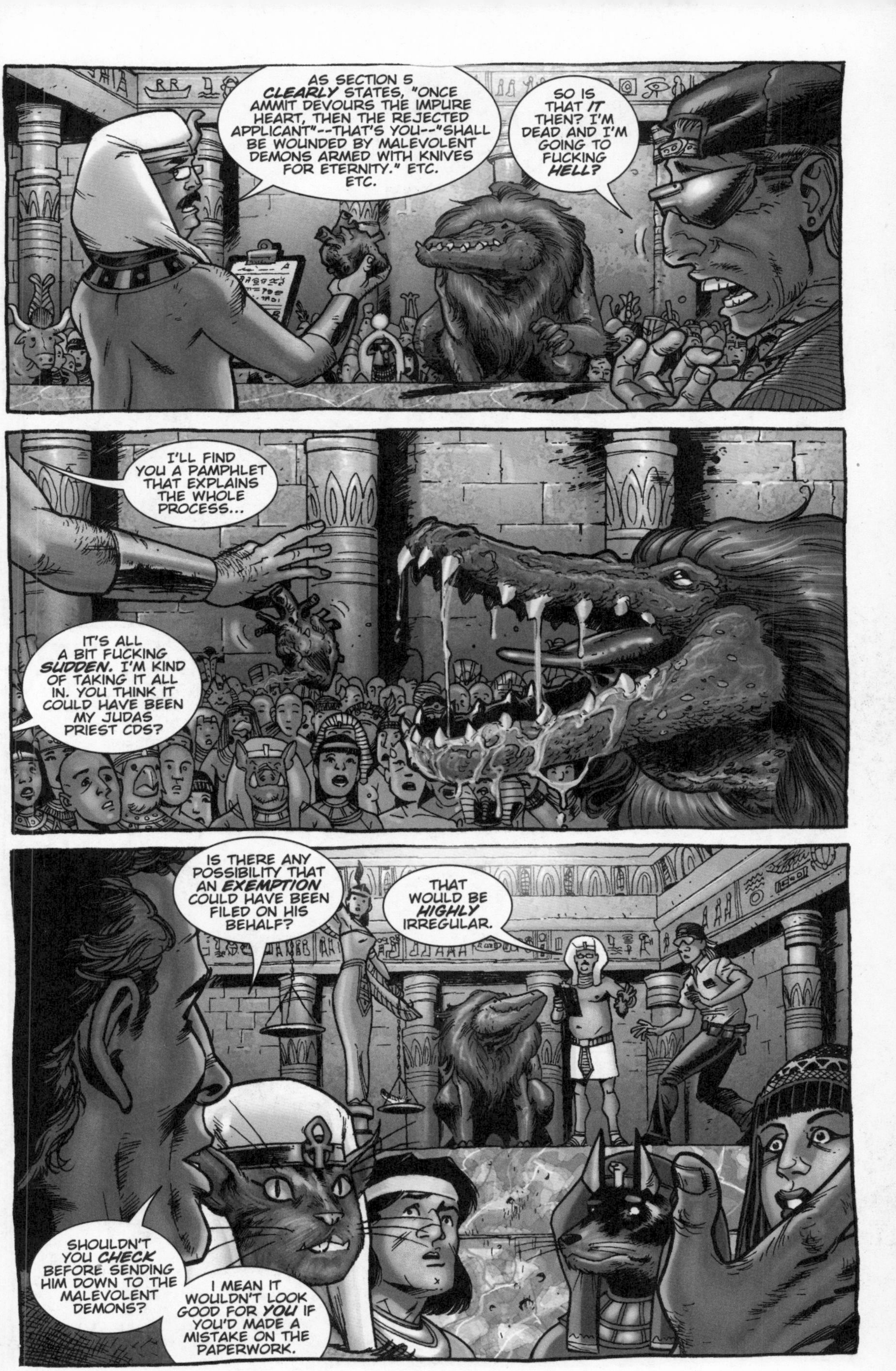
AS SECTION 5 CLEARLY STATES, "ONCE AMMIT DEVOURS THE IMPURE HEART, THEN THE REJECTED APPLICANT"--THAT'S YOU--"SHALL BE WOUNDED BY MALEVOLENT DEMONS ARMED WITH KNIVES FOR ETERNITY." ETC. ETC.
SO IS THAT IT THEN? I'M DEAD AND I'M GOING TO FUCKING HELL?
I'LL FIND YOU A PAMPHLET THAT EXPLAINS THE WHOLE PROCESS...
IT'S ALL A BIT FUCKING SUDDEN. I'M KIND OF TAKING IT ALL IN. YOU THINK IT COULD HAVE BEEN MY JUDAS PRIEST CDS?
IS THERE ANY POSSIBILITY THAT AN EXEMPTION COULD HAVE BEEN FILED ON HIS BEHALF?
THAT WOULD BE HIGHLY IRREGULAR.
SHOULDN'T YOU CHECK BEFORE SENDING HIM DOWN TO THE MALEVOLENT DEMONS?
I MEAN IT WOULDN'T LOOK GOOD FOR YOU IF YOU'D MADE A MISTAKE ON THE PAPERWORK.

THAT BRAINLESS, SPOILED *FRAT BOY* TUT! 3,000 YEARS I'VE WAITED FOR MY RIDE OUT OF HERE AND HE LURES HIM AWAY FOR A *GODDAMN KEG PARTY.*

EONS AGO

KING ATAN, THE *MOB* HAVE BROKEN THROUGH OUR LINES AND THEY'RE ADVANCING ON THE *PALACE.*

SOMEONE IN OUR RANKS BETRAYED THE SECRET OF THE *BUG'S* SOLITARY *WEAKNESS.*

IN TIME IT WILL SLIP FROM MANKIND'S COLLECTIVE MEMORY. BUT FOR *THIS* AGE THE BATTLE IS *LOST.*

FOR NOW, MY SWEET KHEPRON, I HAVE *FAILED* YOU.

HAVE ALL THE ARRANGEMENTS BEEN MADE FOR MY *DEPARTURE?*

YES SIR.

37

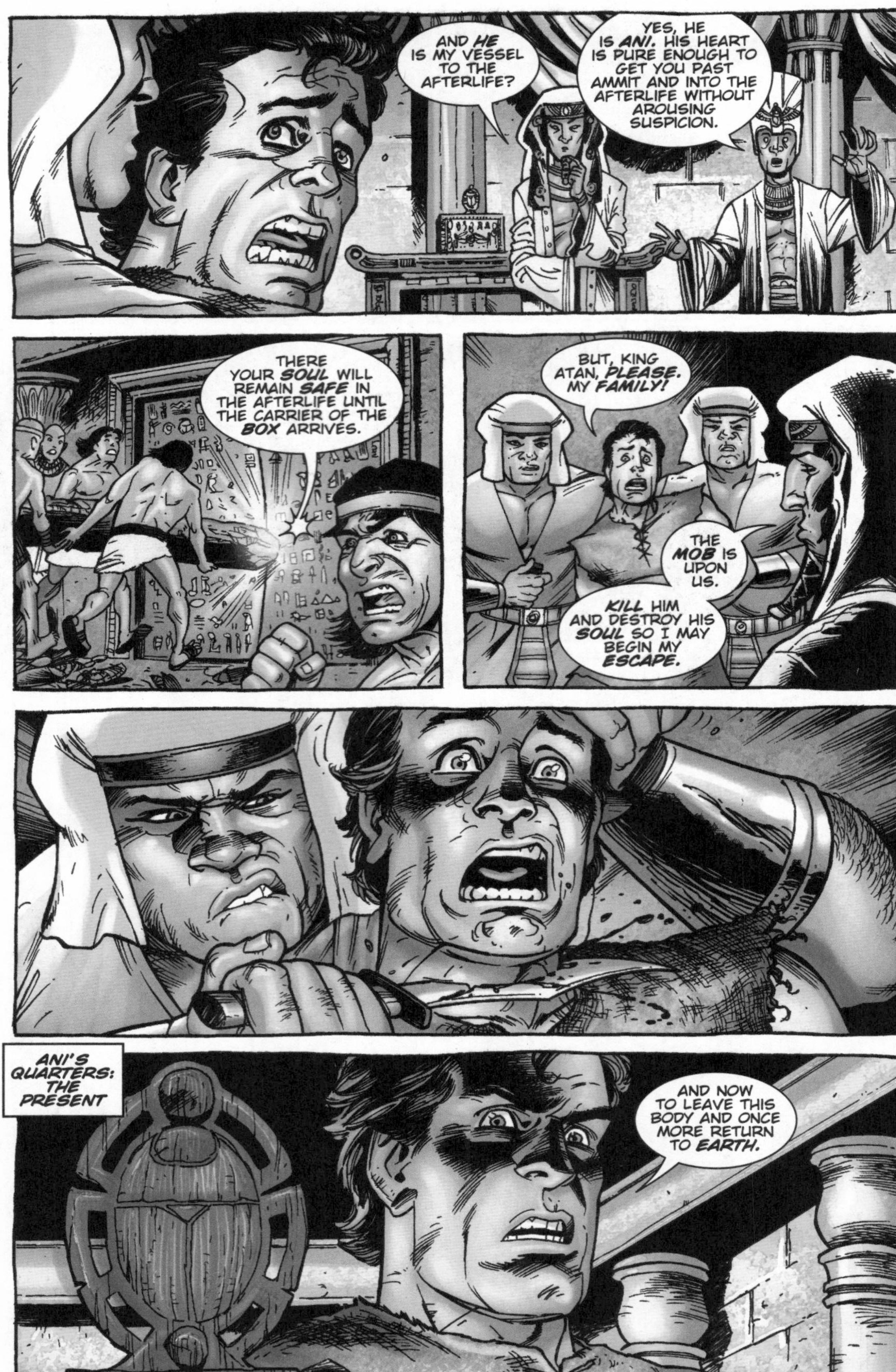
AND HE IS MY VESSEL TO THE AFTERLIFE?
YES, HE IS ANI. HIS HEART IS PURE ENOUGH TO GET YOU PAST AMMIT AND INTO THE AFTERLIFE WITHOUT AROUSING SUSPICION.
THERE YOUR SOUL WILL REMAIN SAFE IN THE AFTERLIFE UNTIL THE CARRIER OF THE BOX ARRIVES.
BUT, KING ATAN, PLEASE. MY FAMILY!
THE MOB IS UPON US.
KILL HIM AND DESTROY HIS SOUL SO I MAY BEGIN MY ESCAPE.
ANI'S QUARTERS: THE PRESENT
AND NOW TO LEAVE THIS BODY AND ONCE MORE RETURN TO EARTH.

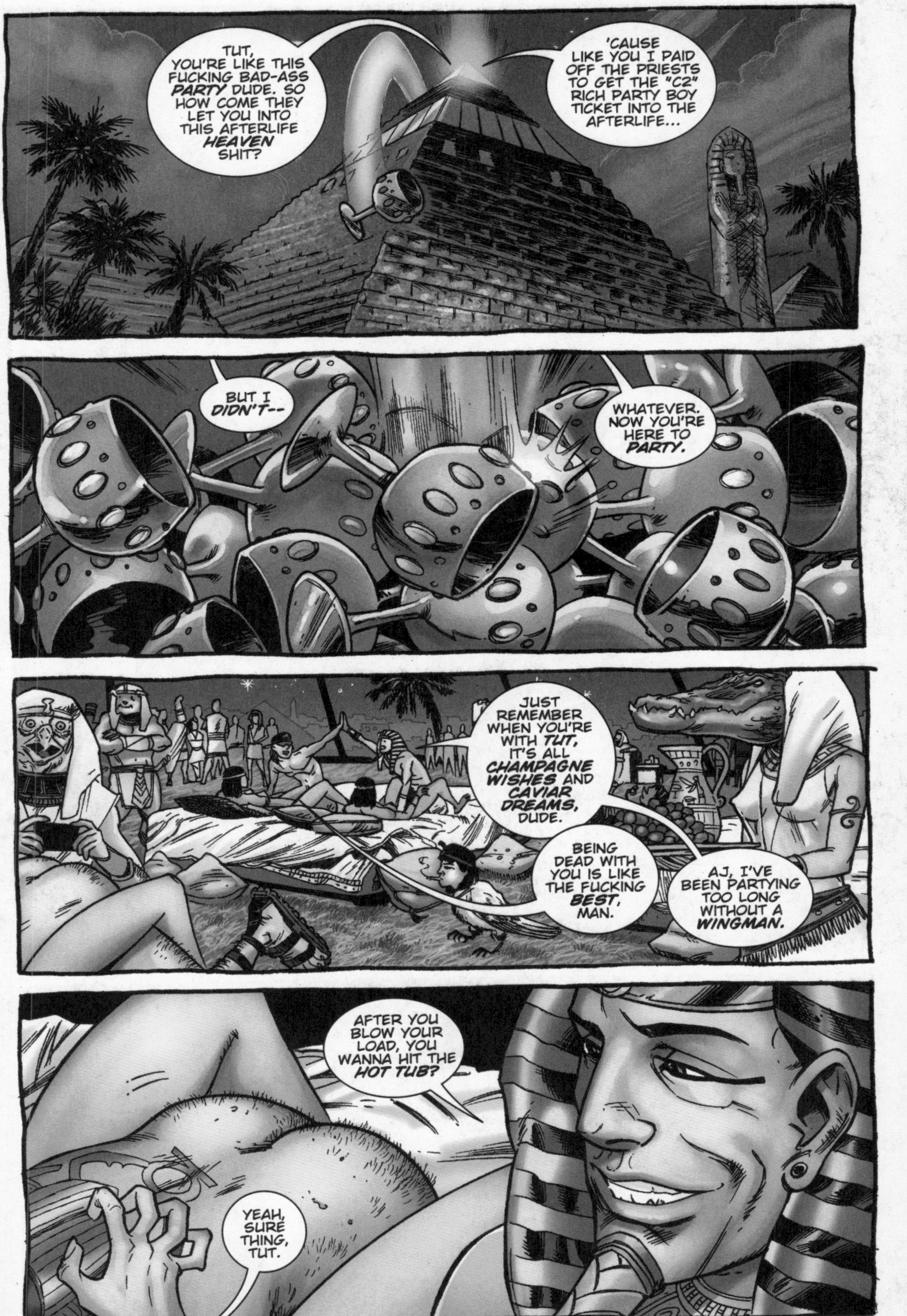
TUT, YOU'RE LIKE THIS FUCKING BAD-ASS *PARTY* DUDE. SO HOW COME THEY LET YOU INTO THIS AFTERLIFE *HEAVEN* SHIT?
'CAUSE LIKE YOU I PAID OFF THE PRIESTS TO GET THE "C2" RICH PARTY BOY TICKET INTO THE AFTERLIFE...
BUT I *DIDN'T--*
WHATEVER. NOW YOU'RE HERE TO *PARTY.*
JUST REMEMBER WHEN YOU'RE WITH *TUT,* IT'S ALL *CHAMPAGNE WISHES* AND *CAVIAR DREAMS,* DUDE.
BEING DEAD WITH YOU IS LIKE THE FUCKING *BEST,* MAN.
AJ, I'VE BEEN PARTYING TOO LONG WITHOUT A *WINGMAN.*
AFTER YOU BLOW YOUR LOAD, YOU WANNA HIT THE *HOT TUB?*
YEAH, SURE THING, TUT.

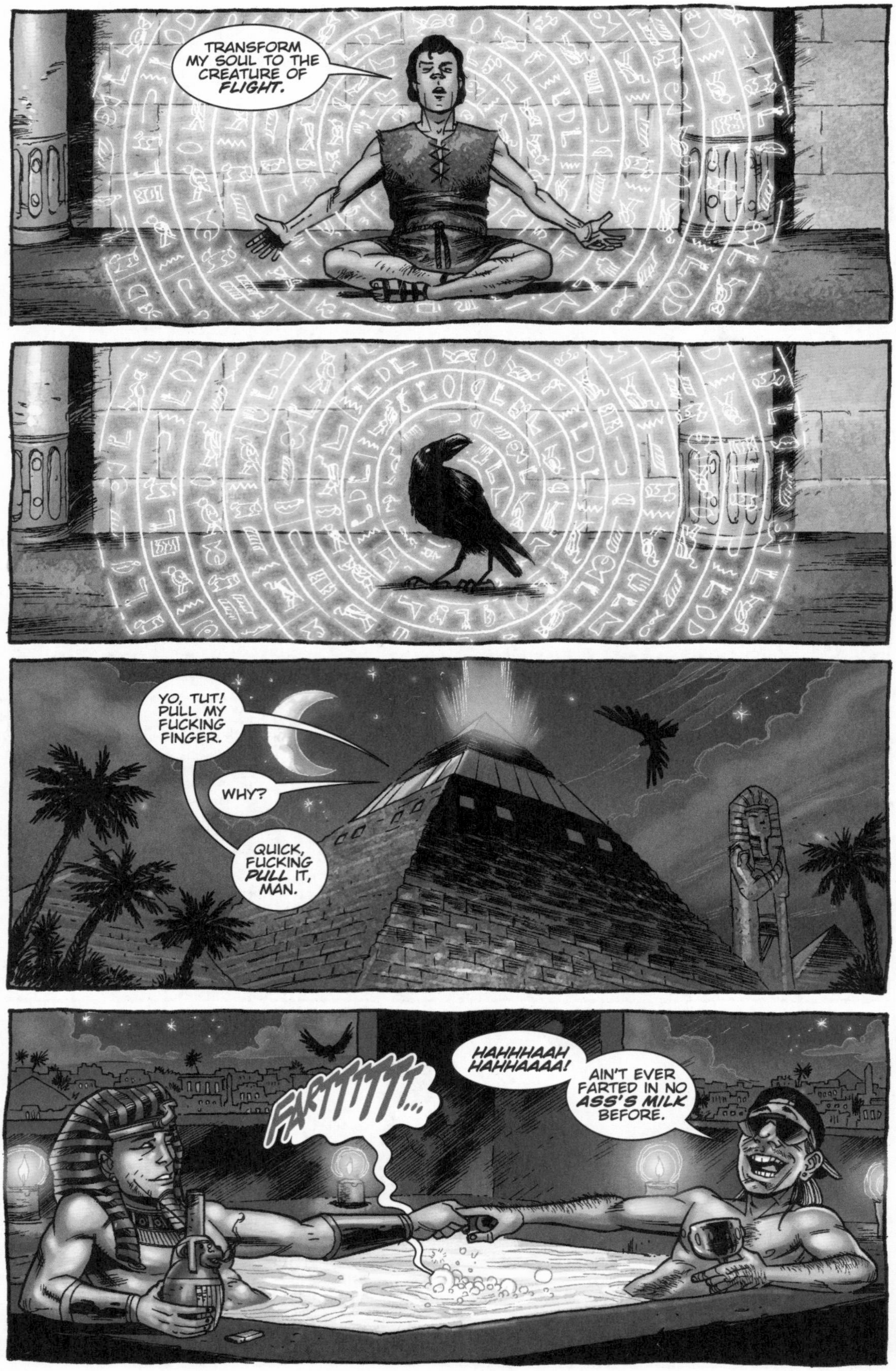
TRANSFORM MY SOUL TO THE CREATURE OF *FLIGHT.*
YO, TUT! PULL MY FUCKING FINGER.
WHY?
QUICK, FUCKING *PULL* IT, MAN.
FARTTTTTT...
HAHHHAAH HAHHAAAA!
AIN'T EVER FARTED IN NO *ASS'S MILK* BEFORE.

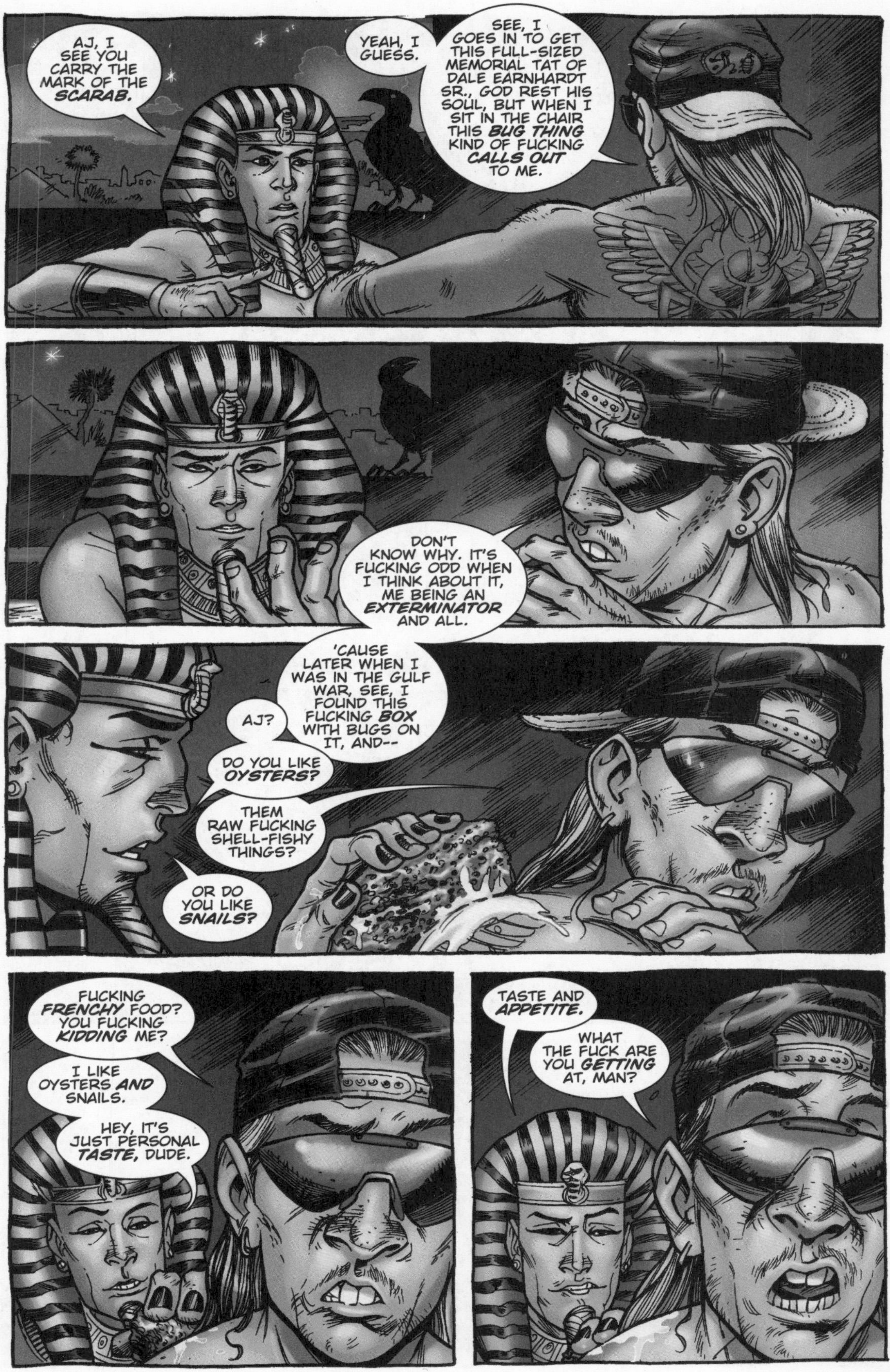
AJ, I SEE YOU CARRY THE MARK OF THE SCARAB.
YEAH, I GUESS.
SEE, I GOES IN TO GET THIS FULL-SIZED MEMORIAL TAT OF DALE EARNHARDT SR., GOD REST HIS SOUL, BUT WHEN I SIT IN THE CHAIR THIS BUG THING KIND OF FUCKING CALLS OUT TO ME.
DON'T KNOW WHY. IT'S FUCKING ODD WHEN I THINK ABOUT IT, ME BEING AN EXTERMINATOR AND ALL.
'CAUSE LATER WHEN I WAS IN THE GULF WAR, SEE, I FOUND THIS FUCKING BOX WITH BUGS ON IT, AND--
AJ?
DO YOU LIKE OYSTERS?
THEM RAW FUCKING SHELL-FISHY THINGS?
OR DO YOU LIKE SNAILS?
FUCKING FRENCHY FOOD? YOU FUCKING KIDDING ME?
I LIKE OYSTERS AND SNAILS.
HEY, IT'S JUST PERSONAL TASTE, DUDE.
TASTE AND APPETITE.
WHAT THE FUCK ARE YOU GETTING AT, MAN?

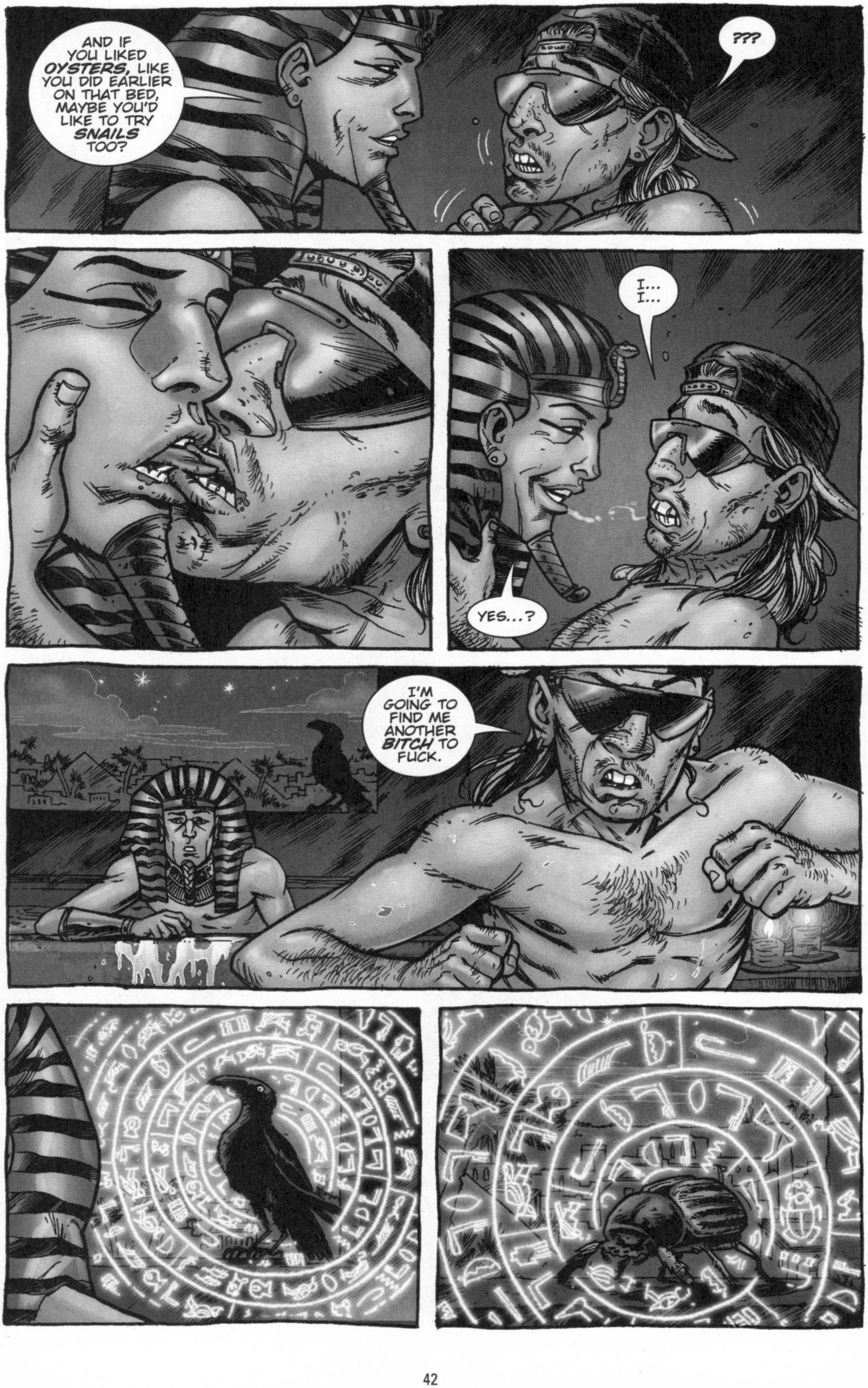
AND IF YOU LIKED OYSTERS, LIKE YOU DID EARLIER ON THAT BED, MAYBE YOU'D LIKE TO TRY SNAILS TOO?
???
I... I...
YES...?
I'M GOING TO FIND ME ANOTHER BITCH TO FUCK.

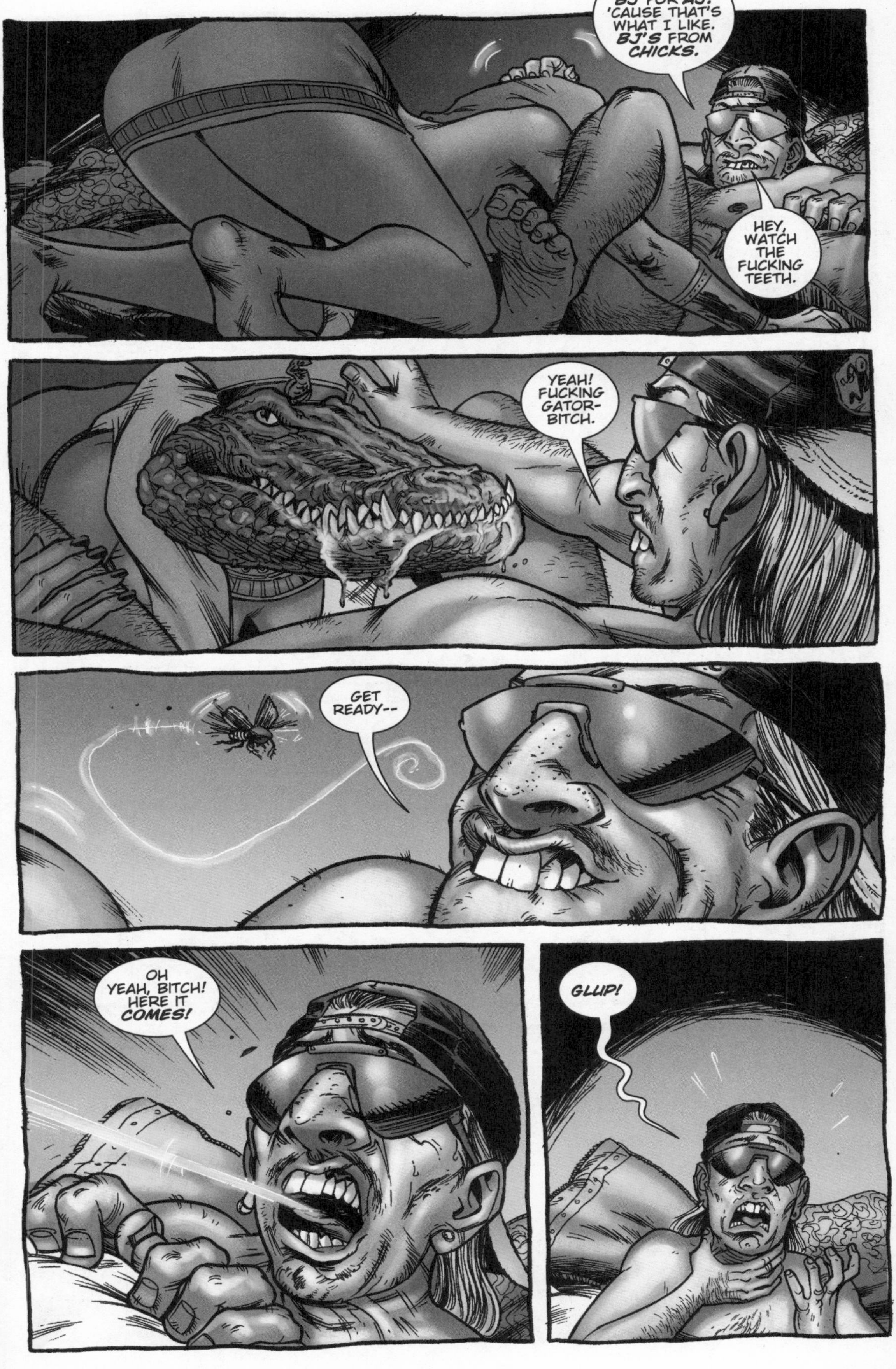
A FUCKING BJ FOR AJ. 'CAUSE THAT'S WHAT I LIKE. BJ'S FROM CHICKS.
HEY, WATCH THE FUCKING TEETH.
YEAH! FUCKING GATOR-BITCH.
GET READY--
OH YEAH, BITCH! HERE IT COMES!
GLUP!

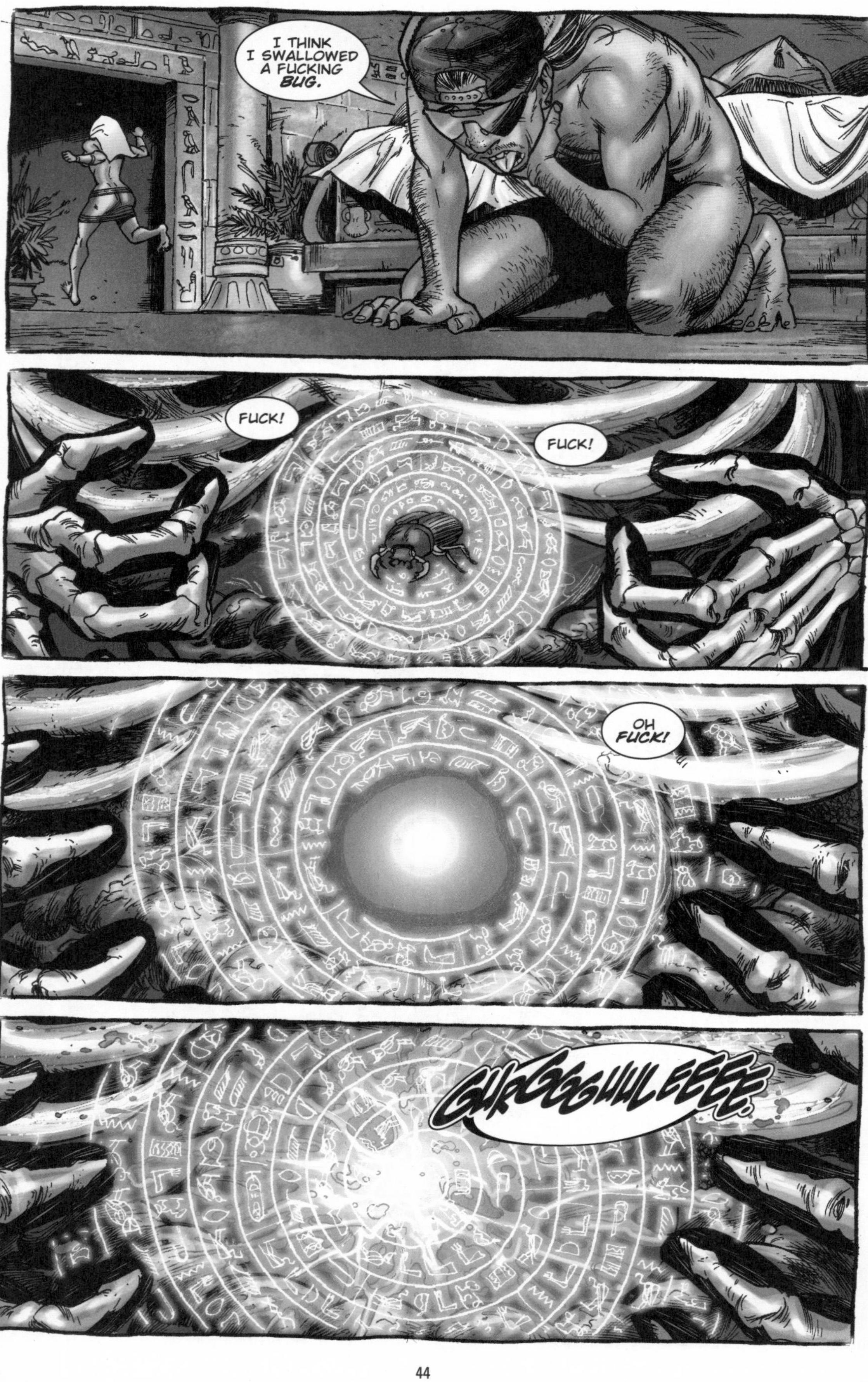
I THINK I SWALLOWED A FUCKING BUG.
FUCK!
FUCK!
OH FUCK!
GURGGGUULEEEE.

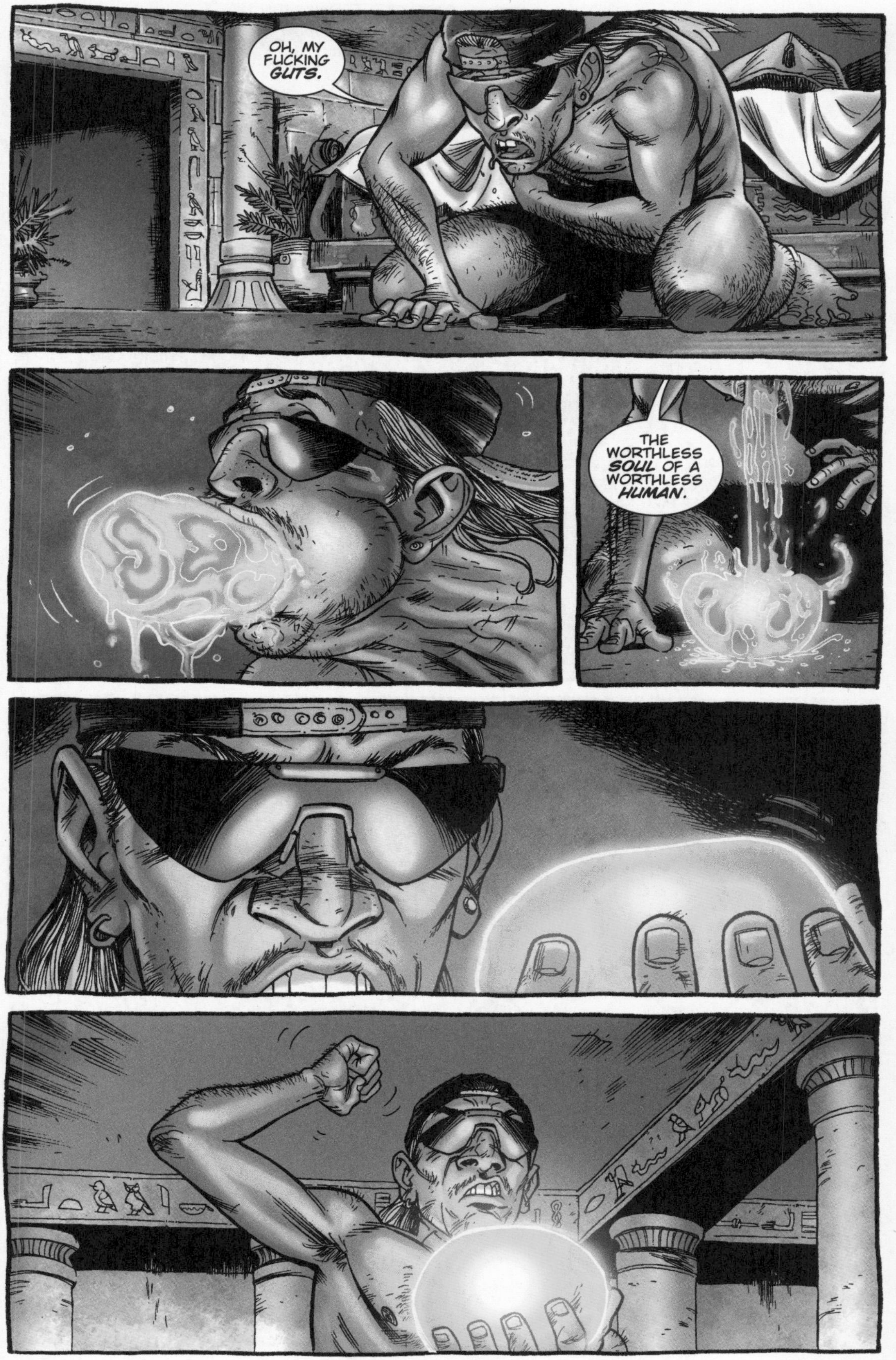
OH, MY FUCKING GUTS.
THE WORTHLESS SOUL OF A WORTHLESS HUMAN.

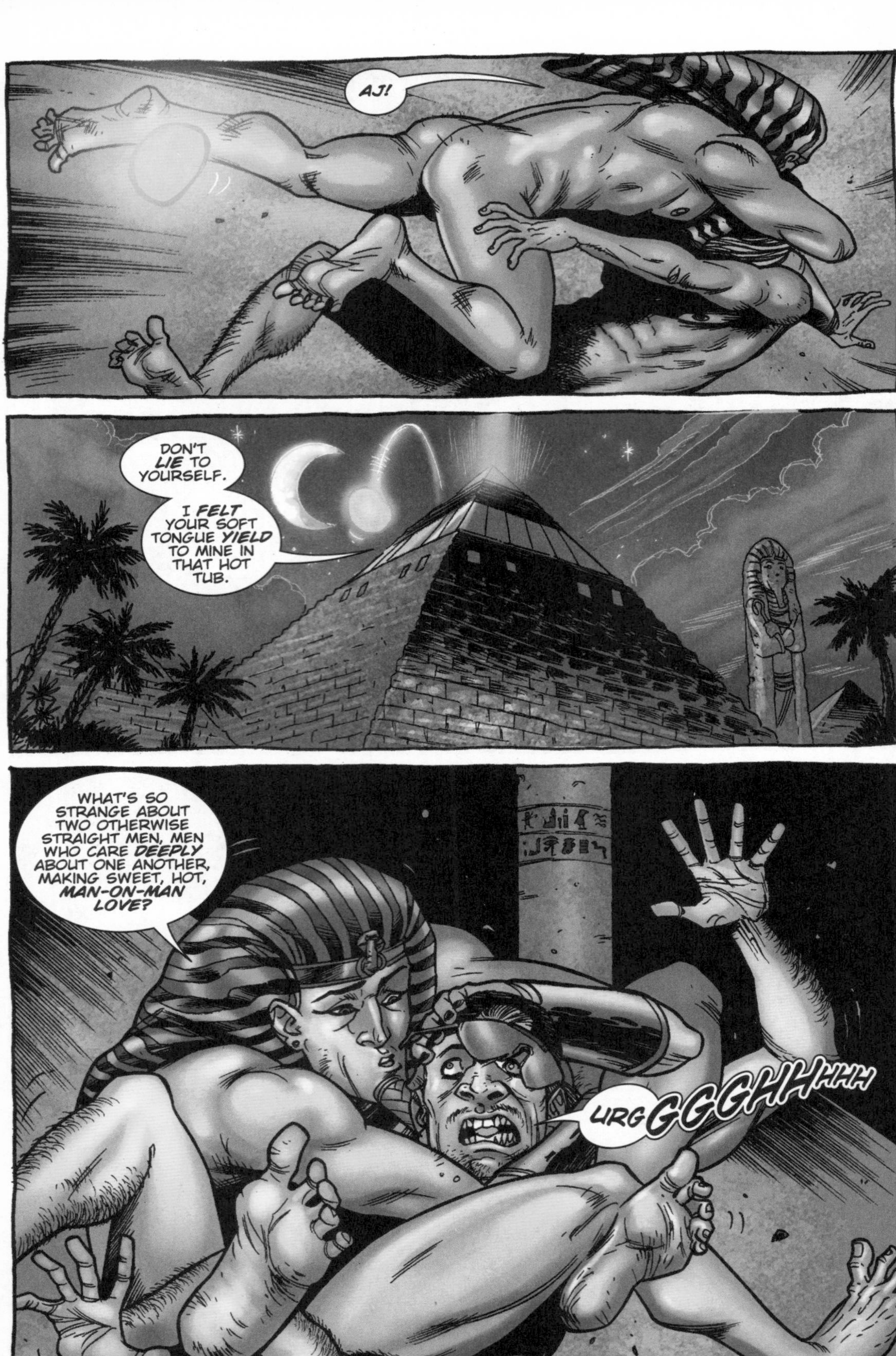
AJ!
DON'T LIE TO YOURSELF.
I FELT YOUR SOFT TONGUE YIELD TO MINE IN THAT HOT TUB.
WHAT'S SO STRANGE ABOUT TWO OTHERWISE STRAIGHT MEN, MEN WHO CARE DEEPLY ABOUT ONE ANOTHER, MAKING SWEET, HOT, MAN-ON-MAN LOVE?
URGGGGHHHHHH

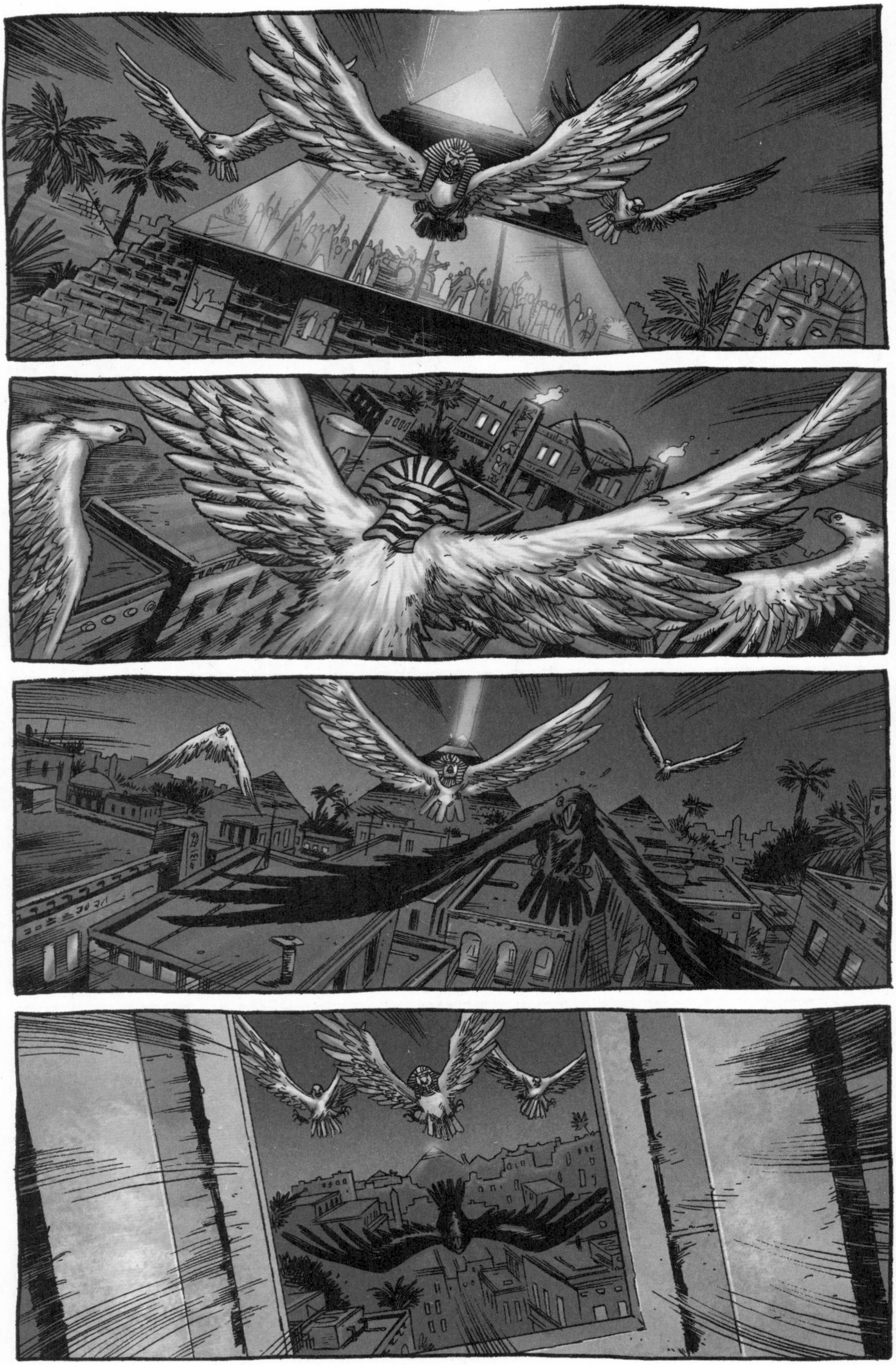

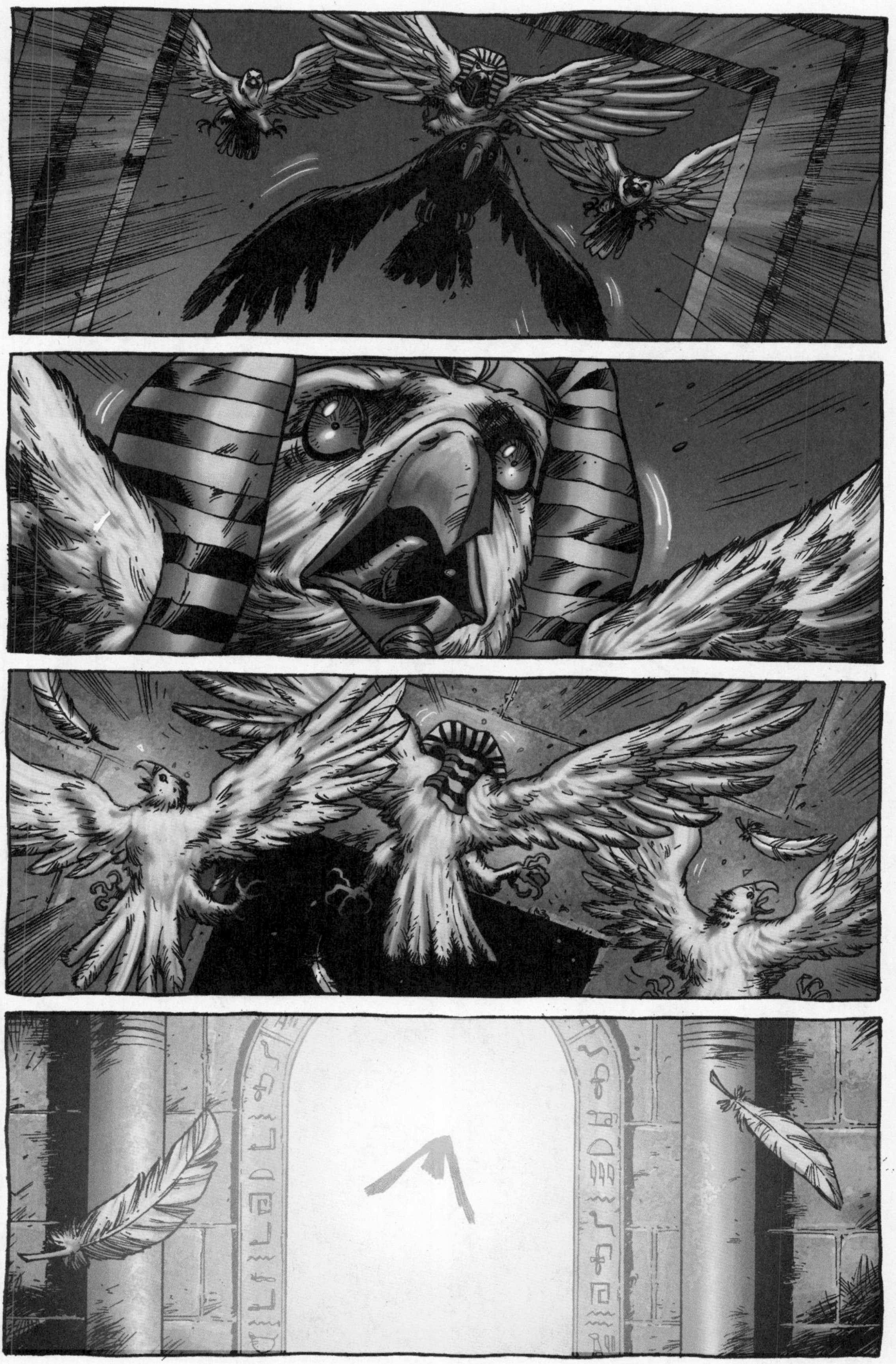

WHAT'S YOUR *NAME*, NAKED WHITE MAN?

HE AIN'T *MOVING*, BRO...

PLEASE GET YOUR DOG'S *TONGUE* OUT OF MY *ASS*.

SO WHAT'S YOUR *NAME*, MISTER?

LEAVE HIM BE, SILAS. DUDE JUST FELL FROM THE *SKY*, LIKE FUCKING *E.T.*

MY NAME--MY NAME IS, ER, *BJ*?

YOU MAY WANNA *RETHINK* THAT, MISTER.

CJ, THEN?

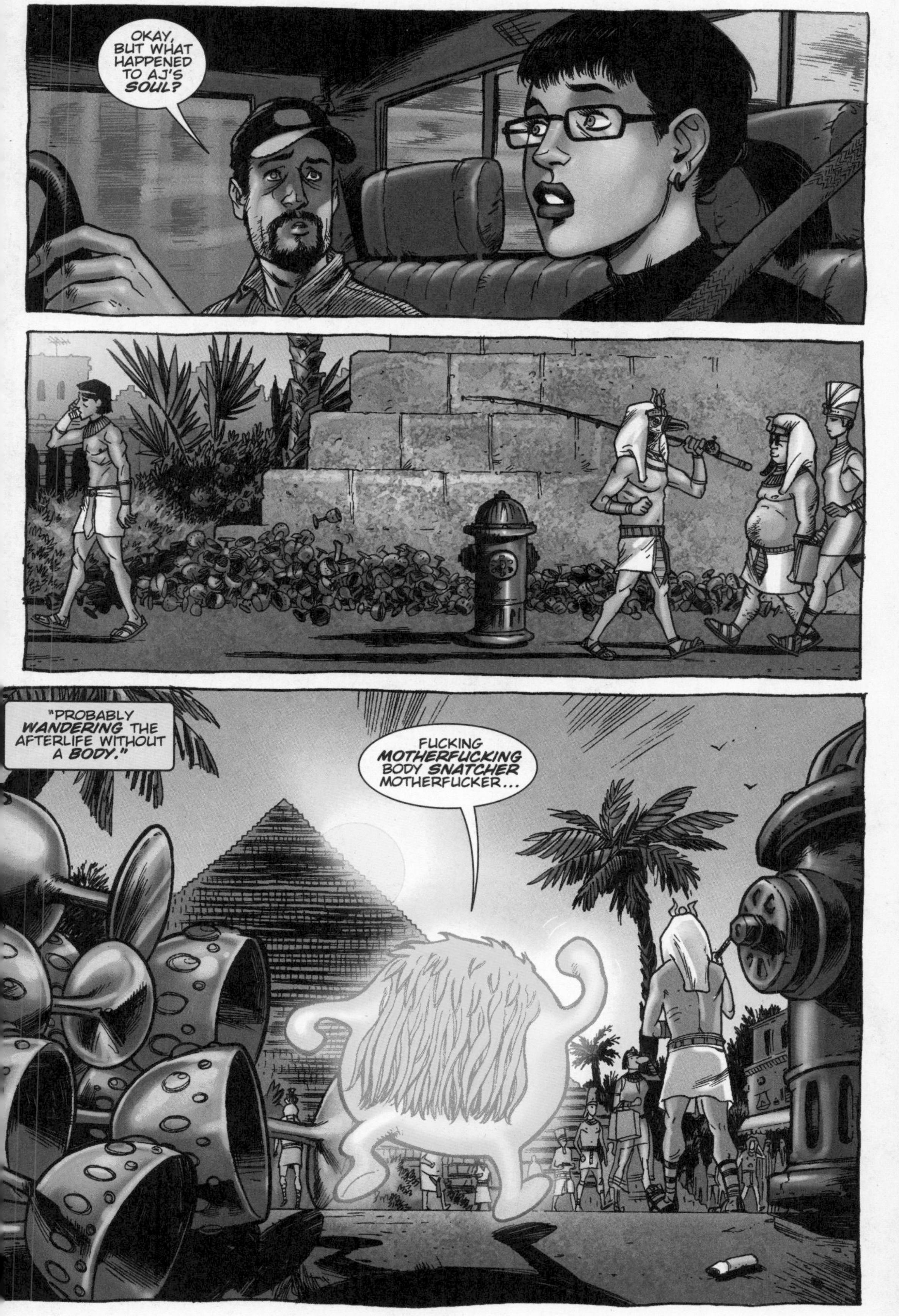
OKAY, BUT WHAT HAPPENED TO AJ'S SOUL?
"PROBABLY WANDERING THE AFTERLIFE WITHOUT A BODY."
FUCKING MOTHERFUCKING BODY SNATCHER MOTHERFUCKER...

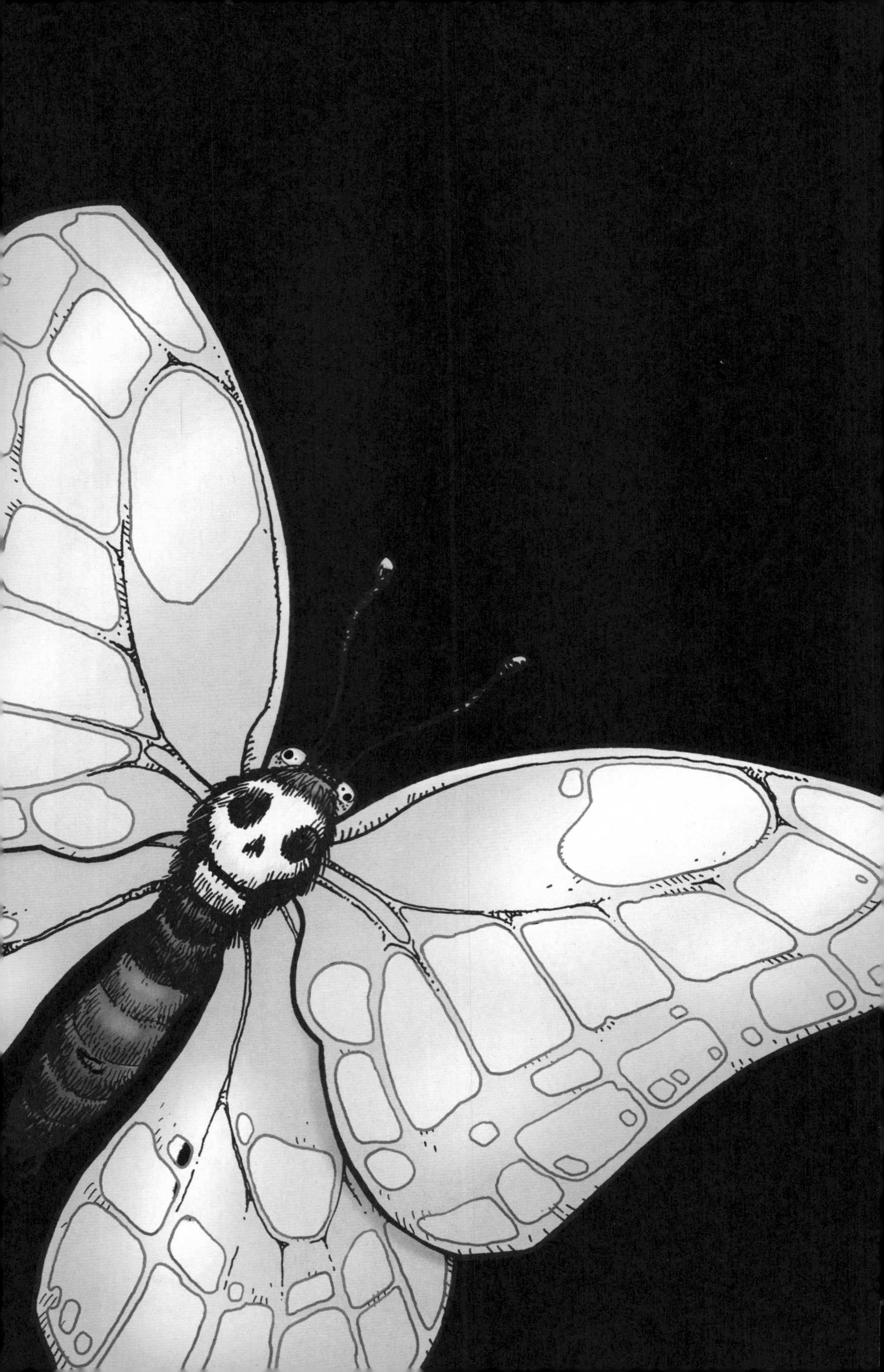

LAURA GOES DOWN cover art by PHILIP BOND and DAVID HAHN

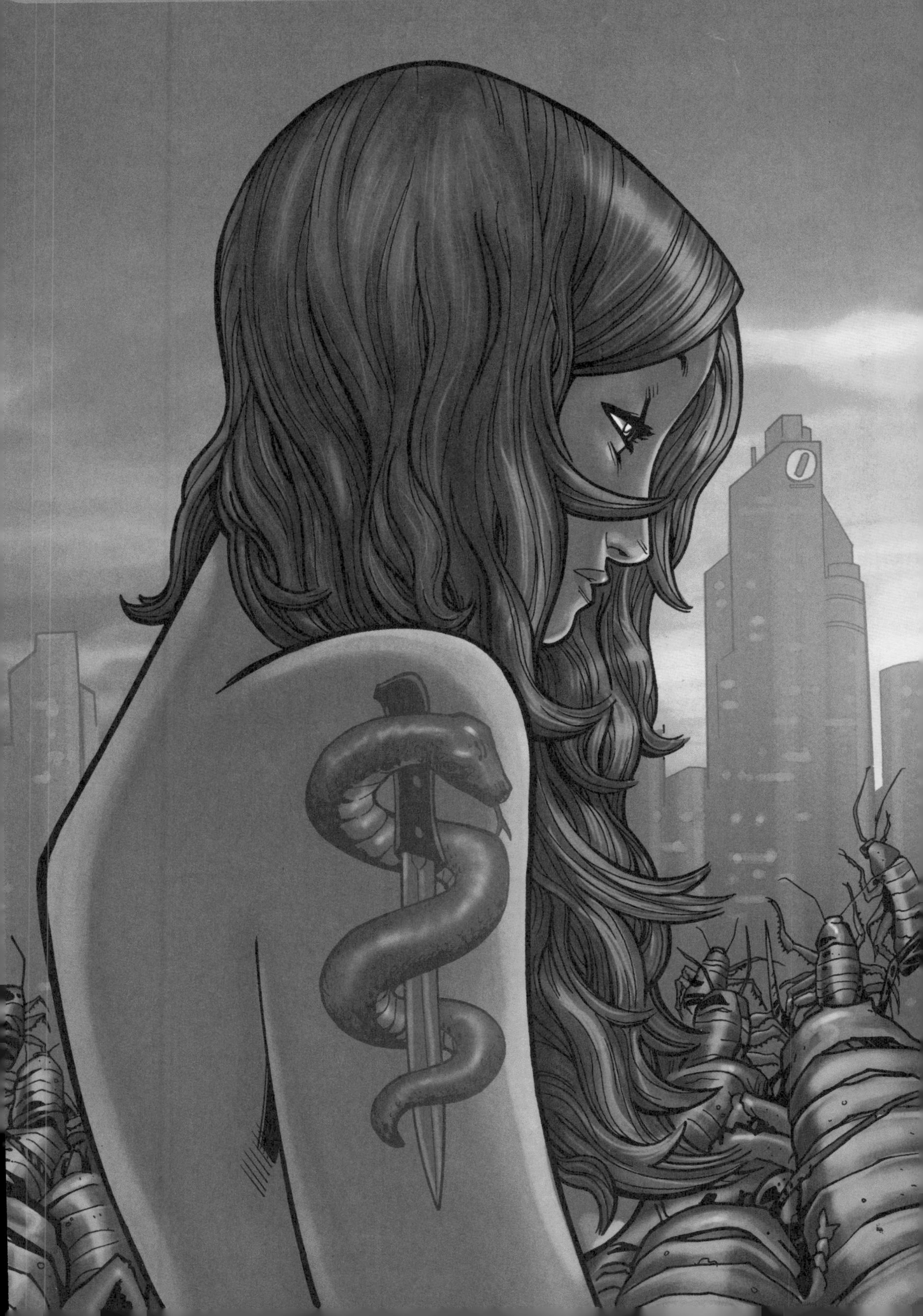

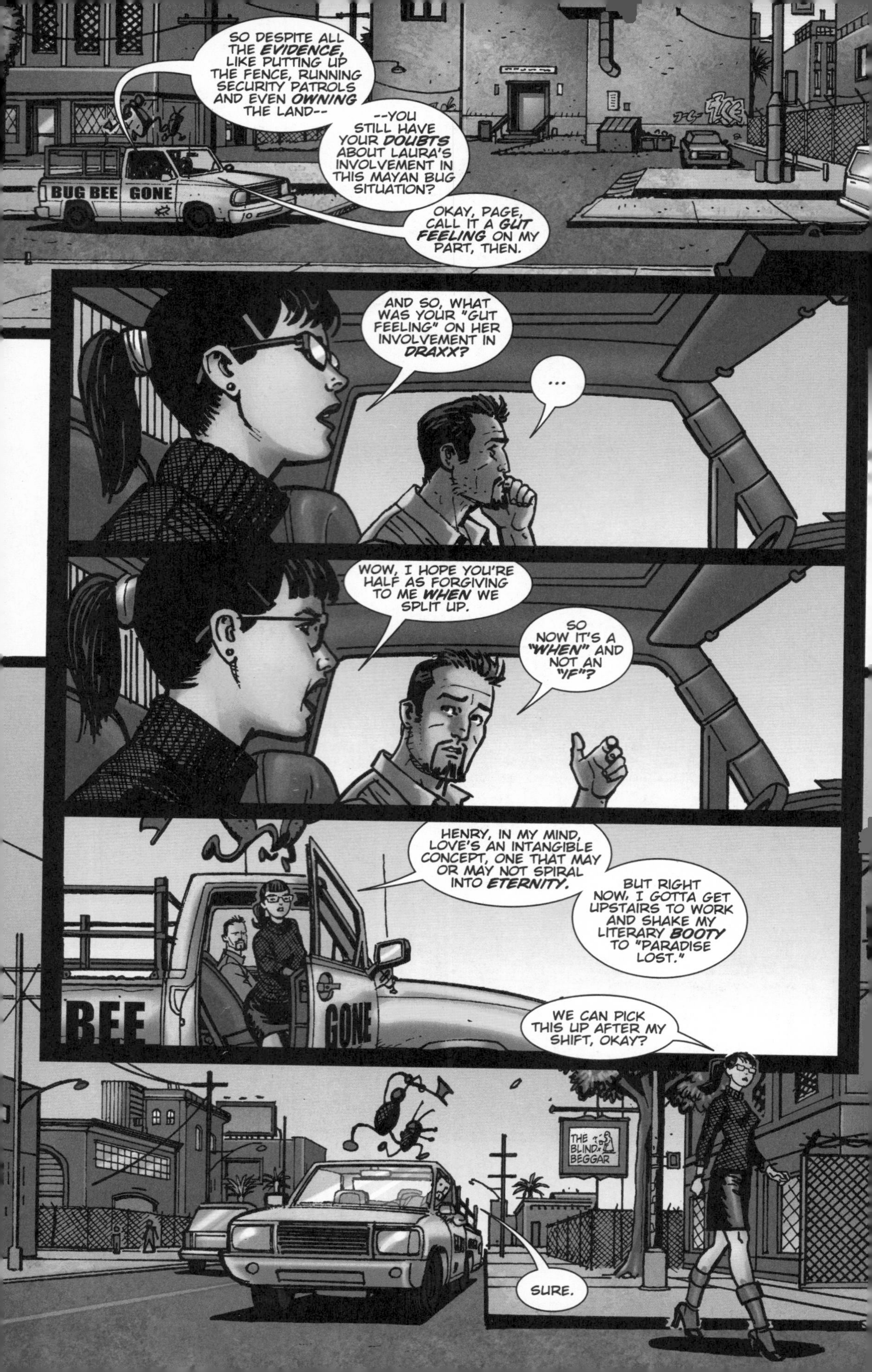
SO DESPITE ALL THE EVIDENCE, LIKE PUTTING UP THE FENCE, RUNNING SECURITY PATROLS AND EVEN OWNING THE LAND--
--YOU STILL HAVE YOUR DOUBTS ABOUT LAURA'S INVOLVEMENT IN THIS MAYAN BUG SITUATION?
OKAY, PAGE, CALL IT A GUT FEELING ON MY PART, THEN.
BUG BEE GONE
AND SO, WHAT WAS YOUR "GUT FEELING" ON HER INVOLVEMENT IN DRAXX?
...
WOW, I HOPE YOU'RE HALF AS FORGIVING TO ME WHEN WE SPLIT UP.
SO NOW IT'S A "WHEN" AND NOT AN "IF"?
HENRY, IN MY MIND, LOVE'S AN INTANGIBLE CONCEPT, ONE THAT MAY OR MAY NOT SPIRAL INTO ETERNITY.
BUT RIGHT NOW, I GOTTA GET UPSTAIRS TO WORK AND SHAKE MY LITERARY BOOTY TO "PARADISE LOST."
BEE GONE
WE CAN PICK THIS UP AFTER MY SHIFT, OKAY?
THE BLIND BEGGAR
SURE.

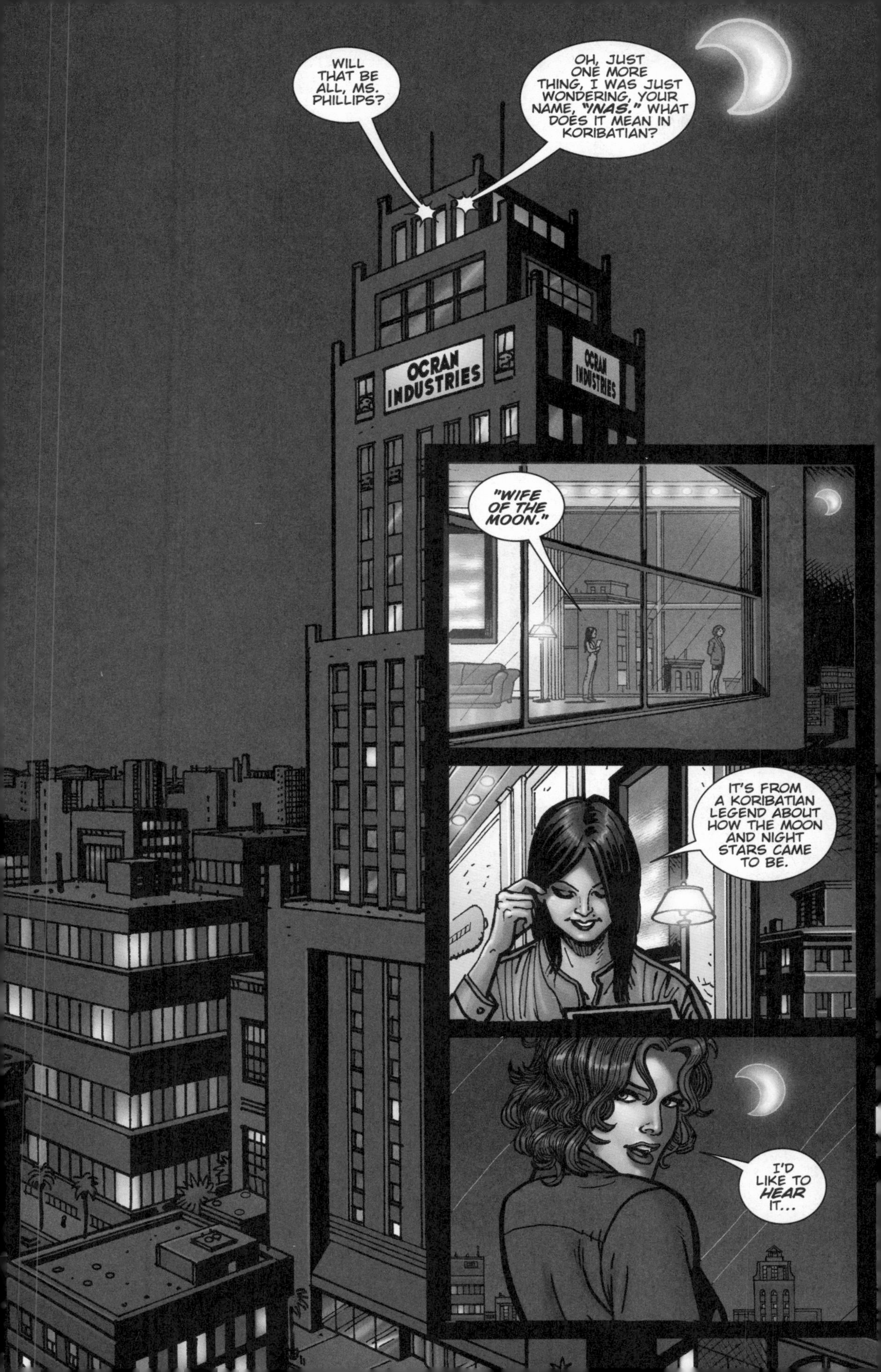
WILL THAT BE ALL, MS. PHILLIPS?
OH, JUST ONE MORE THING, I WAS JUST WONDERING, YOUR NAME, *"INAS."* WHAT DOES IT MEAN IN KORIBATIAN?
OCRAN INDUSTRIES
OCRAN INDUSTRIES
"WIFE OF THE MOON."
IT'S FROM A KORIBATIAN LEGEND ABOUT HOW THE MOON AND NIGHT STARS CAME TO BE.
I'D LIKE TO *HEAR* IT...

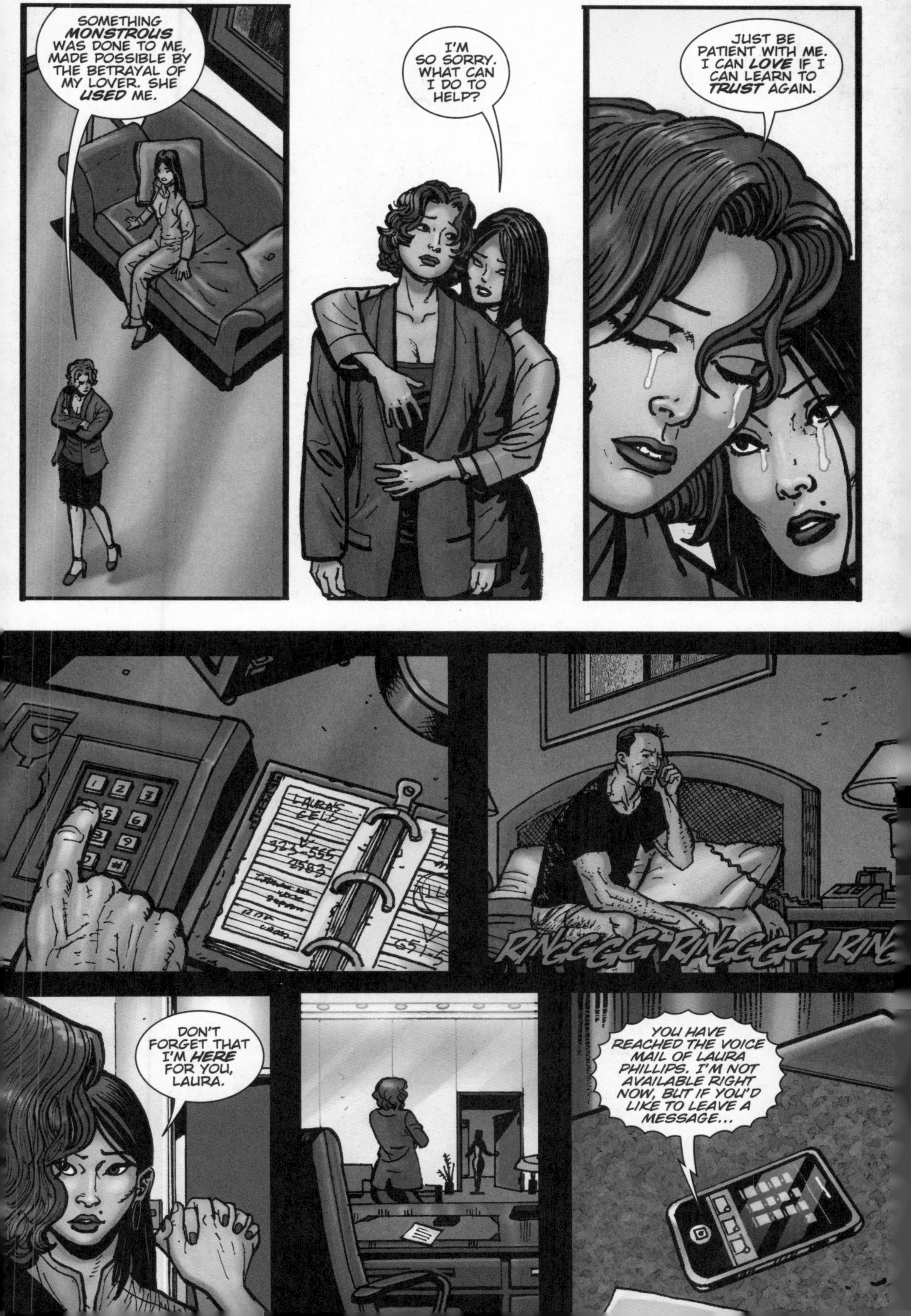
SOMETHING MONSTROUS WAS DONE TO ME, MADE POSSIBLE BY THE BETRAYAL OF MY LOVER. SHE USED ME.
I'M SO SORRY. WHAT CAN I DO TO HELP?
JUST BE PATIENT WITH ME. I CAN LOVE IF I CAN LEARN TO TRUST AGAIN.
LAURA'S CELL
RINGGGG RINGGGG
DON'T FORGET THAT I'M HERE FOR YOU, LAURA.
YOU HAVE REACHED THE VOICE MAIL OF LAURA PHILLIPS. I'M NOT AVAILABLE RIGHT NOW, BUT IF YOU'D LIKE TO LEAVE A MESSAGE...

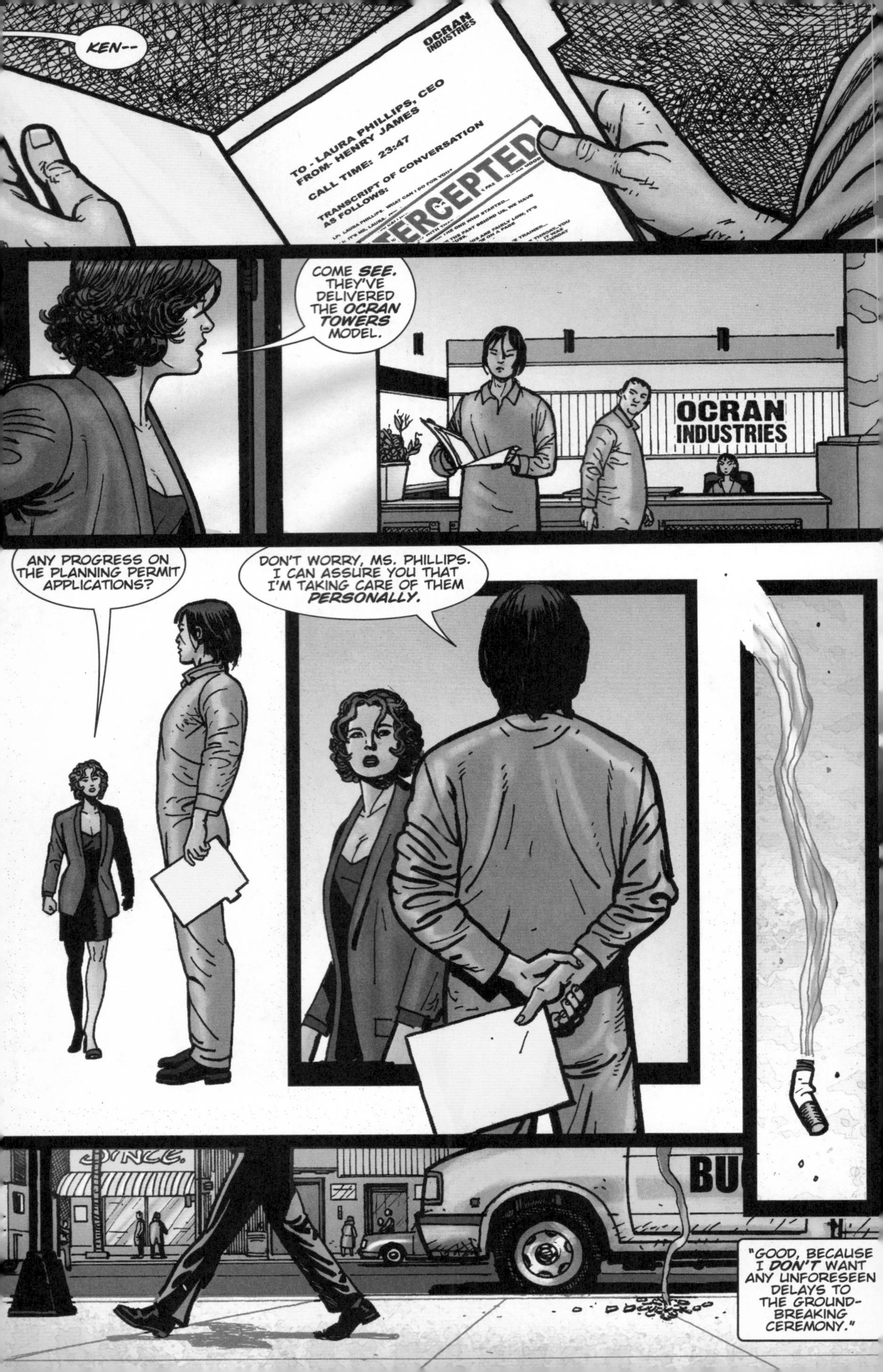
KEN--
OCRAN INDUSTRIES
TO - LAURA PHILLIPS, CEO
FROM- HENRY JAMES
CALL TIME: 23:47
TRANSCRIPT OF CONVERSATION AS FOLLOWS:
COME SEE. THEY'VE DELIVERED THE OCRAN TOWERS MODEL.
OCRAN INDUSTRIES
ANY PROGRESS ON THE PLANNING PERMIT APPLICATIONS?
DON'T WORRY, MS. PHILLIPS. I CAN ASSURE YOU THAT I'M TAKING CARE OF THEM PERSONALLY.
"GOOD, BECAUSE I DON'T WANT ANY UNFORESEEN DELAYS TO THE GROUND-BREAKING CEREMONY."

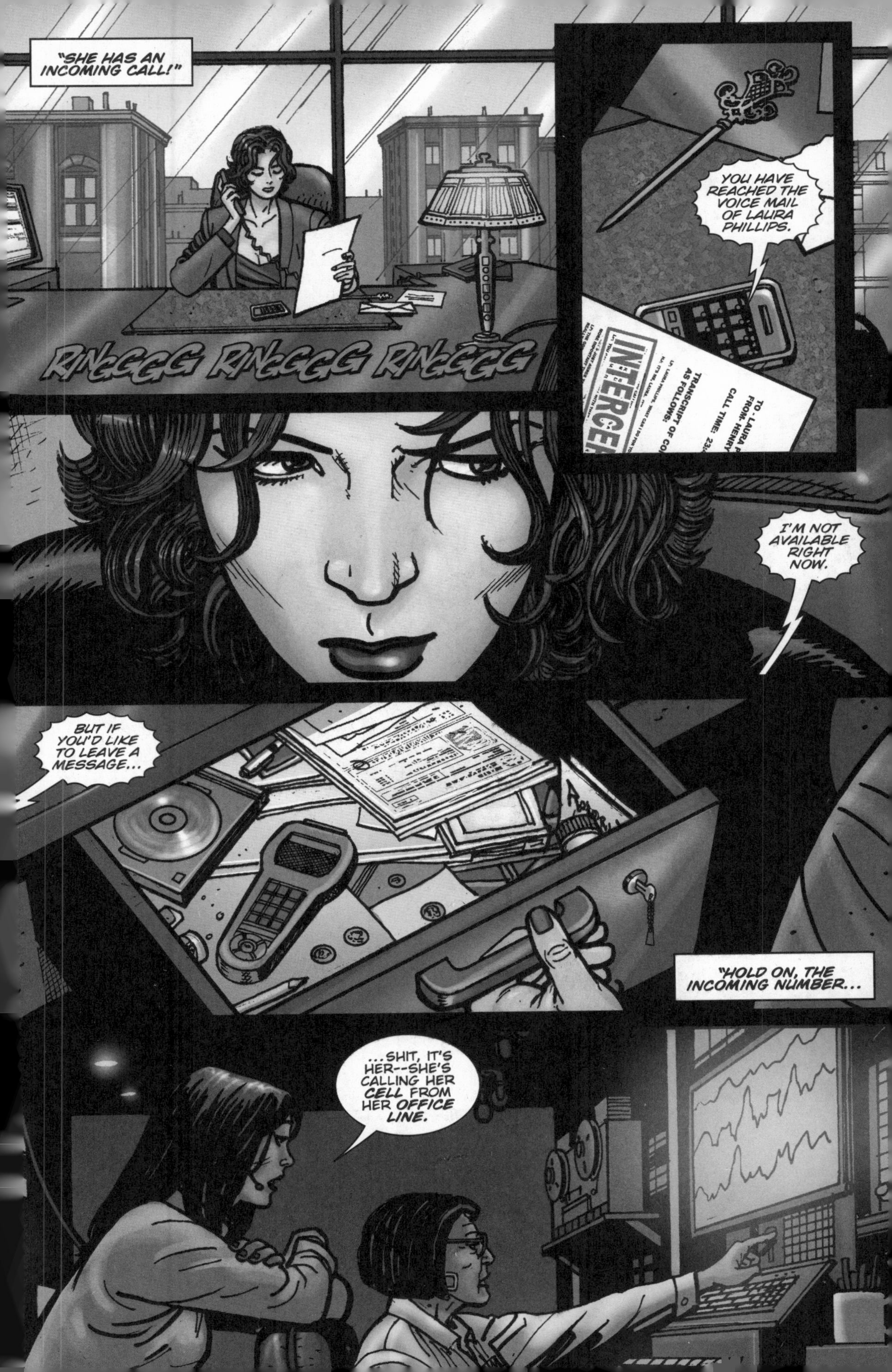
"SHE HAS AN INCOMING CALL!"
RINGGGG RINGGGG RINGGGG
YOU HAVE REACHED THE VOICE MAIL OF LAURA PHILLIPS.
I'M NOT AVAILABLE RIGHT NOW.
BUT IF YOU'D LIKE TO LEAVE A MESSAGE...
"HOLD ON, THE INCOMING NUMBER...
...SHIT, IT'S HER--SHE'S CALLING HER CELL FROM HER OFFICE LINE.

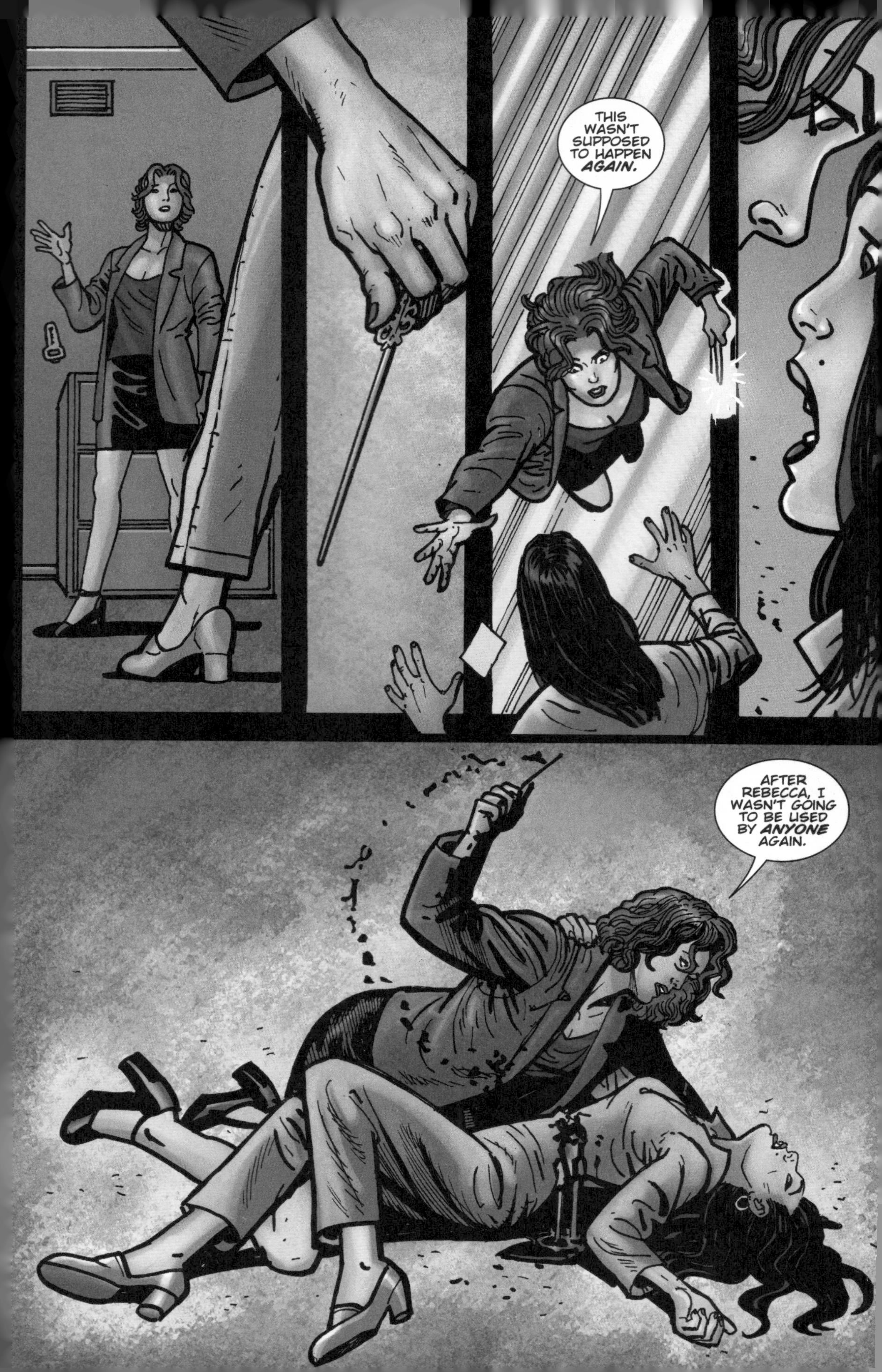
THIS WASN'T SUPPOSED TO HAPPEN *AGAIN.*
AFTER REBECCA, I WASN'T GOING TO BE USED BY *ANYONE* AGAIN.

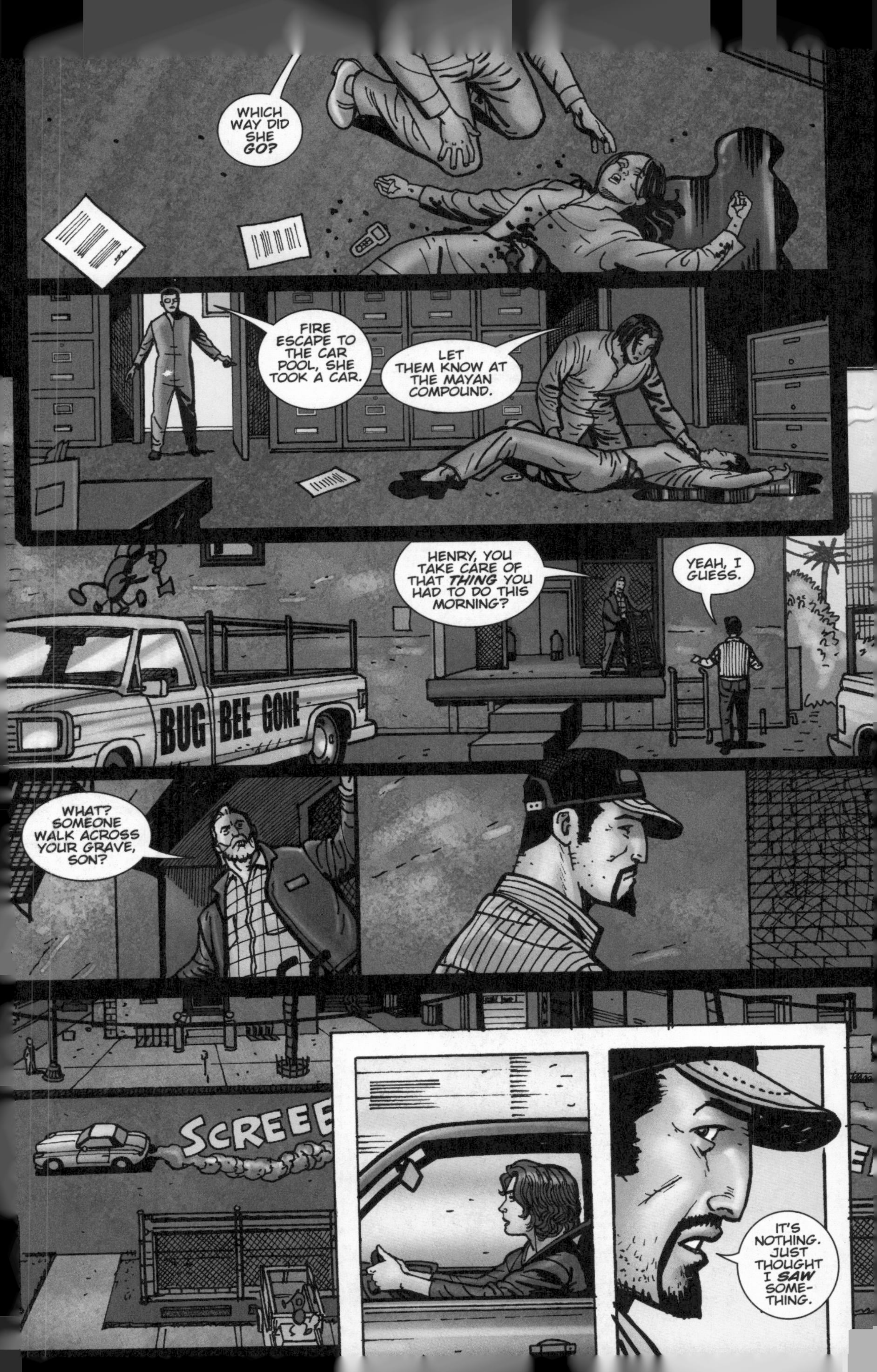
WHICH WAY DID SHE *GO?*
FIRE ESCAPE TO THE CAR POOL, SHE TOOK A CAR.
LET THEM KNOW AT THE MAYAN COMPOUND.
BUG BEE GONE
HENRY, YOU TAKE CARE OF THAT *THING* YOU HAD TO DO THIS MORNING?
YEAH, I GUESS.
WHAT? SOMEONE WALK ACROSS YOUR GRAVE, SON?
SCREEE
IT'S NOTHING. JUST THOUGHT I *SAW* SOME-THING.

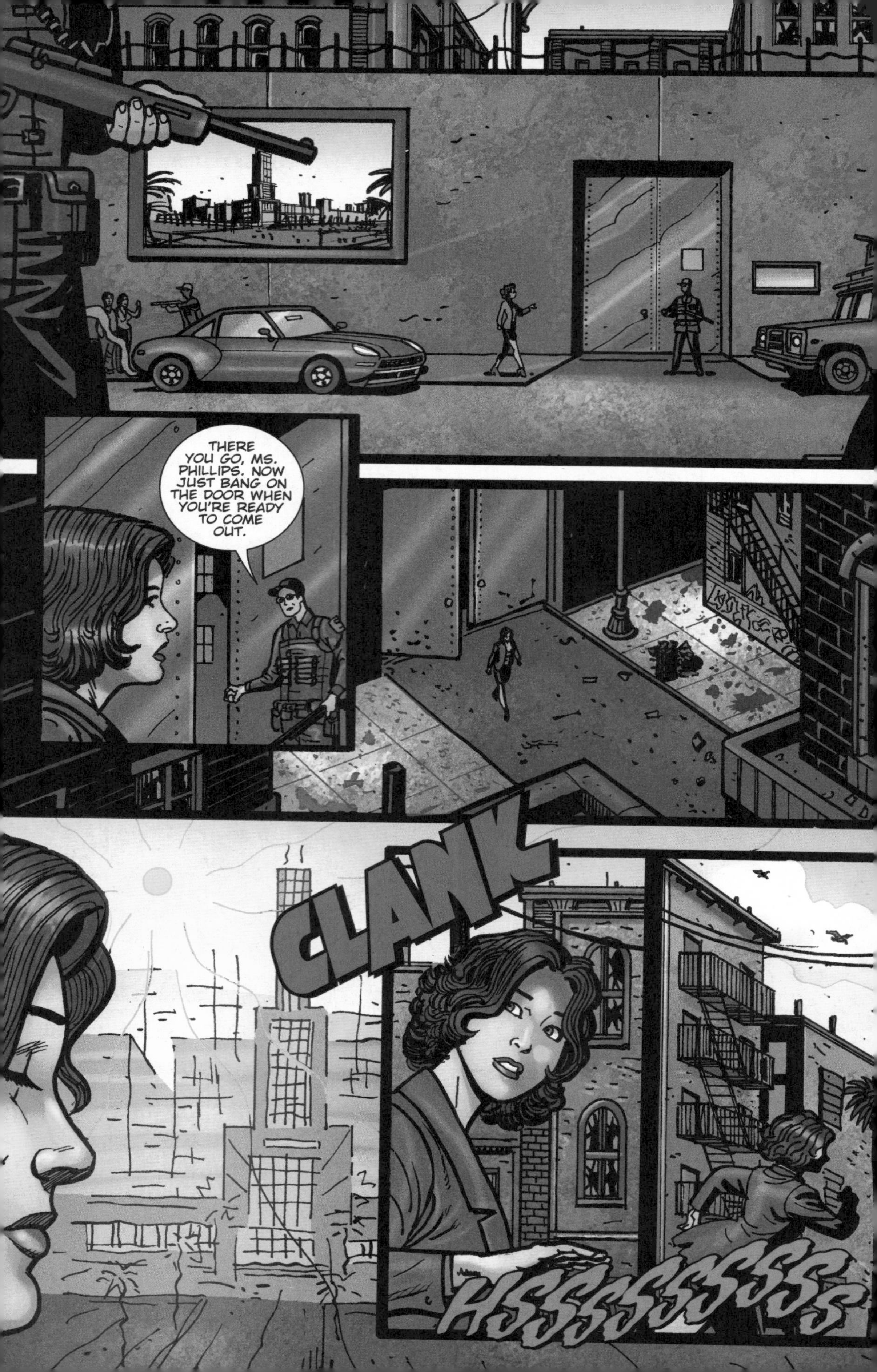
THERE YOU GO, MS. PHILLIPS. NOW JUST BANG ON THE DOOR WHEN YOU'RE READY TO COME OUT.
CLANK
HSSSSSSSSS

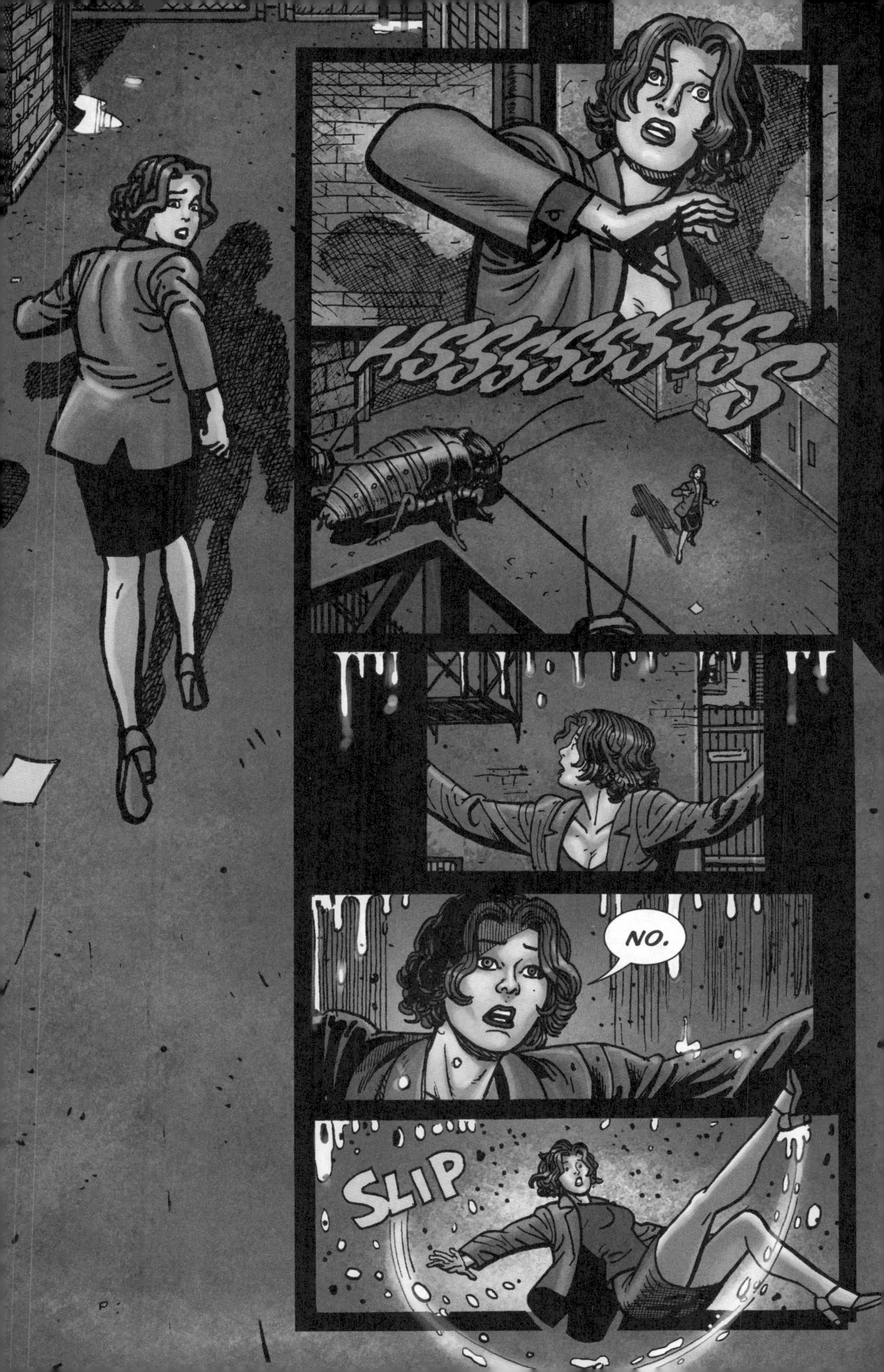
HSSSSSSSSSS
NO.
SLIP

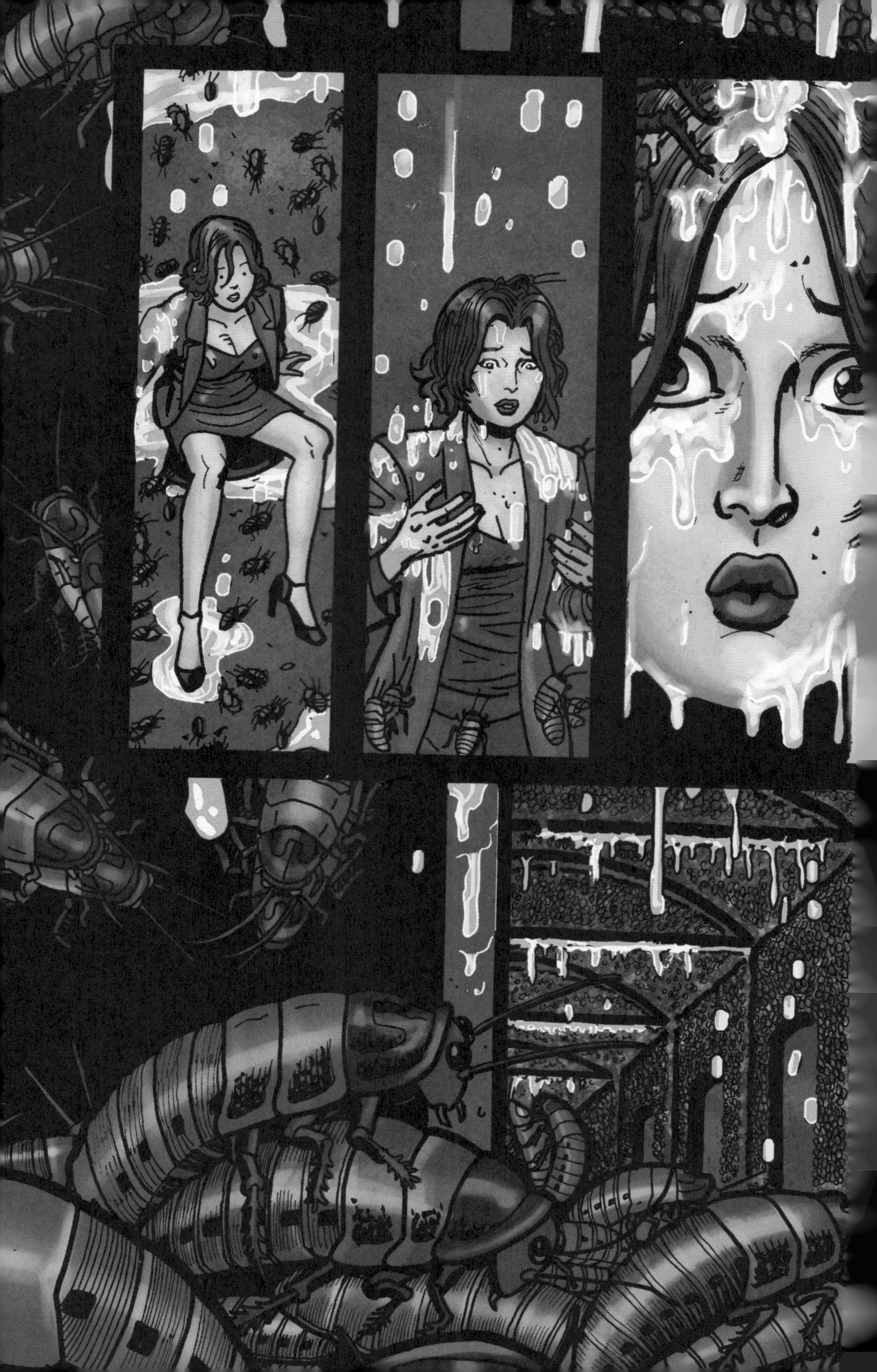

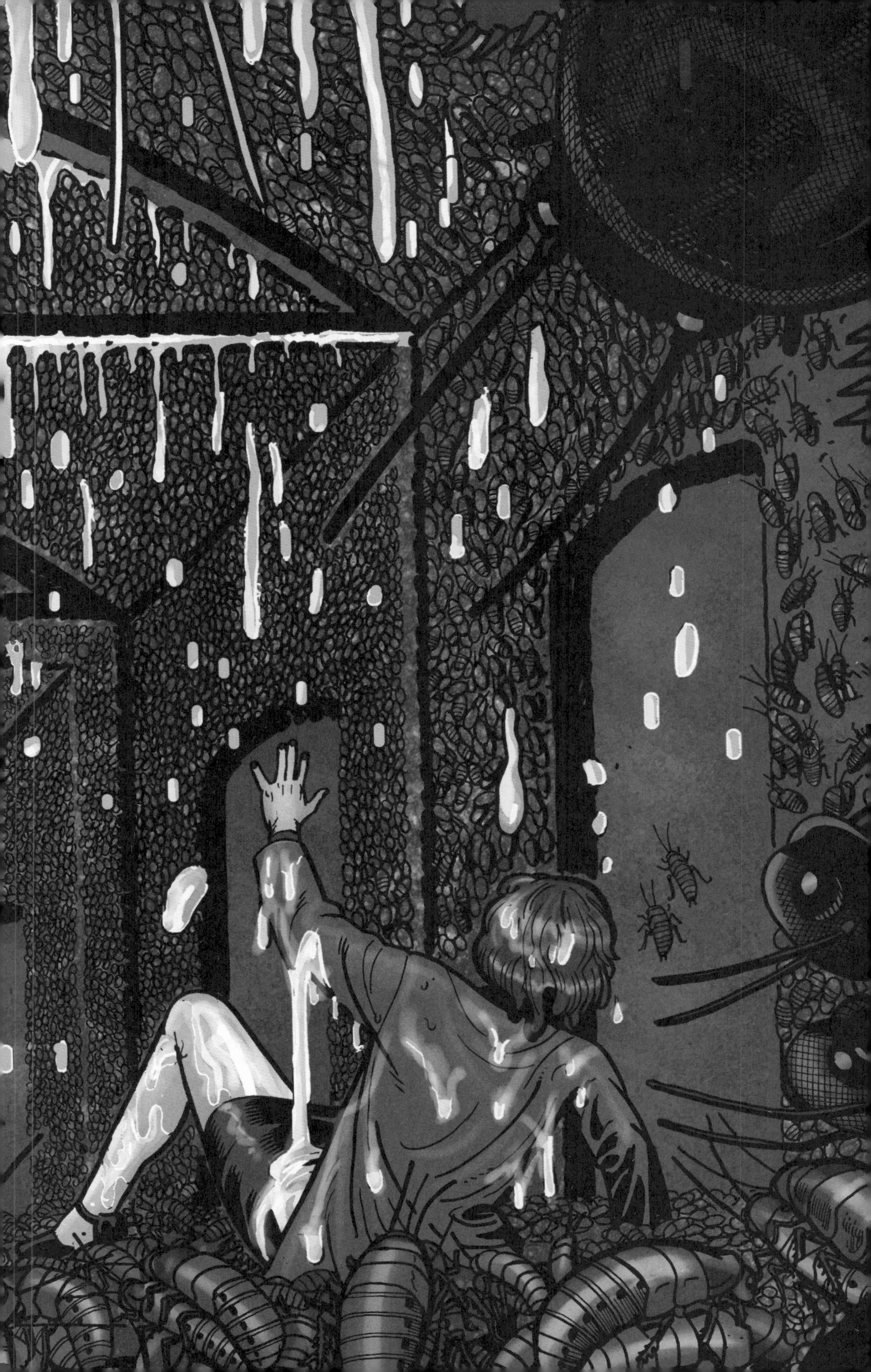

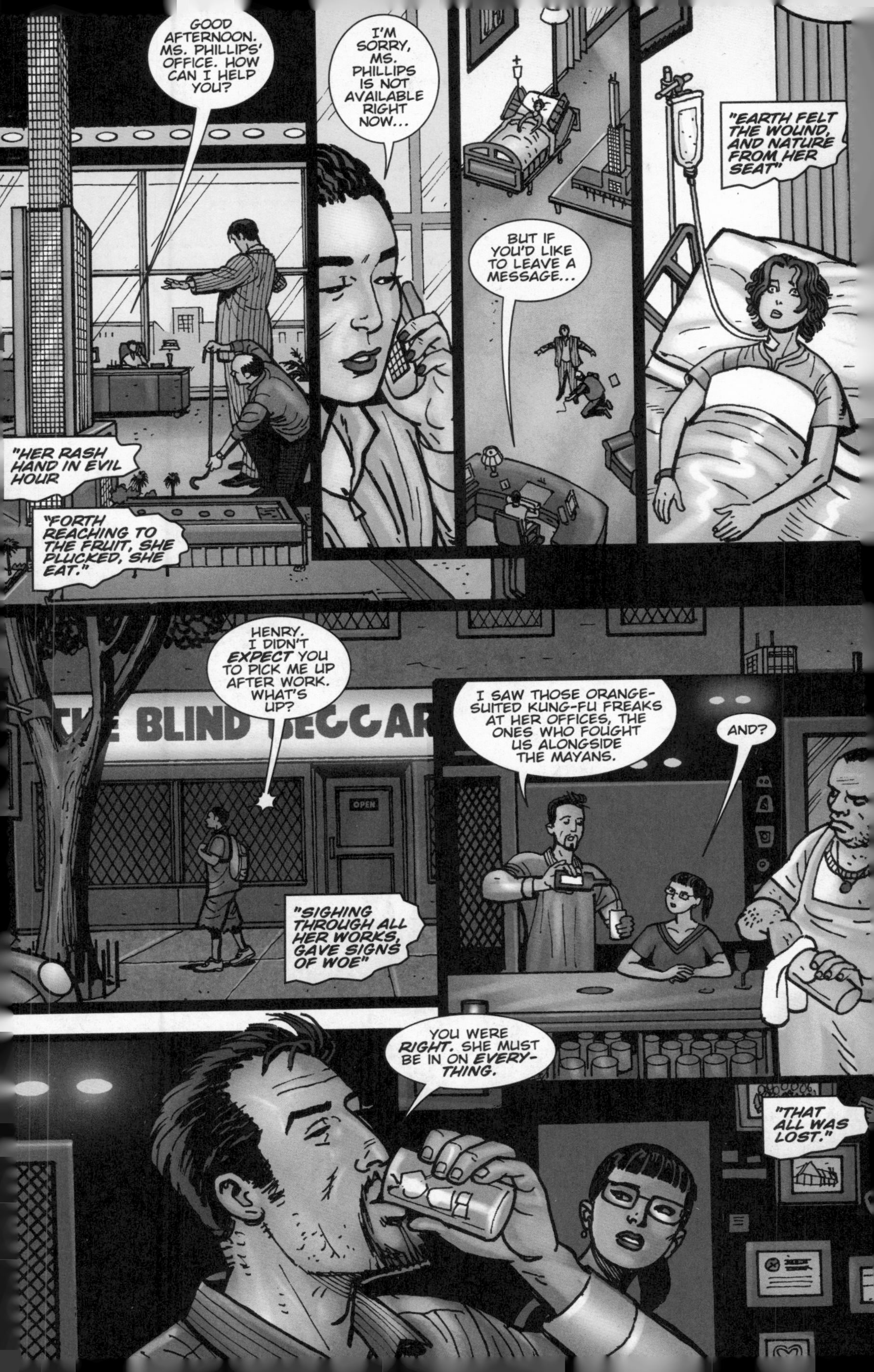
GOOD AFTERNOON. MS. PHILLIPS' OFFICE. HOW CAN I HELP YOU?
I'M SORRY, MS. PHILLIPS IS NOT AVAILABLE RIGHT NOW...
BUT IF YOU'D LIKE TO LEAVE A MESSAGE...
"EARTH FELT THE WOUND, AND NATURE FROM HER SEAT"
"HER RASH HAND IN EVIL HOUR
"FORTH REACHING TO THE FRUIT, SHE PLUCKED, SHE EAT."
HENRY. I DIDN'T EXPECT YOU TO PICK ME UP AFTER WORK. WHAT'S UP?
THE BLIND BEGGAR
OPEN
"SIGHING THROUGH ALL HER WORKS, GAVE SIGNS OF WOE"
I SAW THOSE ORANGE-SUITED KUNG-FU FREAKS AT HER OFFICES, THE ONES WHO FOUGHT US ALONGSIDE THE MAYANS.
AND?
YOU WERE RIGHT. SHE MUST BE IN ON EVERY-THING.
"THAT ALL WAS LOST."

RAISING CHÉ cover art by TONY MOORE

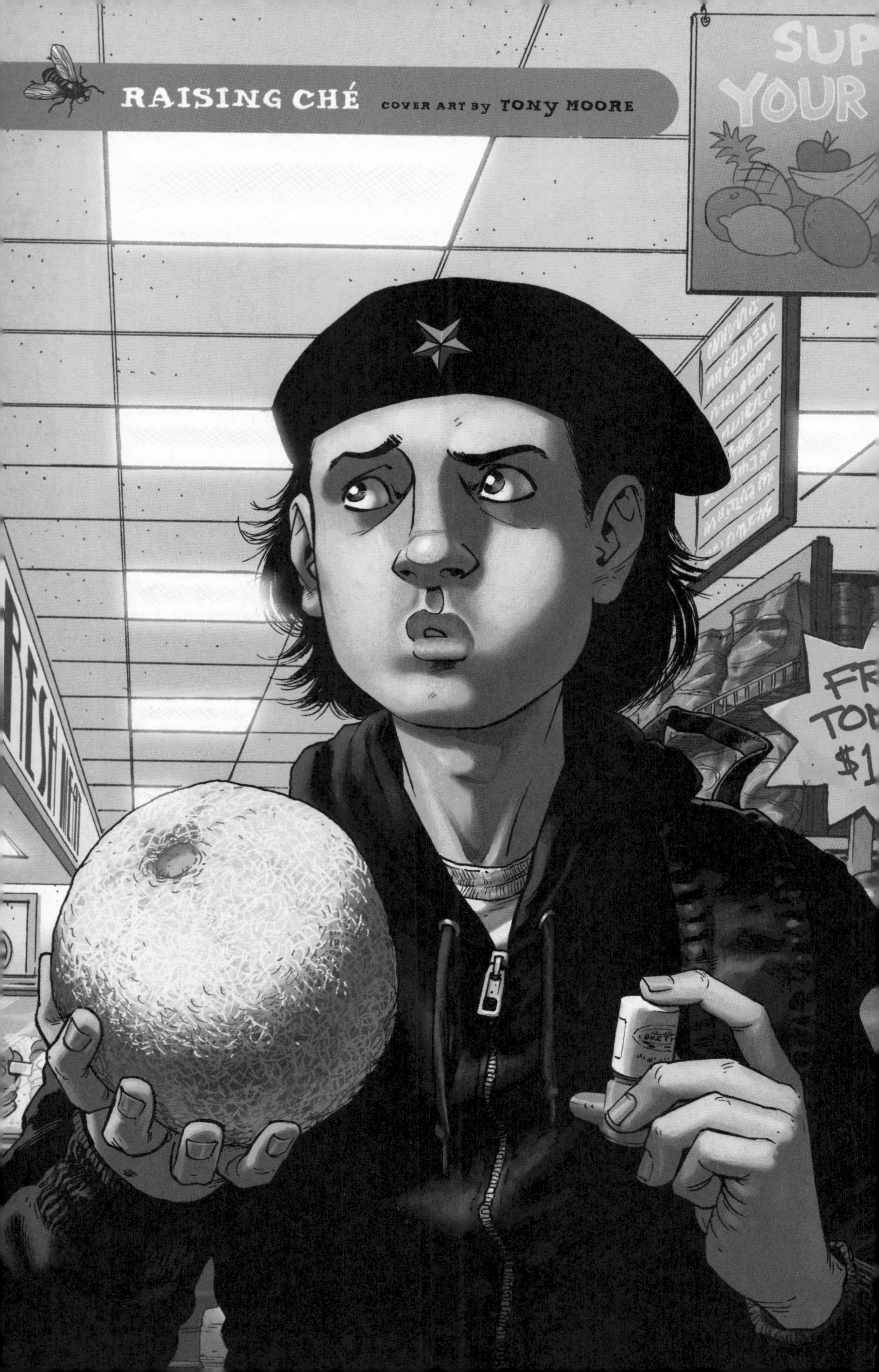

77

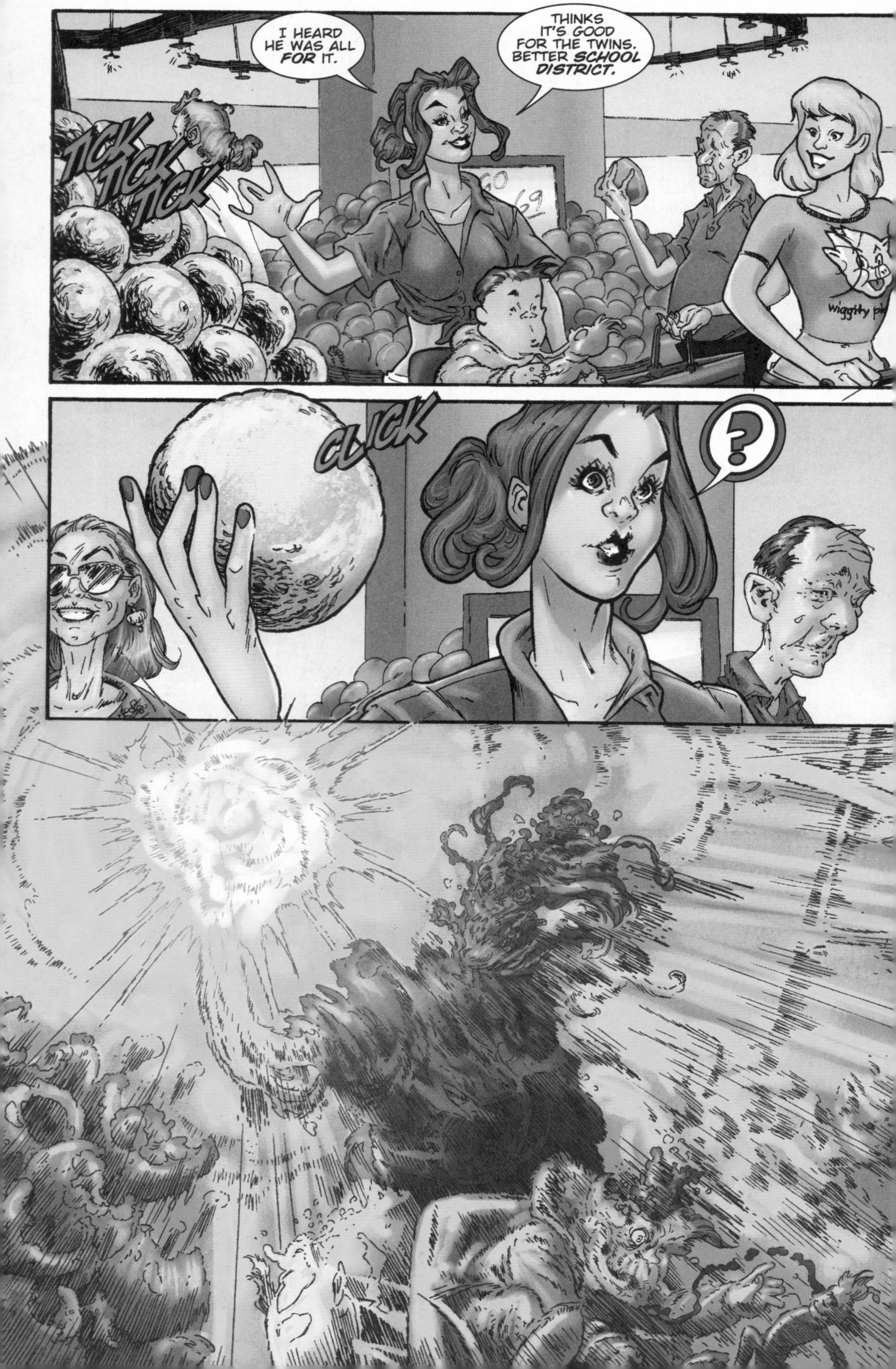
TICK TICK TICK
I HEARD HE WAS ALL FOR IT.
THINKS IT'S GOOD FOR THE TWINS. BETTER SCHOOL DISTRICT.
CLICK
?

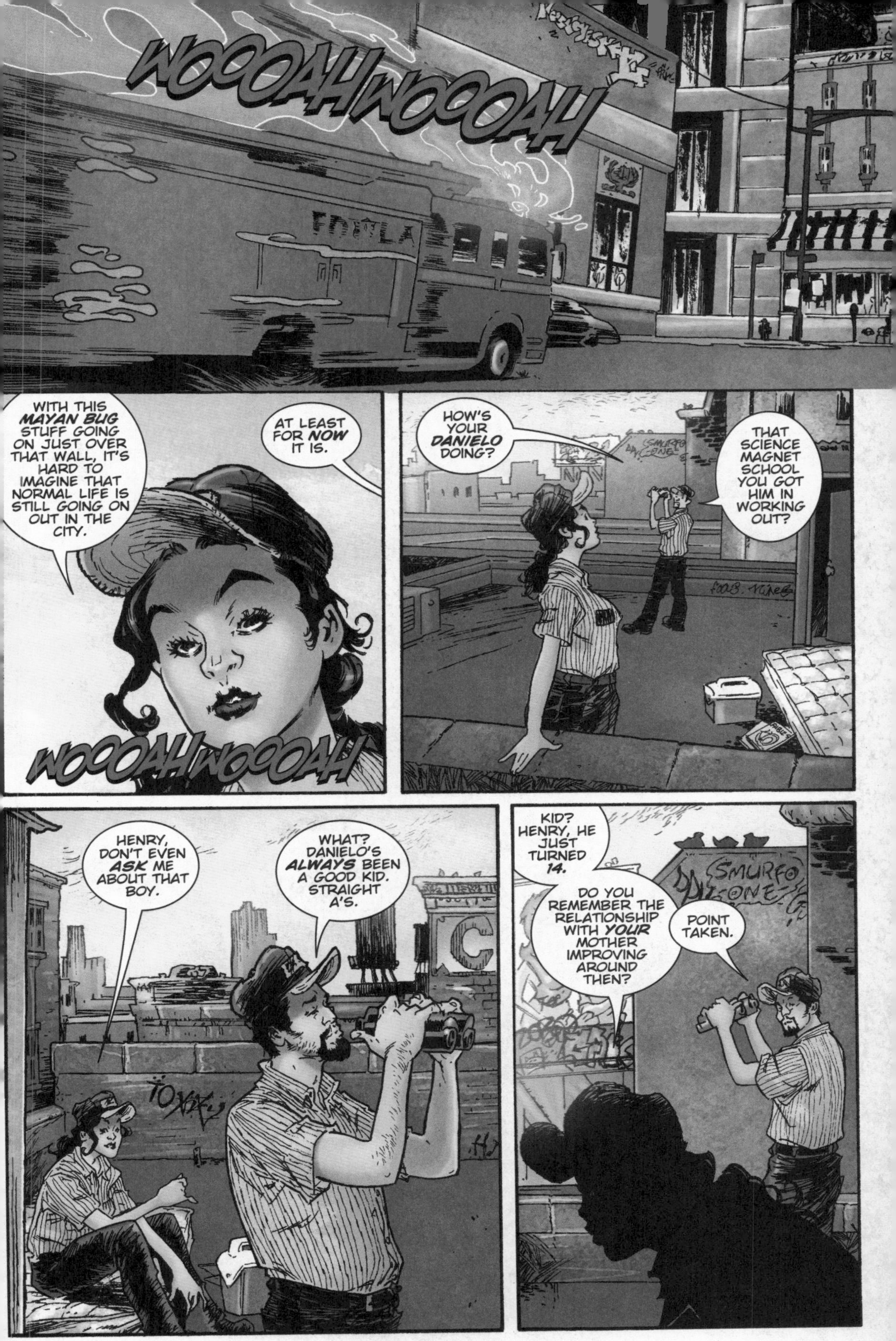
WOOOAH WOOOAH
WITH THIS MAYAN BUG STUFF GOING ON JUST OVER THAT WALL, IT'S HARD TO IMAGINE THAT NORMAL LIFE IS STILL GOING ON OUT IN THE CITY.
AT LEAST FOR NOW IT IS.
WOOOAH WOOOAH
HOW'S YOUR DANIELO DOING?
THAT SCIENCE MAGNET SCHOOL YOU GOT HIM IN WORKING OUT?
HENRY, DON'T EVEN ASK ME ABOUT THAT BOY.
WHAT? DANIELO'S ALWAYS BEEN A GOOD KID. STRAIGHT A'S.
KID? HENRY, HE JUST TURNED 14.
DO YOU REMEMBER THE RELATIONSHIP WITH YOUR MOTHER IMPROVING AROUND THEN?
POINT TAKEN.

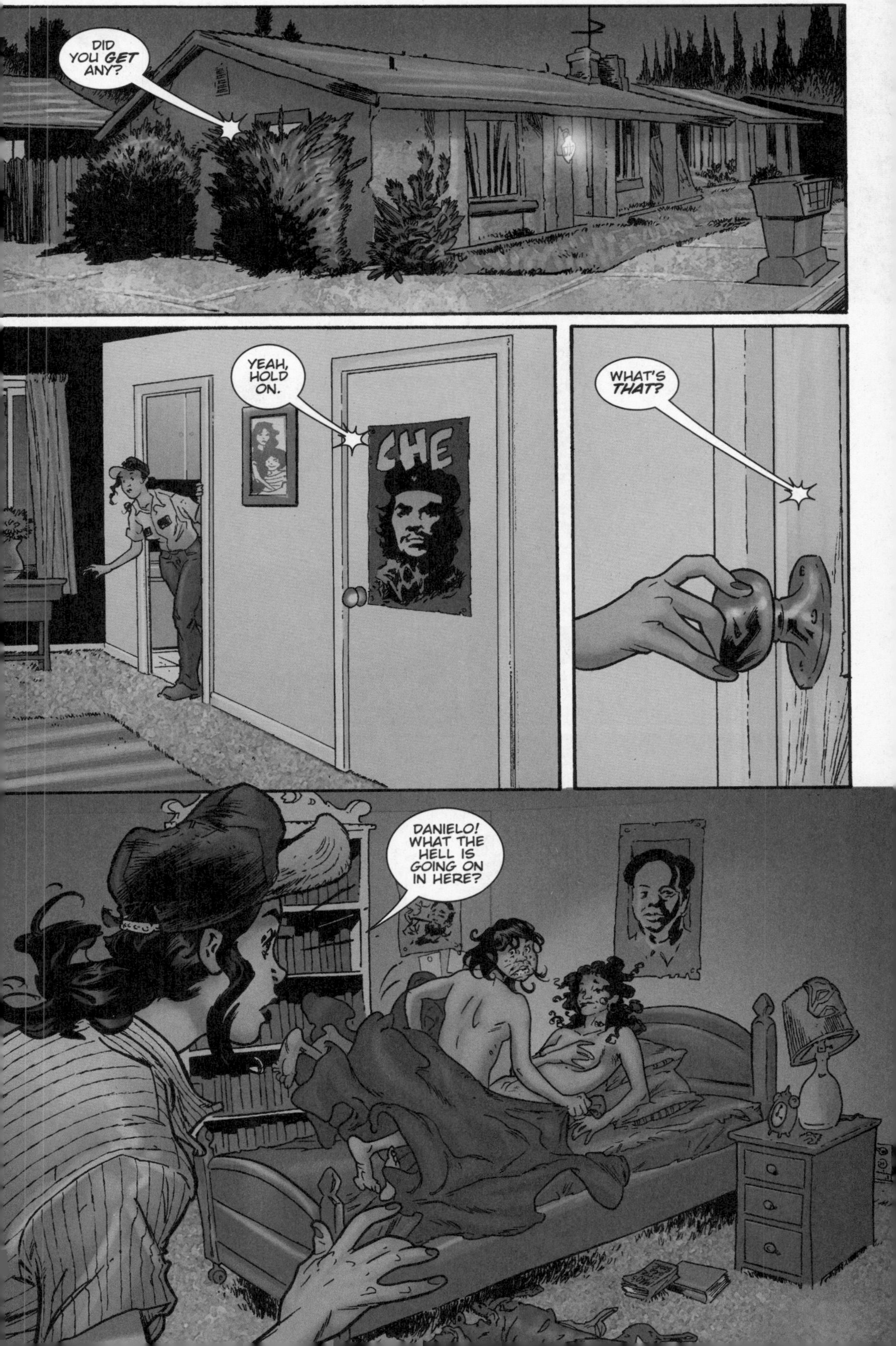
DID YOU GET ANY?
YEAH, HOLD ON.
WHAT'S THAT?
CHE
DANIELO! WHAT THE HELL IS GOING ON IN HERE?

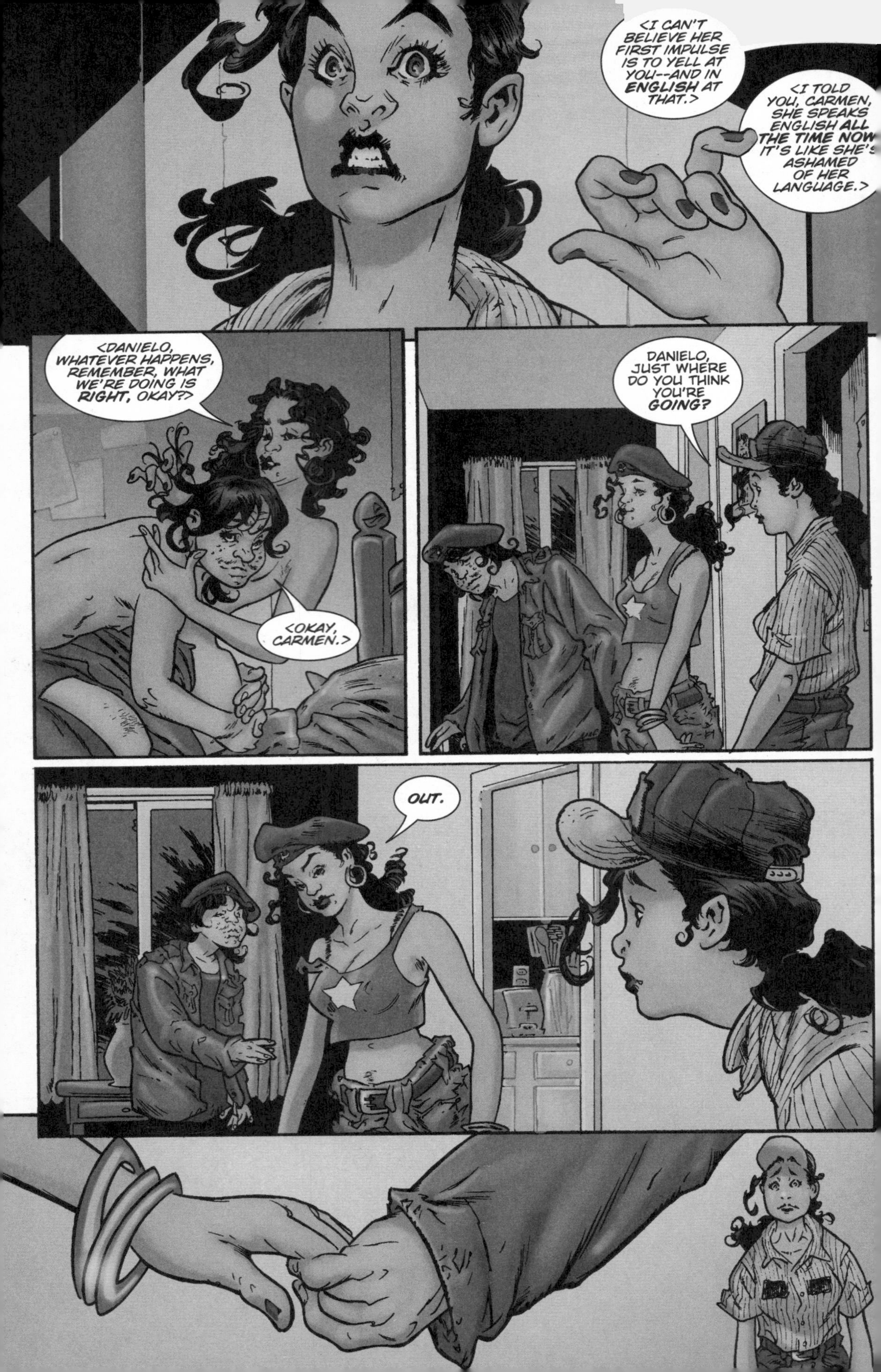
<I CAN'T BELIEVE HER FIRST IMPULSE IS TO YELL AT YOU--AND IN ENGLISH AT THAT.>
<I TOLD YOU, CARMEN, SHE SPEAKS ENGLISH ALL THE TIME NOW. IT'S LIKE SHE'S ASHAMED OF HER LANGUAGE.>
<DANIELO, WHATEVER HAPPENS, REMEMBER, WHAT WE'RE DOING IS RIGHT, OKAY?>
<OKAY, CARMEN.>
DANIELO, JUST WHERE DO YOU THINK YOU'RE GOING?
OUT.

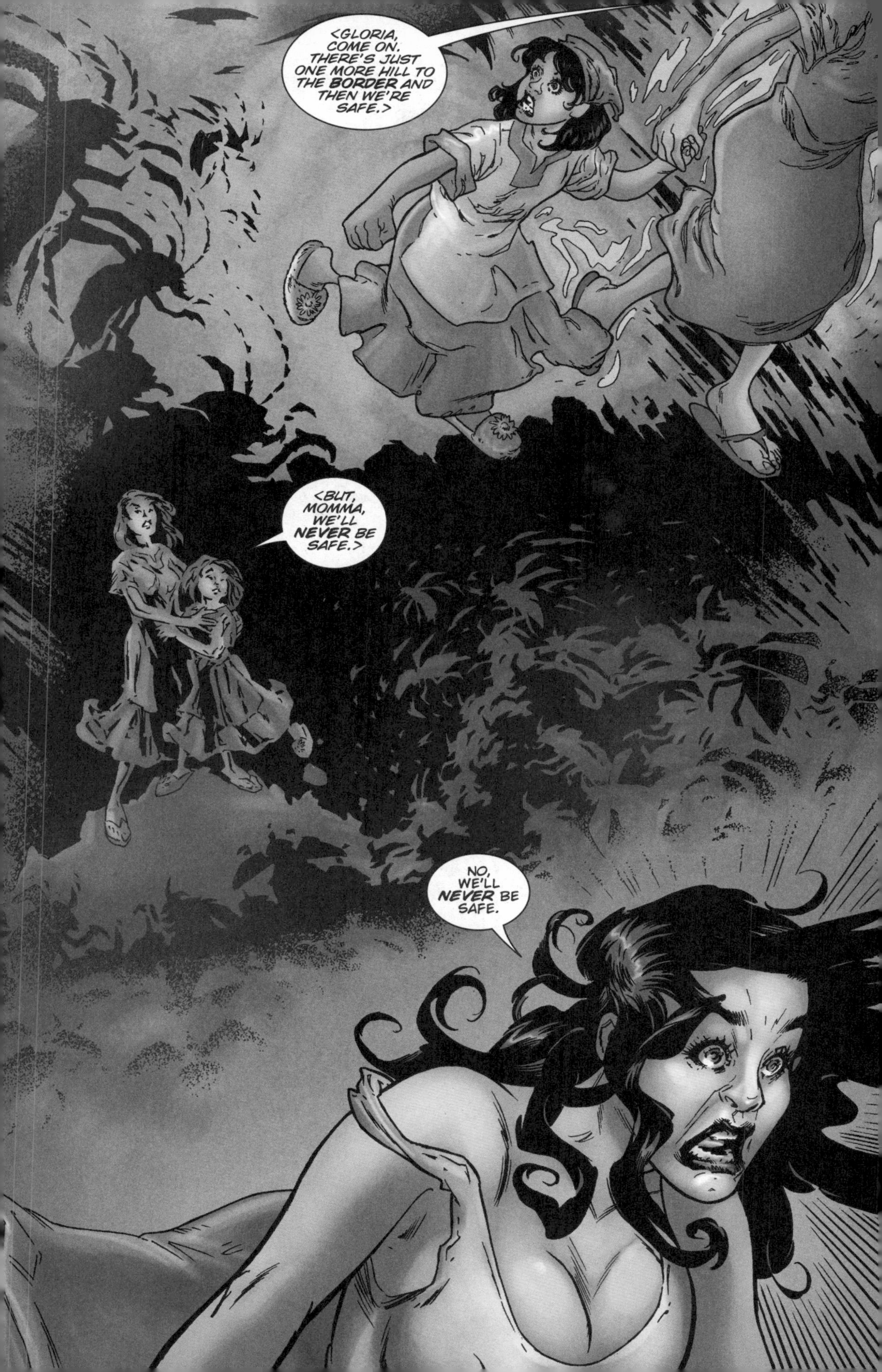
<GLORIA, COME ON. THERE'S JUST ONE MORE HILL TO THE BORDER AND THEN WE'RE SAFE.>
<BUT, MOMMA, WE'LL NEVER BE SAFE.>
NO, WE'LL NEVER BE SAFE.

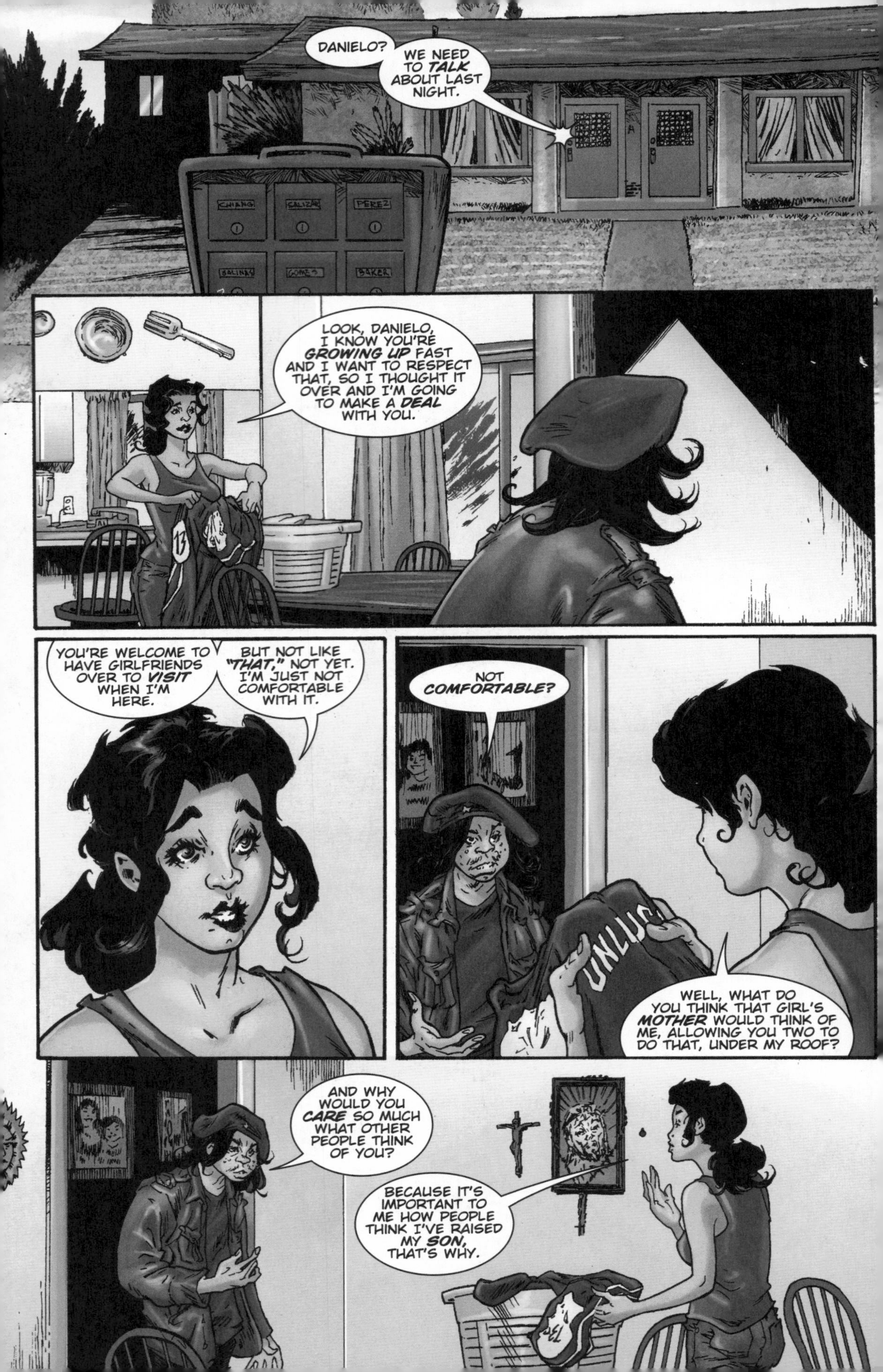
DANIELO?
WE NEED TO *TALK* ABOUT LAST NIGHT.
LOOK, DANIELO, I KNOW YOU'RE *GROWING UP* FAST AND I WANT TO RESPECT THAT, SO I THOUGHT IT OVER AND I'M GOING TO MAKE A *DEAL* WITH YOU.
YOU'RE WELCOME TO HAVE GIRLFRIENDS OVER TO *VISIT* WHEN I'M HERE.
BUT NOT LIKE *"THAT,"* NOT YET. I'M JUST NOT COMFORTABLE WITH IT.
NOT *COMFORTABLE?*
WELL, WHAT DO YOU THINK THAT GIRL'S *MOTHER* WOULD THINK OF ME, ALLOWING YOU TWO TO DO THAT, UNDER MY ROOF?
AND WHY WOULD YOU *CARE* SO MUCH WHAT OTHER PEOPLE THINK OF YOU?
BECAUSE IT'S IMPORTANT TO ME HOW PEOPLE THINK I'VE RAISED MY *SON,* THAT'S WHY.

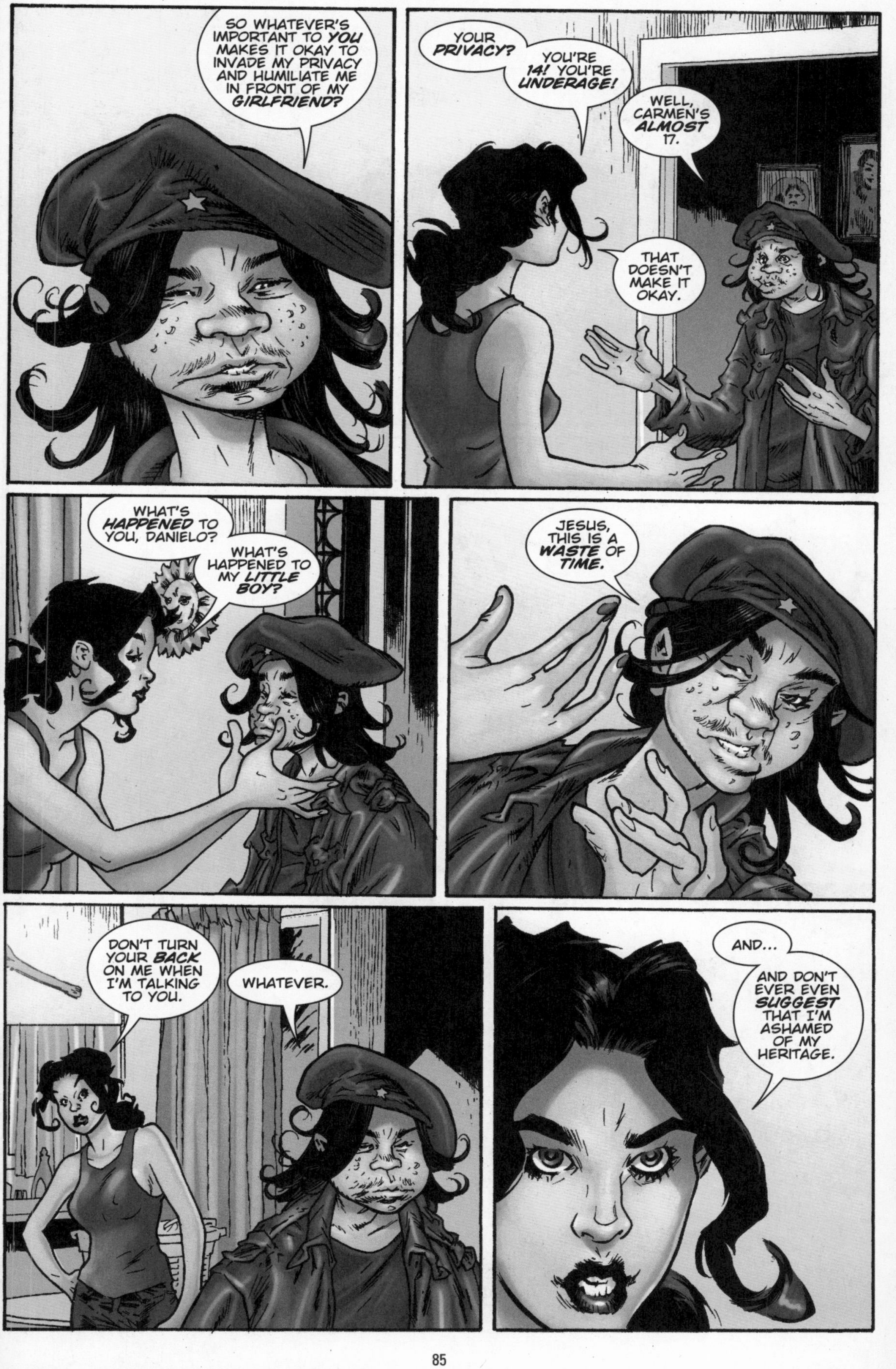
SO WHATEVER'S IMPORTANT TO YOU MAKES IT OKAY TO INVADE MY PRIVACY AND HUMILIATE ME IN FRONT OF MY GIRLFRIEND?
YOUR PRIVACY?
YOU'RE 14! YOU'RE UNDERAGE!
WELL, CARMEN'S ALMOST 17.
THAT DOESN'T MAKE IT OKAY.
WHAT'S HAPPENED TO YOU, DANIELO?
WHAT'S HAPPENED TO MY LITTLE BOY?
JESUS, THIS IS A WASTE OF TIME.
DON'T TURN YOUR BACK ON ME WHEN I'M TALKING TO YOU.
WHATEVER.
AND...
AND DON'T EVER EVEN SUGGEST THAT I'M ASHAMED OF MY HERITAGE.

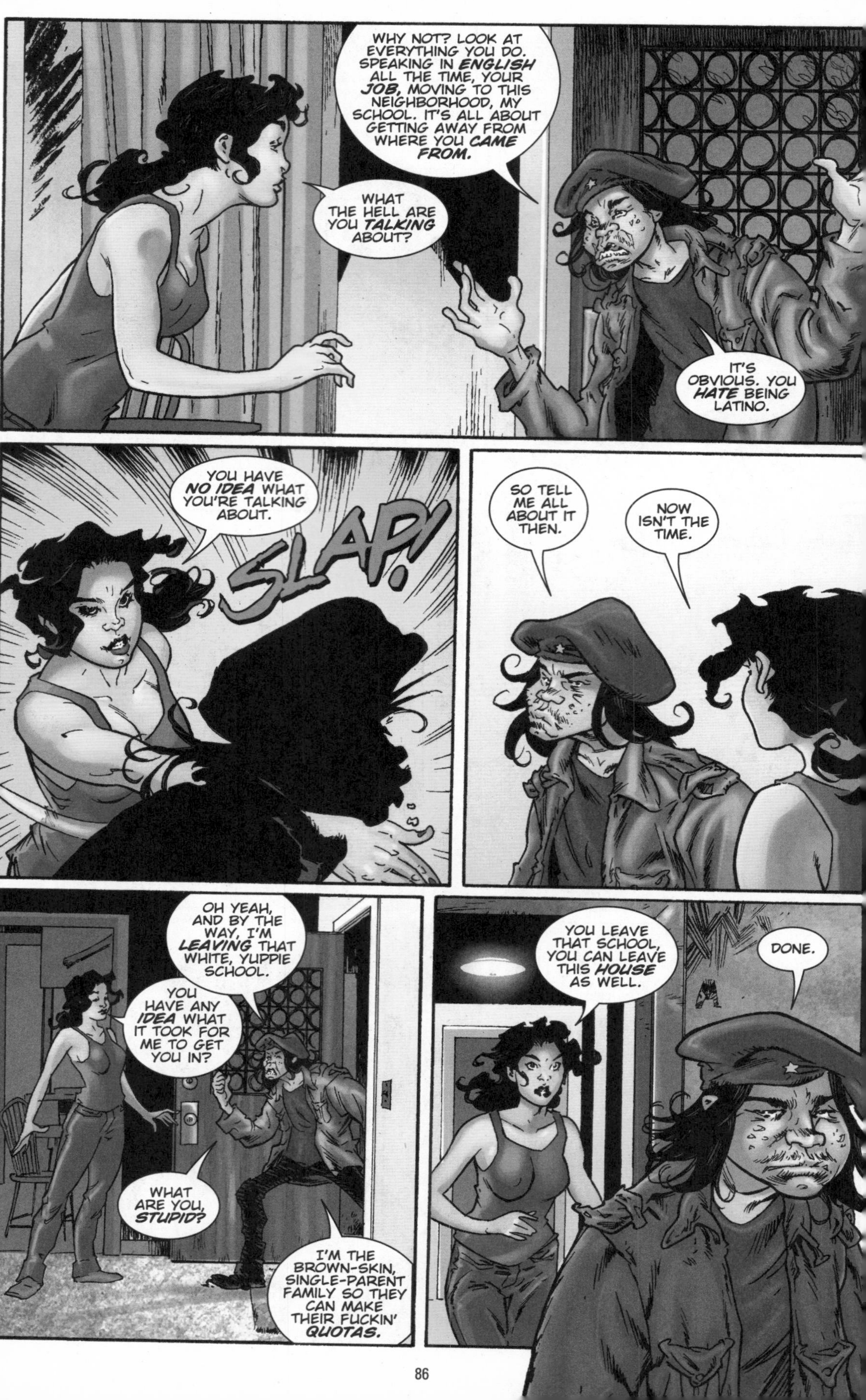
WHY NOT? LOOK AT EVERYTHING YOU DO. SPEAKING IN ENGLISH ALL THE TIME, YOUR JOB, MOVING TO THIS NEIGHBORHOOD, MY SCHOOL. IT'S ALL ABOUT GETTING AWAY FROM WHERE YOU CAME FROM.
WHAT THE HELL ARE YOU TALKING ABOUT?
IT'S OBVIOUS. YOU HATE BEING LATINO.
YOU HAVE NO IDEA WHAT YOU'RE TALKING ABOUT.
SLAP!
SO TELL ME ALL ABOUT IT THEN.
NOW ISN'T THE TIME.
OH YEAH, AND BY THE WAY, I'M LEAVING THAT WHITE, YUPPIE SCHOOL.
YOU HAVE ANY IDEA WHAT IT TOOK FOR ME TO GET YOU IN?
WHAT ARE YOU, STUPID?
I'M THE BROWN-SKIN, SINGLE-PARENT FAMILY SO THEY CAN MAKE THEIR FUCKIN' QUOTAS.
YOU LEAVE THAT SCHOOL, YOU CAN LEAVE THIS HOUSE AS WELL.
DONE.

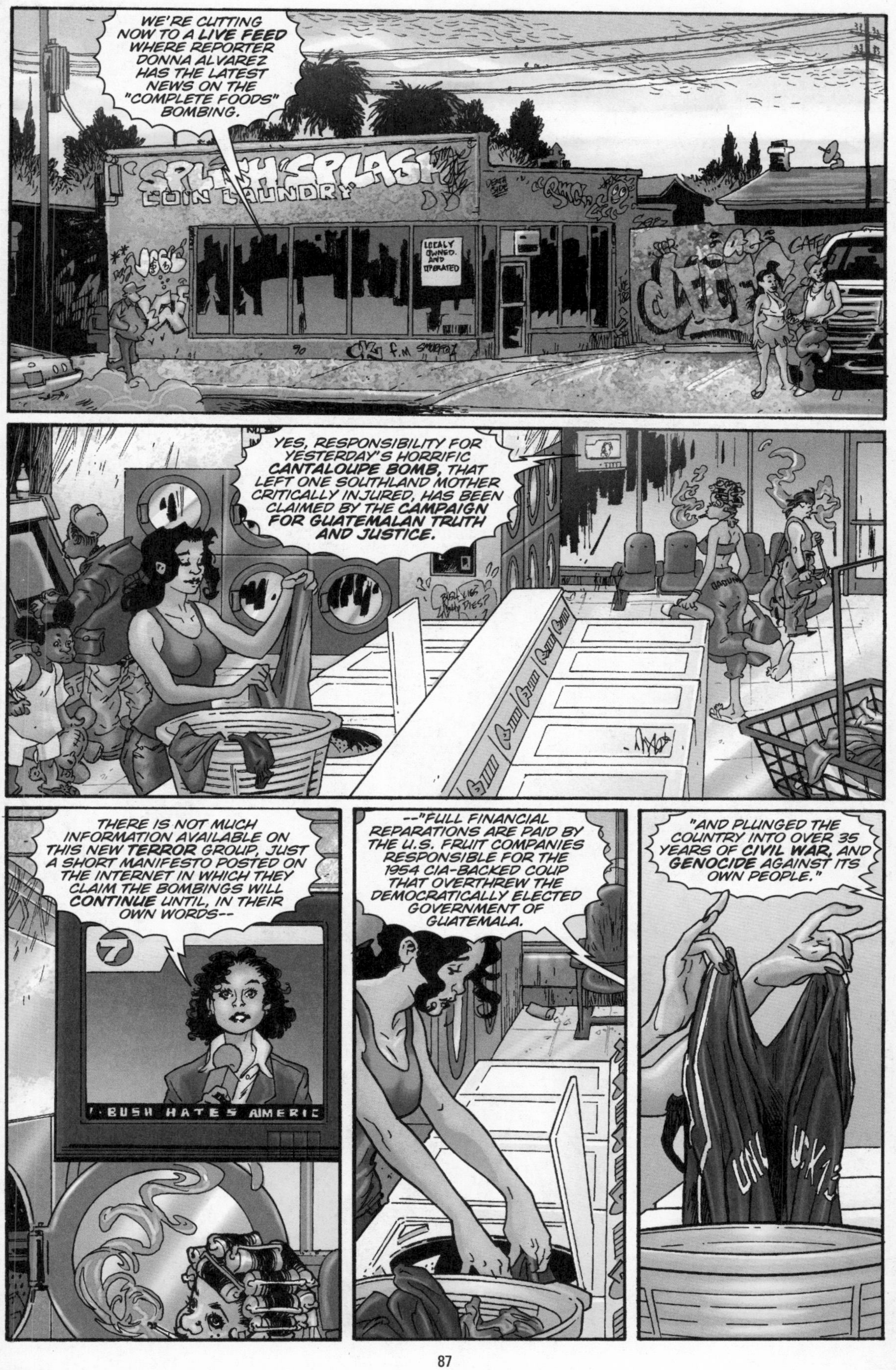
WE'RE CUTTING NOW TO A LIVE FEED WHERE REPORTER DONNA ALVAREZ HAS THE LATEST NEWS ON THE "COMPLETE FOODS" BOMBING.
COIN LAUNDRY
LOCALY OWNED. AND OPERATED
YES, RESPONSIBILITY FOR YESTERDAY'S HORRIFIC CANTALOUPE BOMB, THAT LEFT ONE SOUTHLAND MOTHER CRITICALLY INJURED, HAS BEEN CLAIMED BY THE CAMPAIGN FOR GUATEMALAN TRUTH AND JUSTICE.
THERE IS NOT MUCH INFORMATION AVAILABLE ON THIS NEW TERROR GROUP, JUST A SHORT MANIFESTO POSTED ON THE INTERNET IN WHICH THEY CLAIM THE BOMBINGS WILL CONTINUE UNTIL, IN THEIR OWN WORDS--
BUSH HATES AMERIC
--"FULL FINANCIAL REPARATIONS ARE PAID BY THE U.S. FRUIT COMPANIES RESPONSIBLE FOR THE 1954 CIA-BACKED COUP THAT OVERTHREW THE DEMOCRATICALLY ELECTED GOVERNMENT OF GUATEMALA.
"AND PLUNGED THE COUNTRY INTO OVER 35 YEARS OF CIVIL WAR, AND GENOCIDE AGAINST ITS OWN PEOPLE."

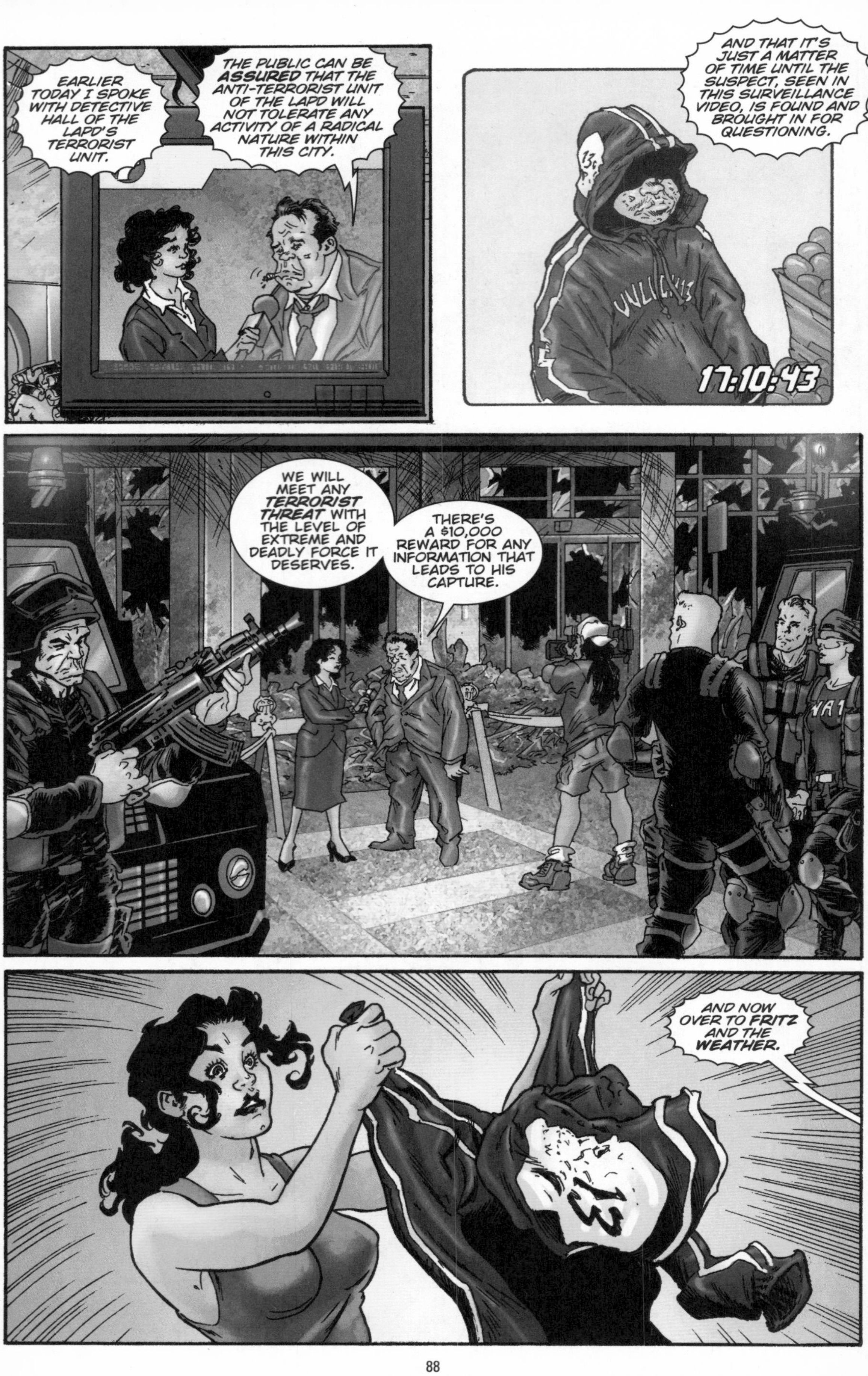
EARLIER TODAY I SPOKE WITH DETECTIVE HALL OF THE LAPD'S TERRORIST UNIT.
THE PUBLIC CAN BE ASSURED THAT THE ANTI-TERRORIST UNIT OF THE LAPD WILL NOT TOLERATE ANY ACTIVITY OF A RADICAL NATURE WITHIN THIS CITY.
AND THAT IT'S JUST A MATTER OF TIME UNTIL THE SUSPECT, SEEN IN THIS SURVEILLANCE VIDEO, IS FOUND AND BROUGHT IN FOR QUESTIONING.
17:10:43
WE WILL MEET ANY TERRORIST THREAT WITH THE LEVEL OF EXTREME AND DEADLY FORCE IT DESERVES.
THERE'S A $10,000 REWARD FOR ANY INFORMATION THAT LEADS TO HIS CAPTURE.
AND NOW OVER TO FRITZ AND THE WEATHER.

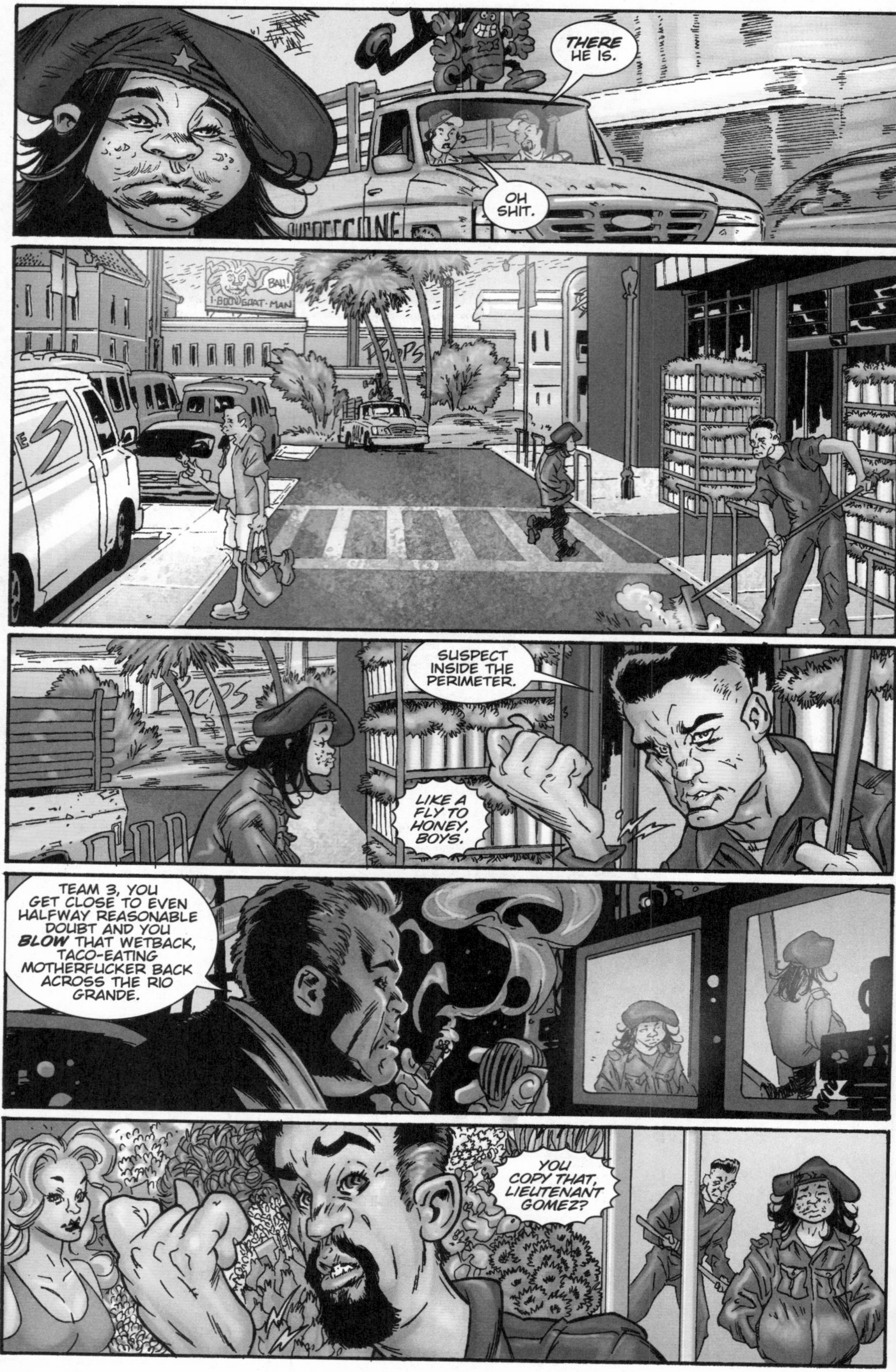
THERE HE IS.
OH SHIT.
BAH!
SUSPECT INSIDE THE PERIMETER.
LIKE A FLY TO HONEY, BOYS.
TEAM 3, YOU GET CLOSE TO EVEN HALFWAY REASONABLE DOUBT AND YOU BLOW THAT WETBACK, TACO-EATING MOTHERFUCKER BACK ACROSS THE RIO GRANDE.
YOU COPY THAT, LIEUTENANT GOMEZ?

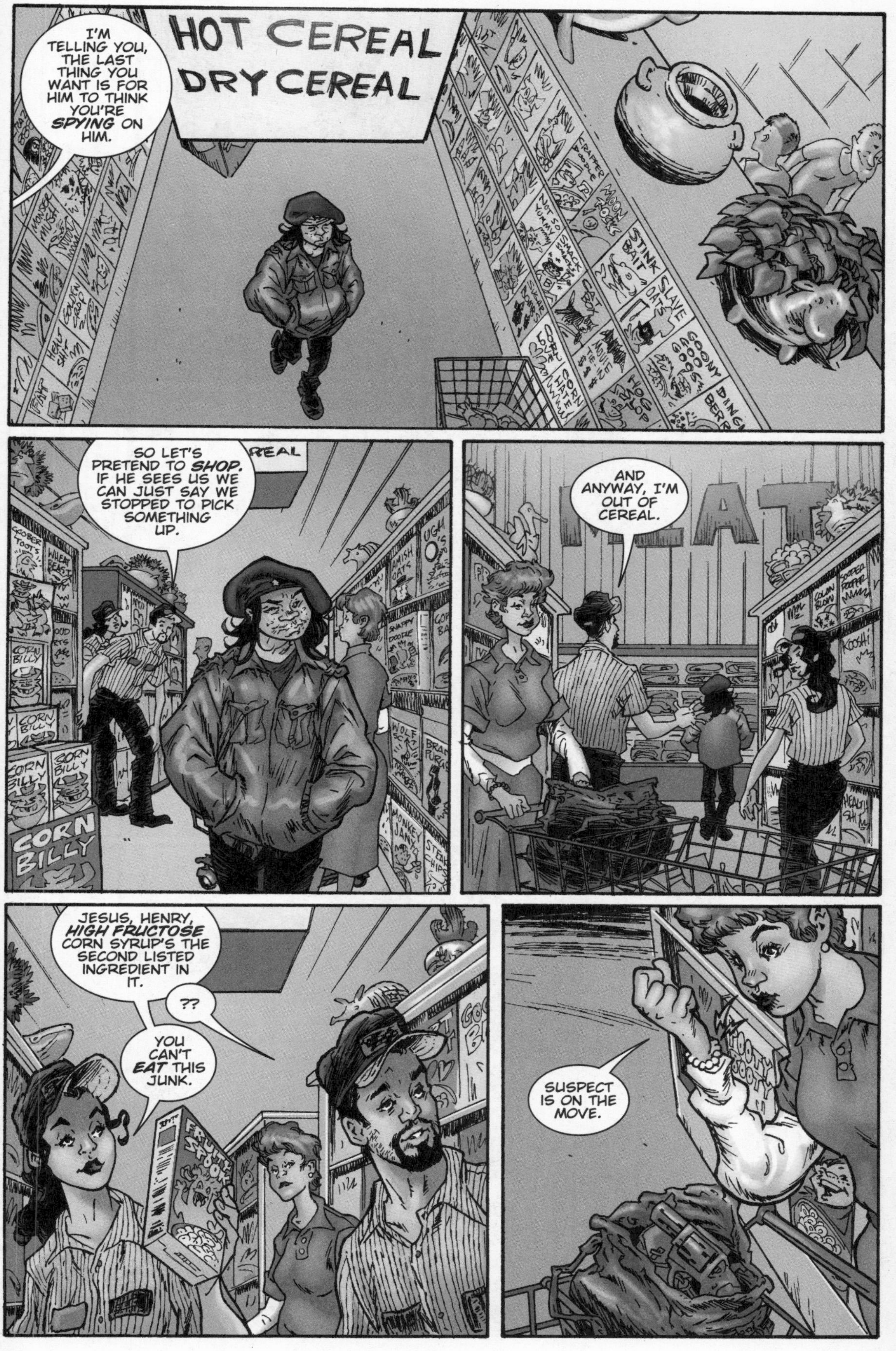
HOT CEREAL
DRY CEREAL
I'M TELLING YOU, THE LAST THING YOU WANT IS FOR HIM TO THINK YOU'RE SPYING ON HIM.
SO LET'S PRETEND TO SHOP. IF HE SEES US WE CAN JUST SAY WE STOPPED TO PICK SOMETHING UP.
AND ANYWAY, I'M OUT OF CEREAL.
JESUS, HENRY, HIGH FRUCTOSE CORN SYRUP'S THE SECOND LISTED INGREDIENT IN IT.
??
YOU CAN'T EAT THIS JUNK.
SUSPECT IS ON THE MOVE.

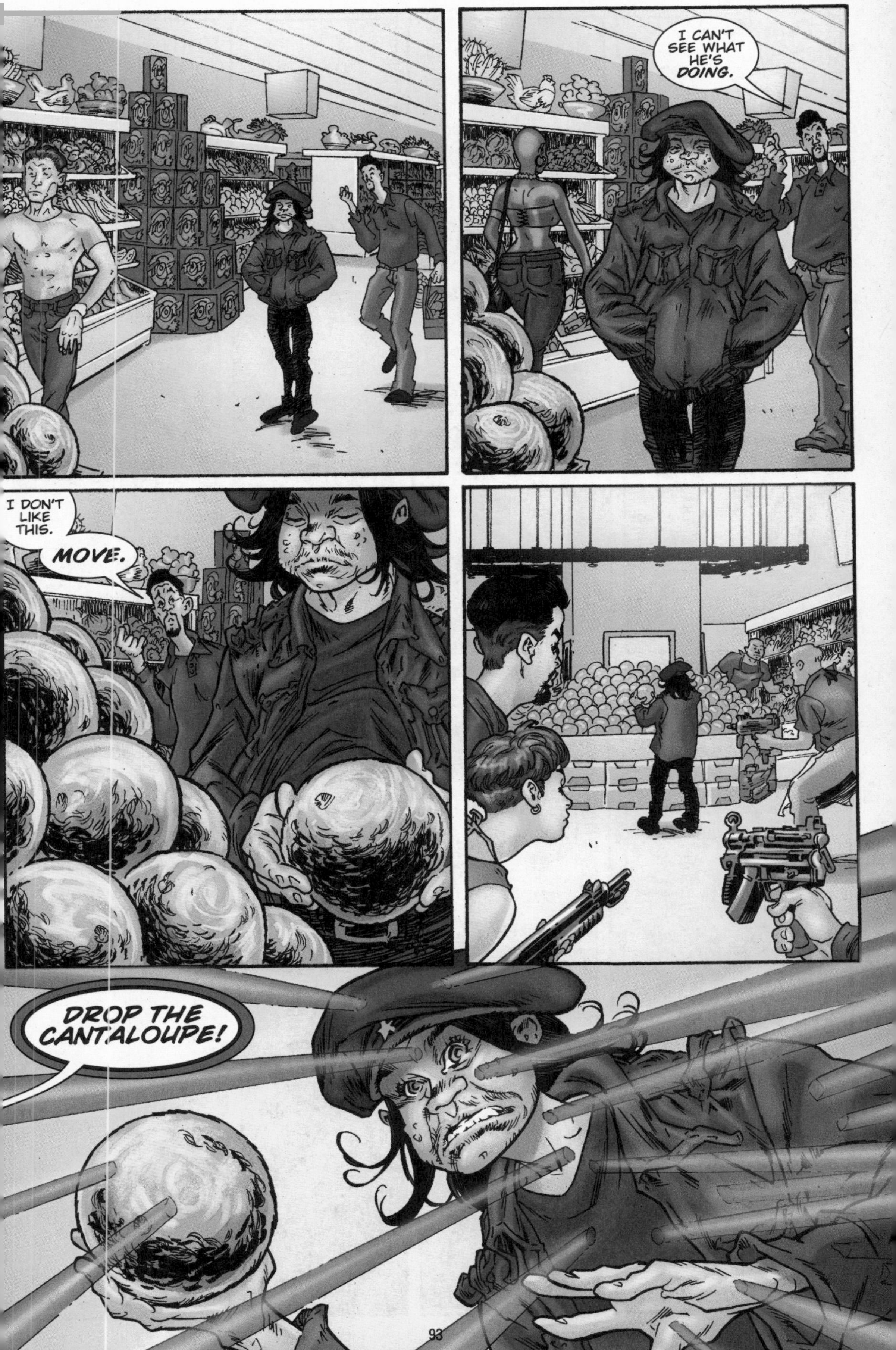
I CAN'T SEE WHAT HE'S DOING.
I DON'T LIKE THIS.
MOVE.
DROP THE CANTALOUPE!

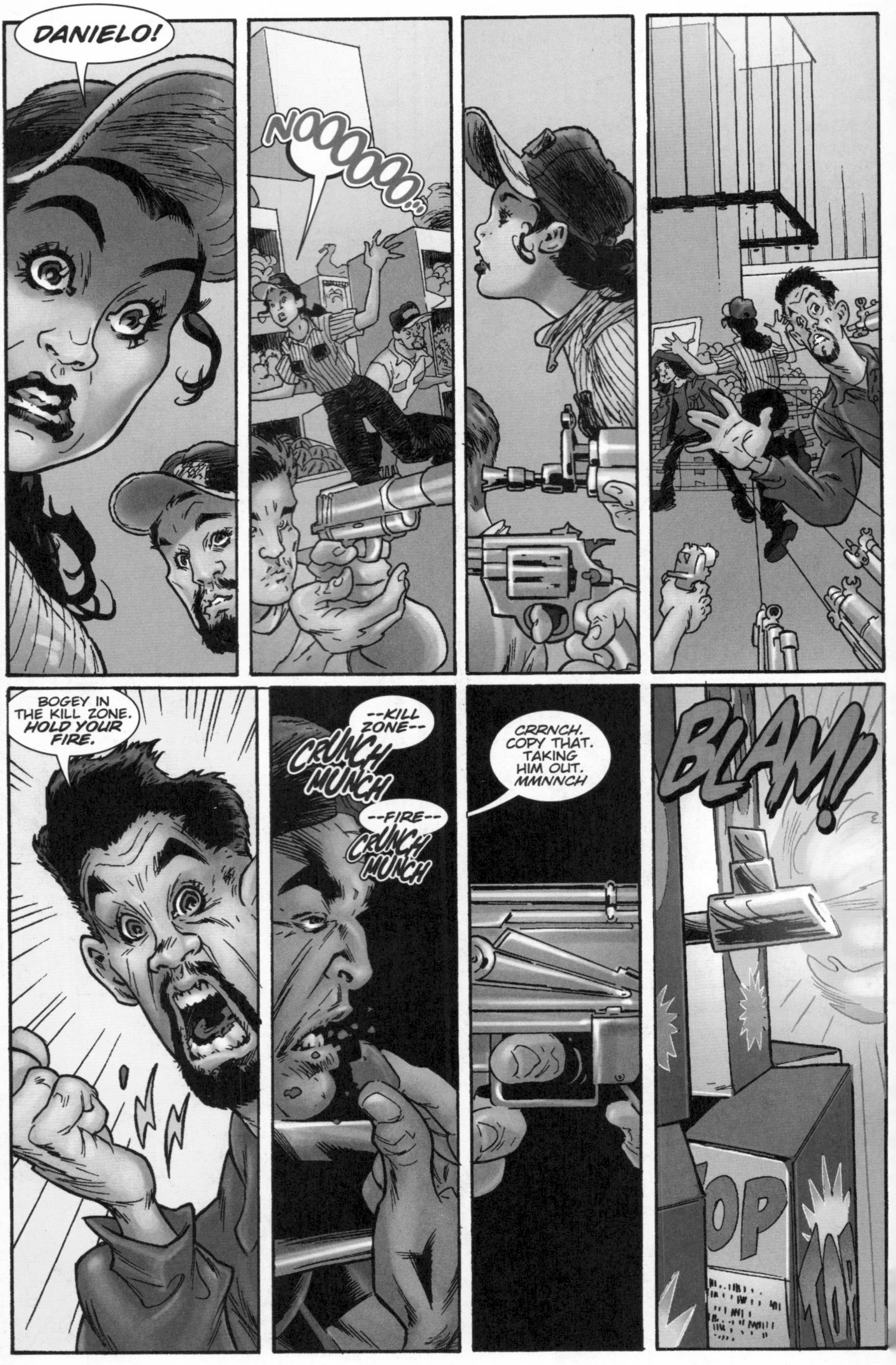
DANIELO!
NOOOOOO..
BOGEY IN THE KILL ZONE. HOLD YOUR FIRE.
--KILL ZONE--
CRUNCH MUNCH
--FIRE--
CRUNCH MUNCH
CRRNCH. COPY THAT. TAKING HIM OUT. MMNNCH
BLAM!

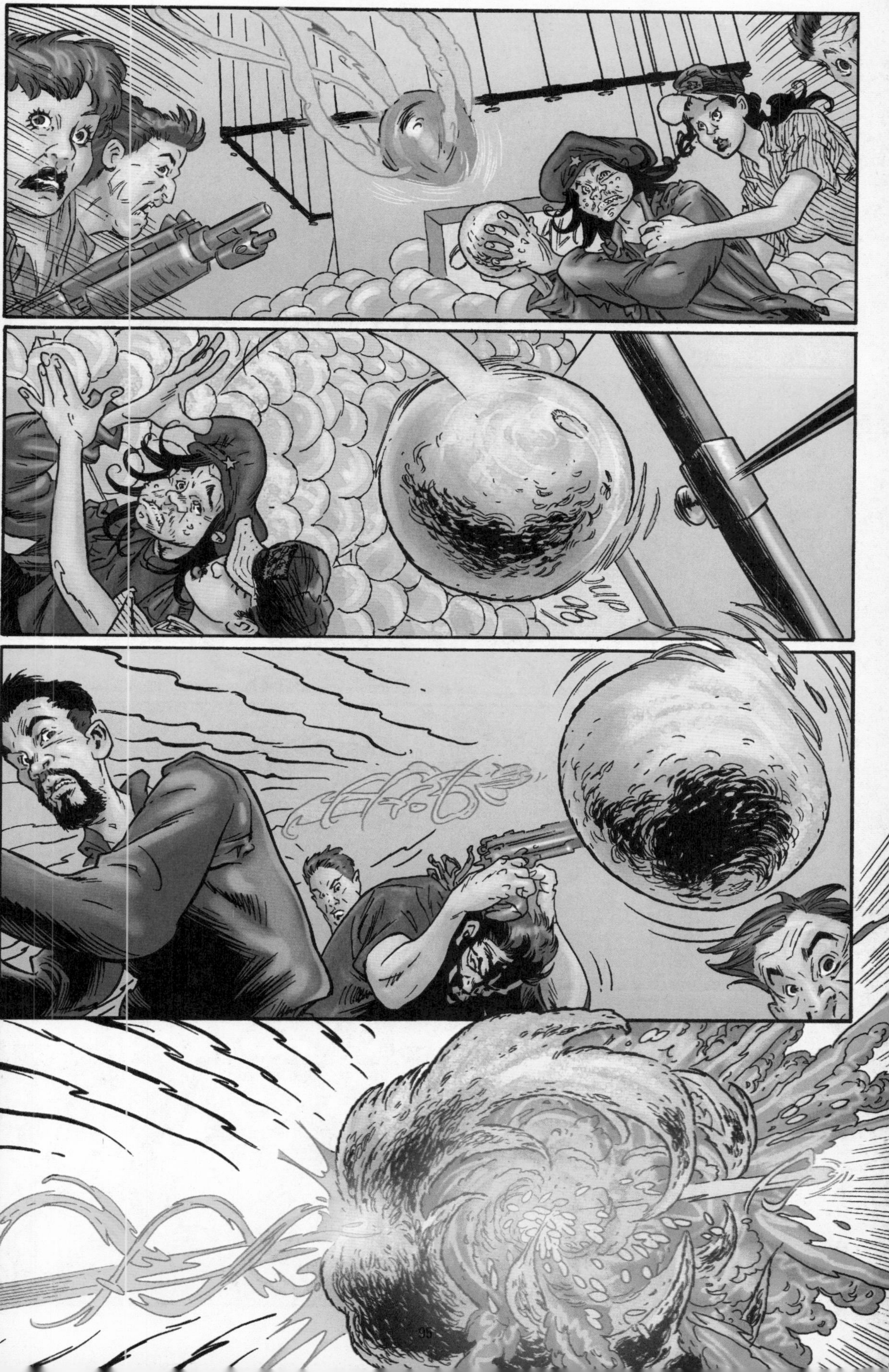

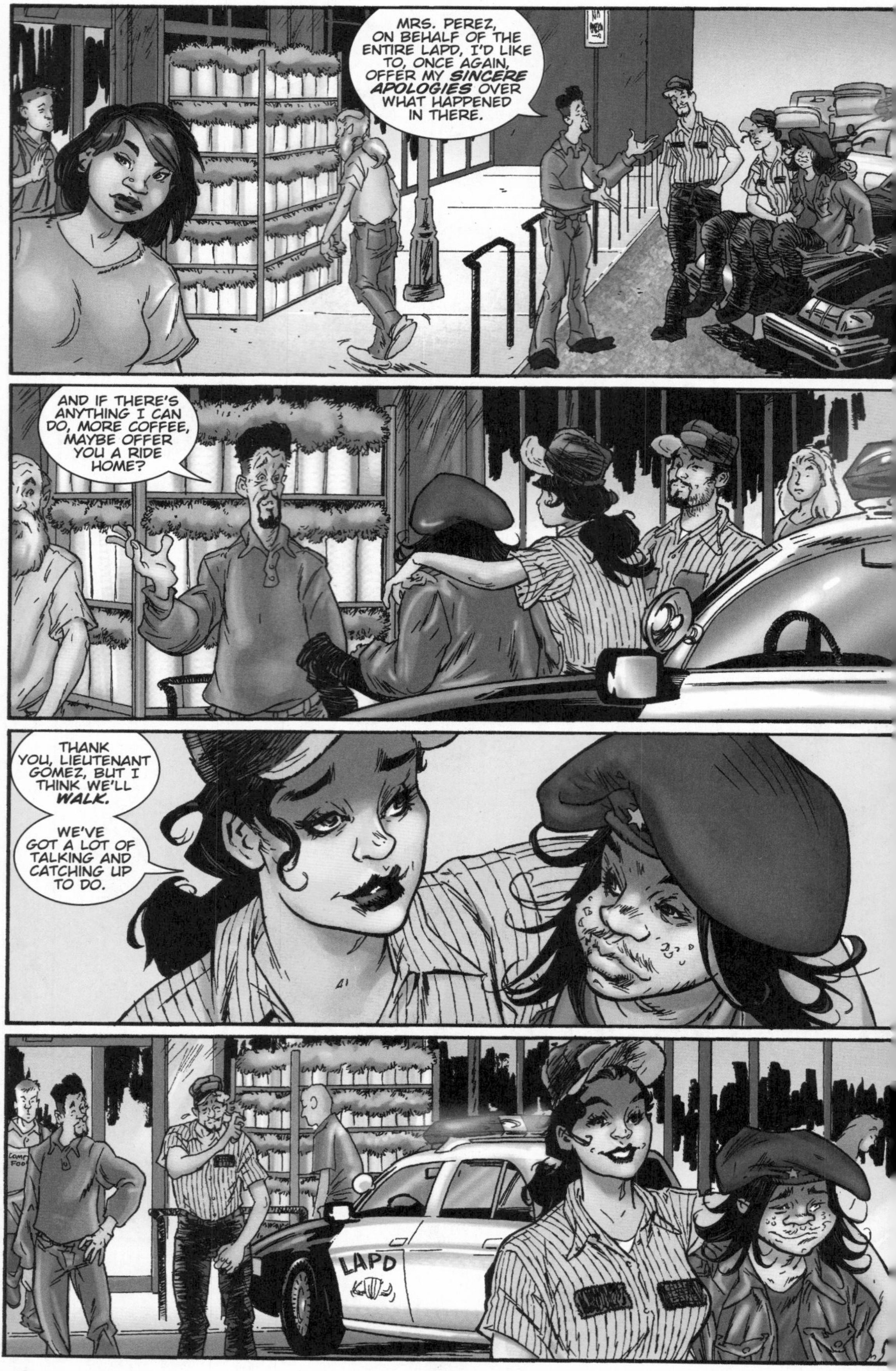
MRS. PEREZ, ON BEHALF OF THE ENTIRE LAPD, I'D LIKE TO, ONCE AGAIN, OFFER MY SINCERE APOLOGIES OVER WHAT HAPPENED IN THERE.
AND IF THERE'S ANYTHING I CAN DO, MORE COFFEE, MAYBE OFFER YOU A RIDE HOME?
THANK YOU, LIEUTENANT GOMEZ, BUT I THINK WE'LL WALK.
WE'VE GOT A LOT OF TALKING AND CATCHING UP TO DO.
LAPD

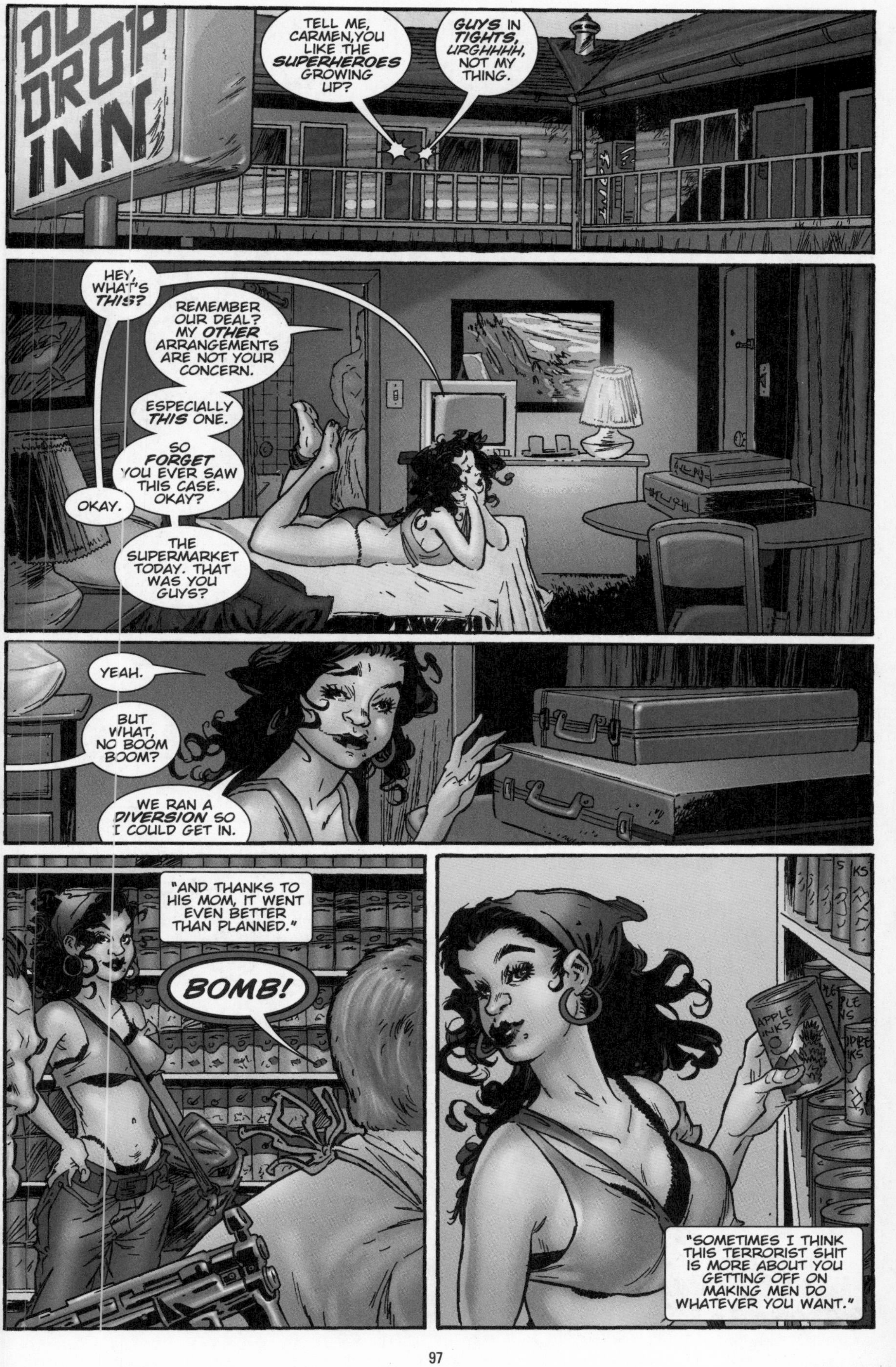
DU DROP INN
TELL ME, CARMEN, YOU LIKE THE SUPERHEROES GROWING UP?
GUYS IN TIGHTS, URGHHHH, NOT MY THING.
HEY, WHAT'S THIS?
REMEMBER OUR DEAL? MY OTHER ARRANGEMENTS ARE NOT YOUR CONCERN.
ESPECIALLY THIS ONE.
SO FORGET YOU EVER SAW THIS CASE. OKAY?
OKAY.
THE SUPERMARKET TODAY. THAT WAS YOU GUYS?
YEAH.
BUT WHAT, NO BOOM BOOM?
WE RAN A DIVERSION SO I COULD GET IN.
"AND THANKS TO HIS MOM, IT WENT EVEN BETTER THAN PLANNED."
BOMB!
APPLE INKS
"SOMETIMES I THINK THIS TERRORIST SHIT IS MORE ABOUT YOU GETTING OFF ON MAKING MEN DO WHATEVER YOU WANT."

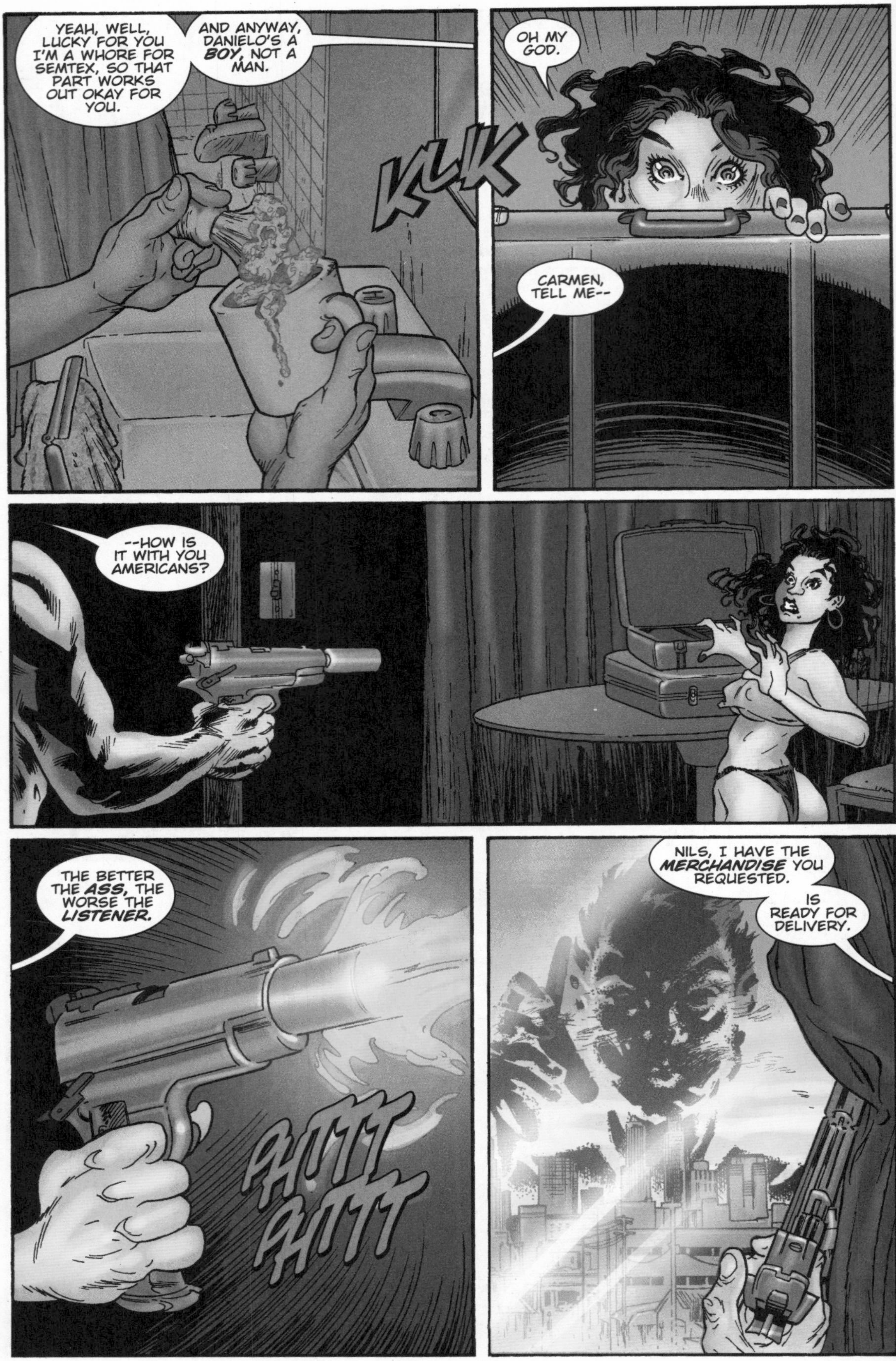
YEAH, WELL, LUCKY FOR YOU I'M A WHORE FOR SEMTEX, SO THAT PART WORKS OUT OKAY FOR YOU.
AND ANYWAY, DANIELO'S A BOY, NOT A MAN.
KLIK
OH MY GOD.
CARMEN, TELL ME--
--HOW IS IT WITH YOU AMERICANS?
THE BETTER THE ASS, THE WORSE THE LISTENER.
PHTTT PHTTT
NILS, I HAVE THE MERCHANDISE YOU REQUESTED.
IS READY FOR DELIVERY.

UG BROTHERS FOREVER CHAPTER ONE / COVER ART BY PHILIP BOND

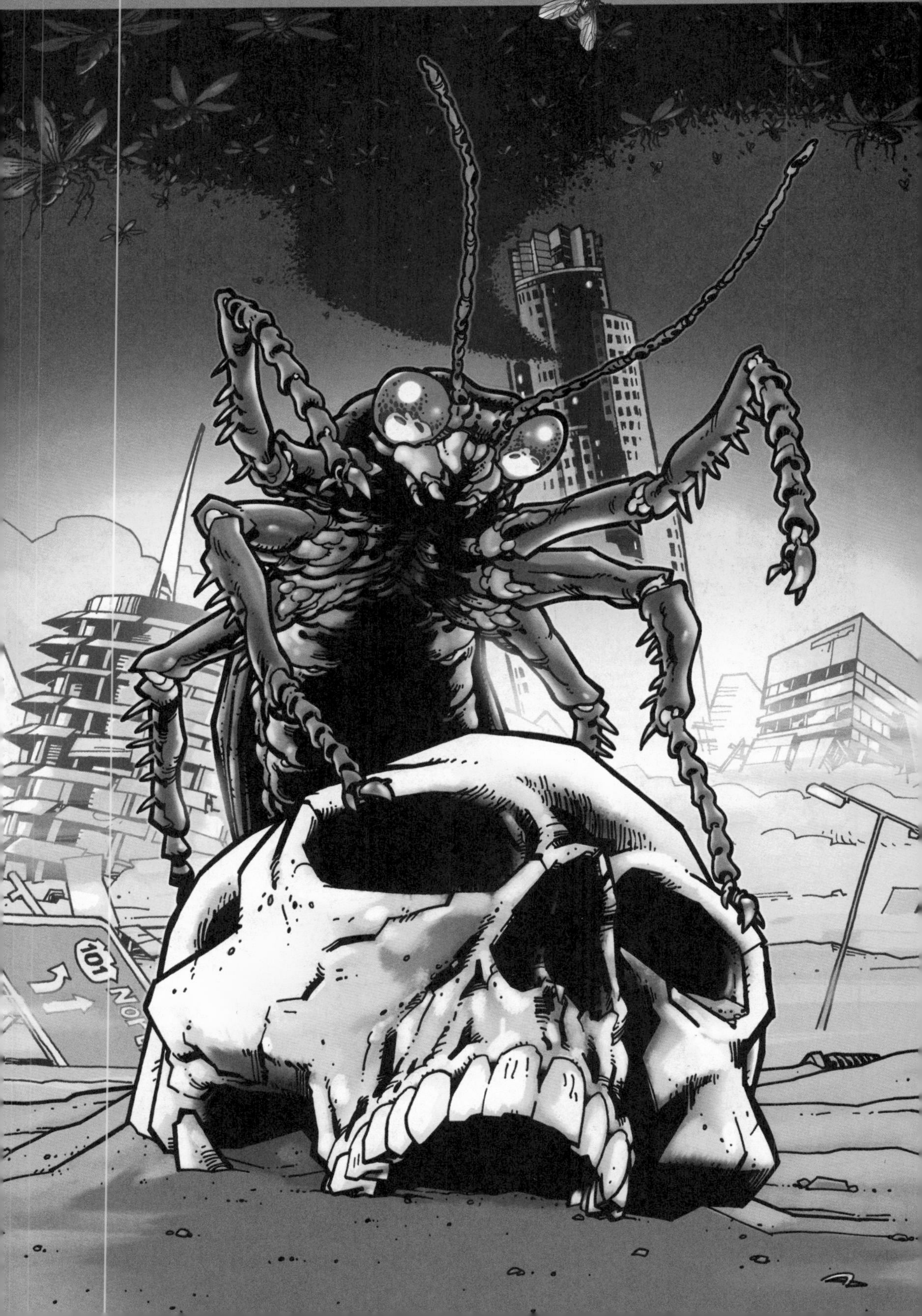

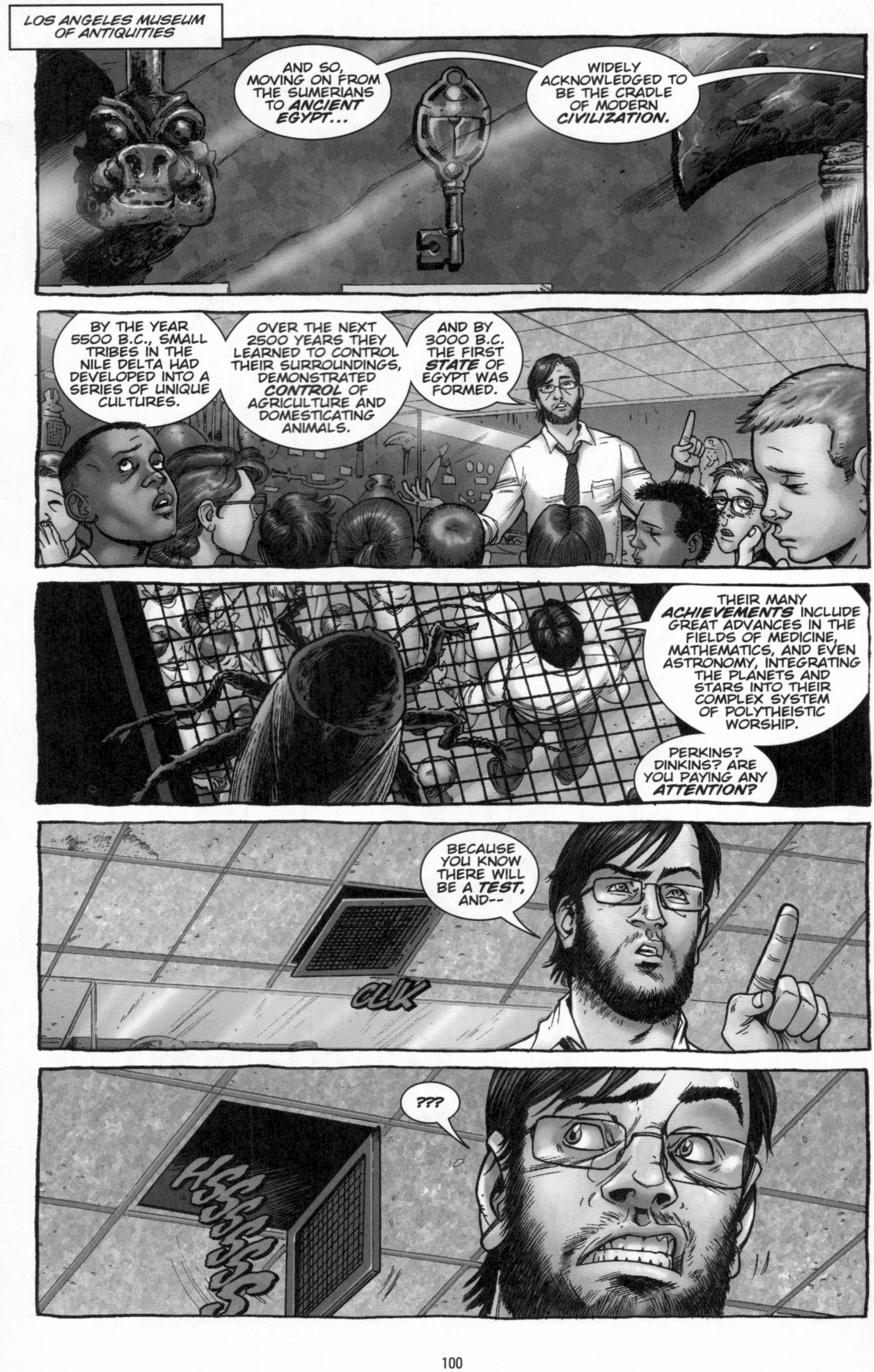
LOS ANGELES MUSEUM OF ANTIQUITIES
AND SO, MOVING ON FROM THE SUMERIANS TO ANCIENT EGYPT...
WIDELY ACKNOWLEDGED TO BE THE CRADLE OF MODERN CIVILIZATION.
BY THE YEAR 5500 B.C., SMALL TRIBES IN THE NILE DELTA HAD DEVELOPED INTO A SERIES OF UNIQUE CULTURES.
OVER THE NEXT 2500 YEARS THEY LEARNED TO CONTROL THEIR SURROUNDINGS, DEMONSTRATED CONTROL OF AGRICULTURE AND DOMESTICATING ANIMALS.
AND BY 3000 B.C. THE FIRST STATE OF EGYPT WAS FORMED.
THEIR MANY ACHIEVEMENTS INCLUDE GREAT ADVANCES IN THE FIELDS OF MEDICINE, MATHEMATICS, AND EVEN ASTRONOMY, INTEGRATING THE PLANETS AND STARS INTO THEIR COMPLEX SYSTEM OF POLYTHEISTIC WORSHIP.
PERKINS? DINKINS? ARE YOU PAYING ANY ATTENTION?
BECAUSE YOU KNOW THERE WILL BE A TEST, AND--
CLIK
???
HSSSSSSS

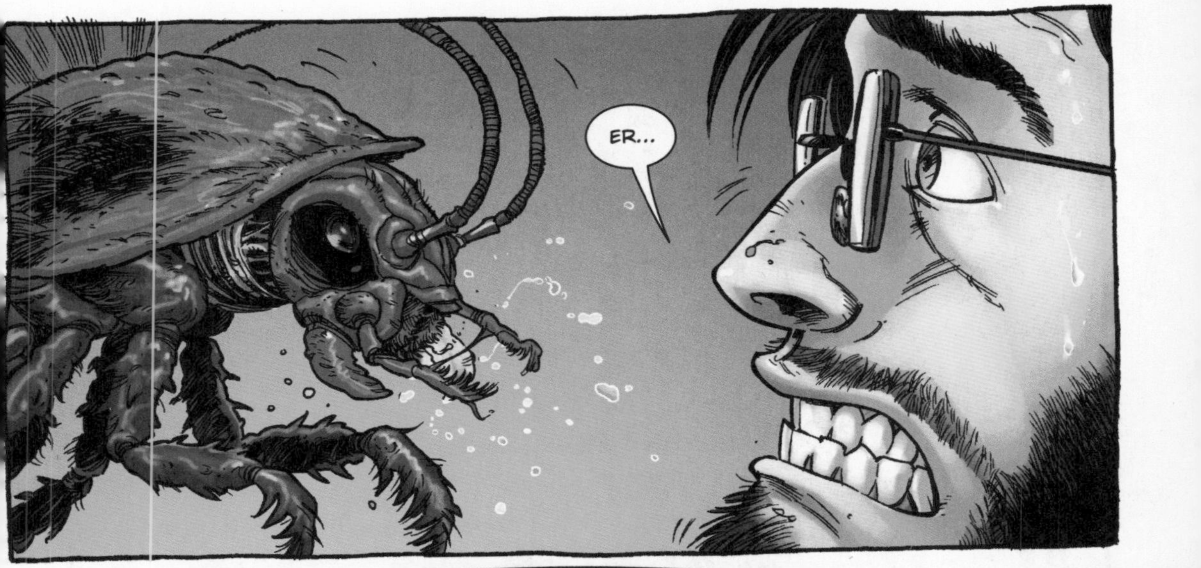
ER...

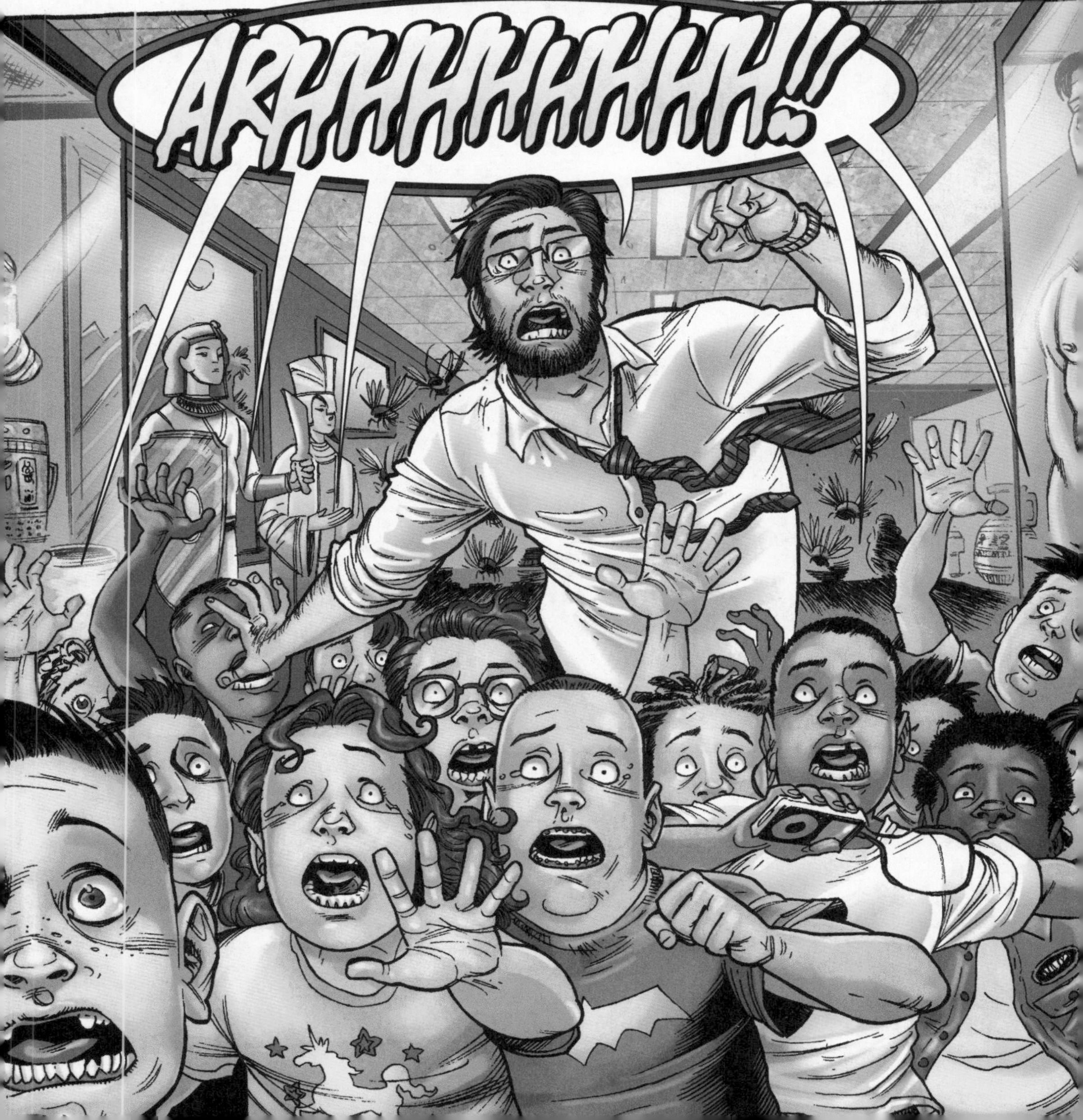
ARHHHHHHHHH!!

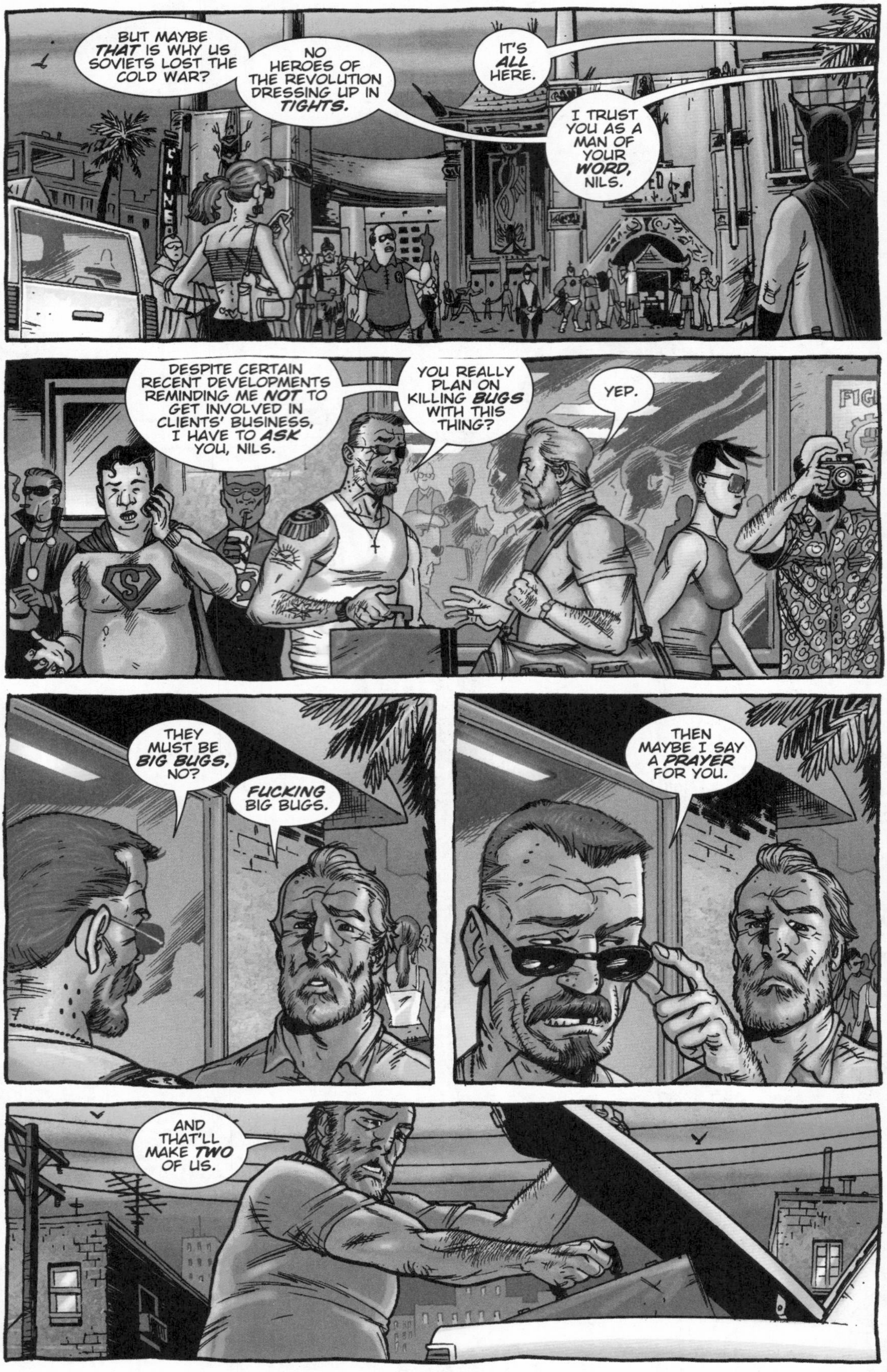
BUT MAYBE THAT IS WHY US SOVIETS LOST THE COLD WAR?
NO HEROES OF THE REVOLUTION DRESSING UP IN TIGHTS.
IT'S ALL HERE.
I TRUST YOU AS A MAN OF YOUR WORD, NILS.
DESPITE CERTAIN RECENT DEVELOPMENTS REMINDING ME NOT TO GET INVOLVED IN CLIENTS' BUSINESS, I HAVE TO ASK YOU, NILS.
YOU REALLY PLAN ON KILLING BUGS WITH THIS THING?
YEP.
THEY MUST BE BIG BUGS, NO?
FUCKING BIG BUGS.
THEN MAYBE I SAY A PRAYER FOR YOU.
AND THAT'LL MAKE TWO OF US.

THE ONLY THING THEY TOOK WAS THIS *KEY*, YEAH?

THAT'S *CORRECT*, DETECTIVE.

SO PROFESSOR, ANY SUSPICIOUS *VISITORS* TO THE MUSEUM RECENTLY?

ACTUALLY, LAST THURSDAY THERE *WERE* TWO MEN, MAYBE OF SOUTH PACIFIC ORIGIN, BOTH DRESSED IN IDENTICAL *ORANGE JUMPSUITS*.

AND APART FROM THEIR APPERANCE DID THEY ACTUALLY *DO* ANYTHING THAT YOU'D CLASS AS *SUSPICIOUS*?

DETECTIVE, AS AN EDUCATIONAL FACILITY IN LOS ANGELES, OUTSIDE OF THE OCCASIONAL SCHOOL GROUP, *WEEKS* CAN PASS BETWEEN ACTUAL VISITORS.

THEREFORE, *ANYONE* WHO COMES THROUGH THE DOORS TENDS TO STAND OUT.

DETECTIVE, THE TEACHER'S STILL IN A FETAL POSITION. BUT ONE OF THE RUG RATS STOPPED BLUBBERING LONG ENOUGH TO DRAW *THIS*.

YOU SAY YOU GOT ROBBED BY FUCKING *BUGS*?

OKAY, PROFESSOR WOLFE, SO ALONG WITH THE *ACTUAL* EGYPTIAN *BOX*, THE *FIRST* KEY WAS STOLEN FROM HENRY'S APARTMENT.

BUG-BEE-GONE

EXCELLENCE IN EXTERMINATING

AND IF YOU THINK *THIS* WAS THE SECOND KEY, WHAT ABOUT THE *THIRD?*

ROBBERY AT MUSEUM

YES, NILS. LAST WEEK REUTERS REPORTED A *SWISS BANKER* WITH A FETISH FOR COLLECTING EGYPTIAN ARTIFACTS TURNED UP *DEAD*.

AND YOU THINK HE WAS KILLED FOR THE THIRD KEY?

LIKE THE NAZI GOLD THAT MADE HIM RICH, *MOST* OF HIS COLLECTION WAS STOLEN. THEY'LL NEVER ADMIT TO JUST WHAT WAS TAKEN.

BUT WHY *NOW?* WHY ALL THE FOCUS ON THE KEYS?

ATAN MUST SEE AN OPPORTUNITY TO USE THE KEYS TO OPEN THE BOX AND BRING KHEPRON BACK.

WHICH IS?

WELL, WE'RE NOT SURE. BUT WE DO HAVE AN IDEA IT'S SOMETHING TO DO WITH THE GOD *ENANNA*.

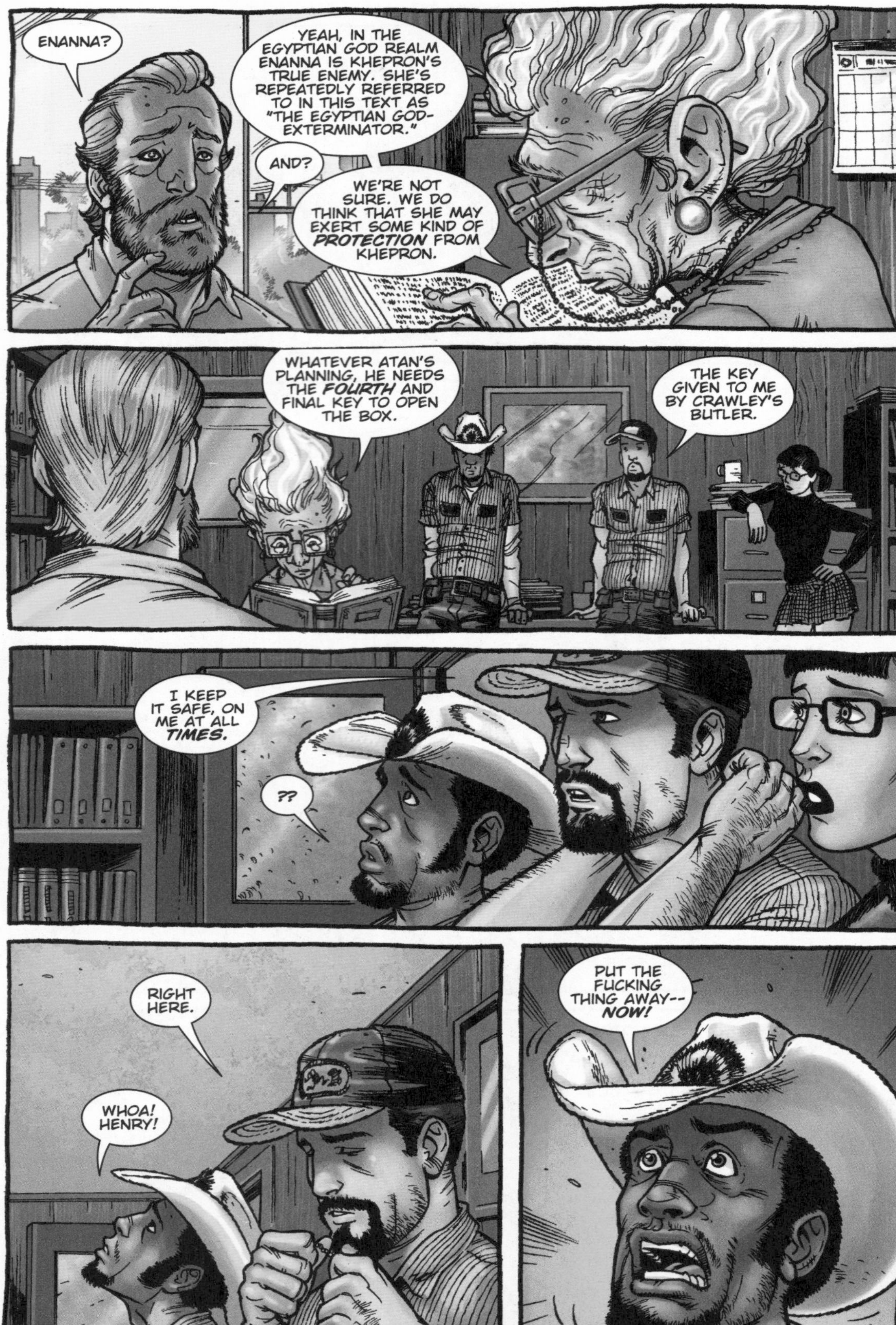
ENANNA?
YEAH, IN THE EGYPTIAN GOD REALM ENANNA IS KHEPRON'S TRUE ENEMY. SHE'S REPEATEDLY REFERRED TO IN THIS TEXT AS "THE EGYPTIAN GOD-EXTERMINATOR."
AND?
WE'RE NOT SURE. WE DO THINK THAT SHE MAY EXERT SOME KIND OF PROTECTION FROM KHEPRON.
WHATEVER ATAN'S PLANNING, HE NEEDS THE FOURTH AND FINAL KEY TO OPEN THE BOX.
THE KEY GIVEN TO ME BY CRAWLEY'S BUTLER.
I KEEP IT SAFE, ON ME AT ALL TIMES.
??
RIGHT HERE.
WHOA! HENRY!
PUT THE FUCKING THING AWAY-- NOW!

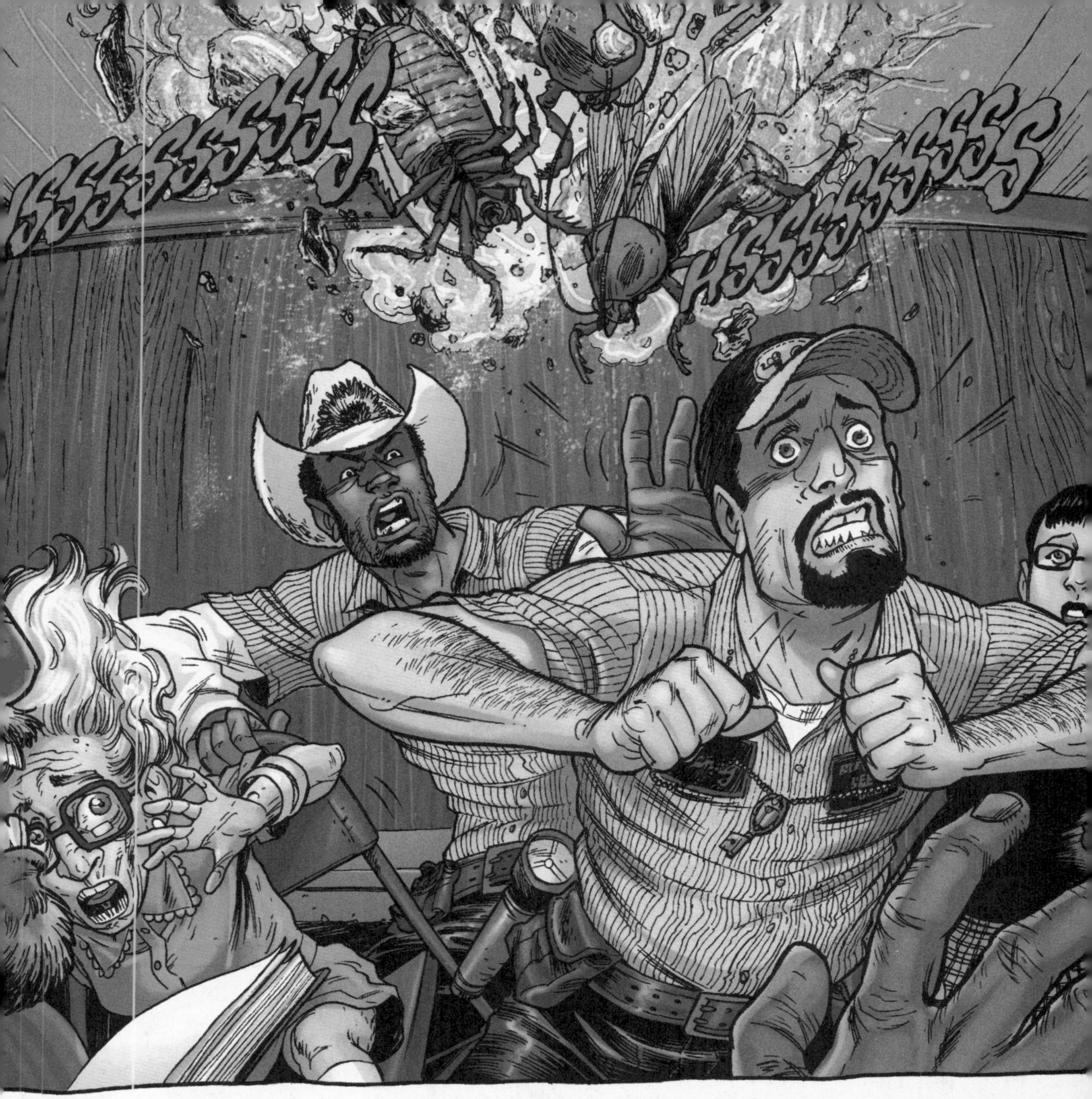
HSSSSSSSSSS
HSSSSSSSSSSS

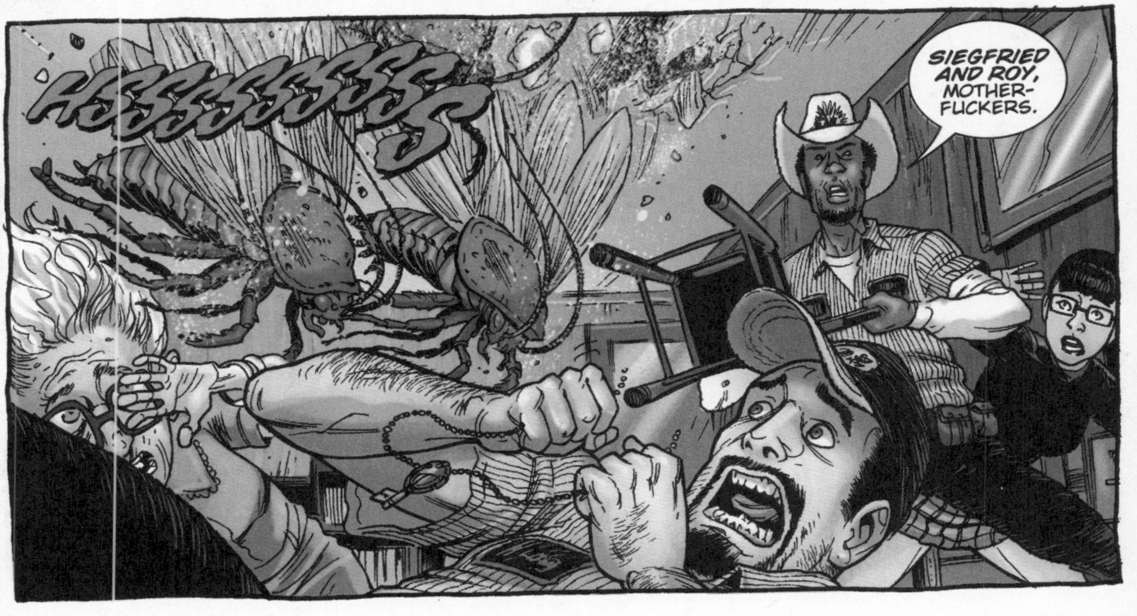
HSSSSSSSSSS
SIEGFRIED AND ROY, MOTHER-FUCKERS.

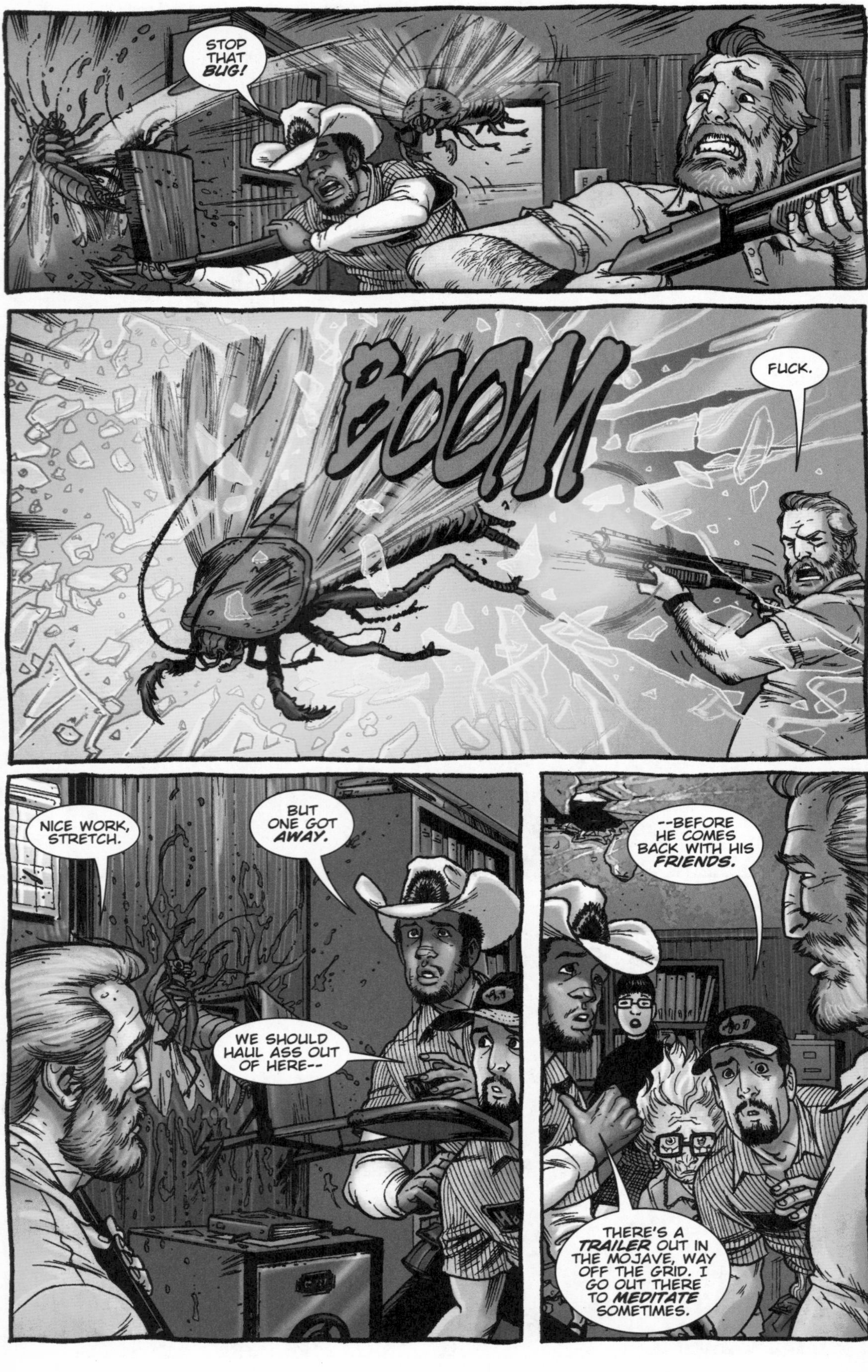
STOP THAT BUG!
BOOM
FUCK.
NICE WORK, STRETCH.
BUT ONE GOT AWAY.
WE SHOULD HAUL ASS OUT OF HERE--
--BEFORE HE COMES BACK WITH HIS FRIENDS.
THERE'S A TRAILER OUT IN THE MOJAVE, WAY OFF THE GRID. I GO OUT THERE TO MEDITATE SOMETIMES.

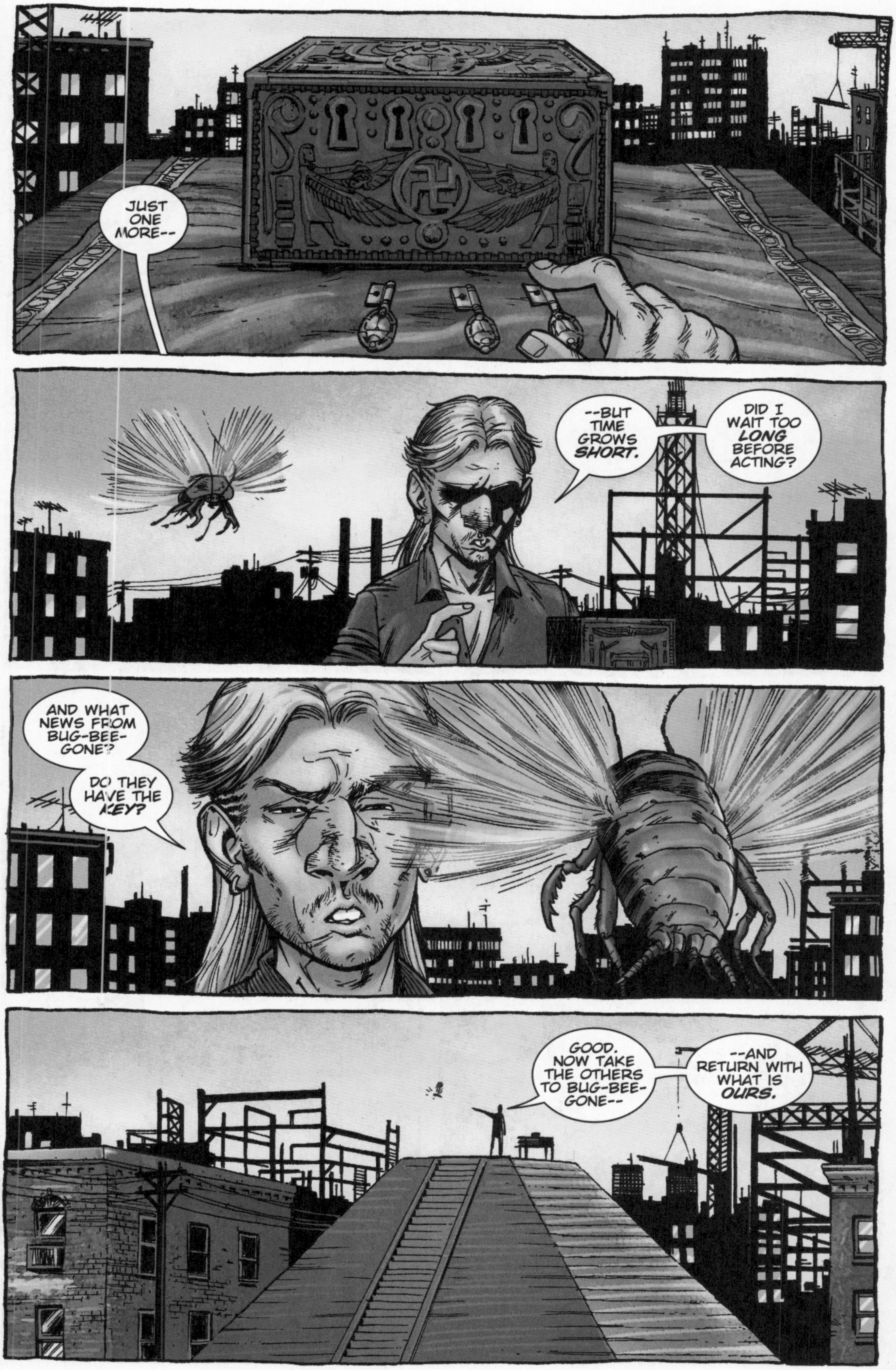
JUST ONE MORE--
--BUT TIME GROWS SHORT.
DID I WAIT TOO LONG BEFORE ACTING?
AND WHAT NEWS FROM BUG-BEE-GONE?
DO THEY HAVE THE KEY?
GOOD. NOW TAKE THE OTHERS TO BUG-BEE-GONE--
--AND RETURN WITH WHAT IS OURS.

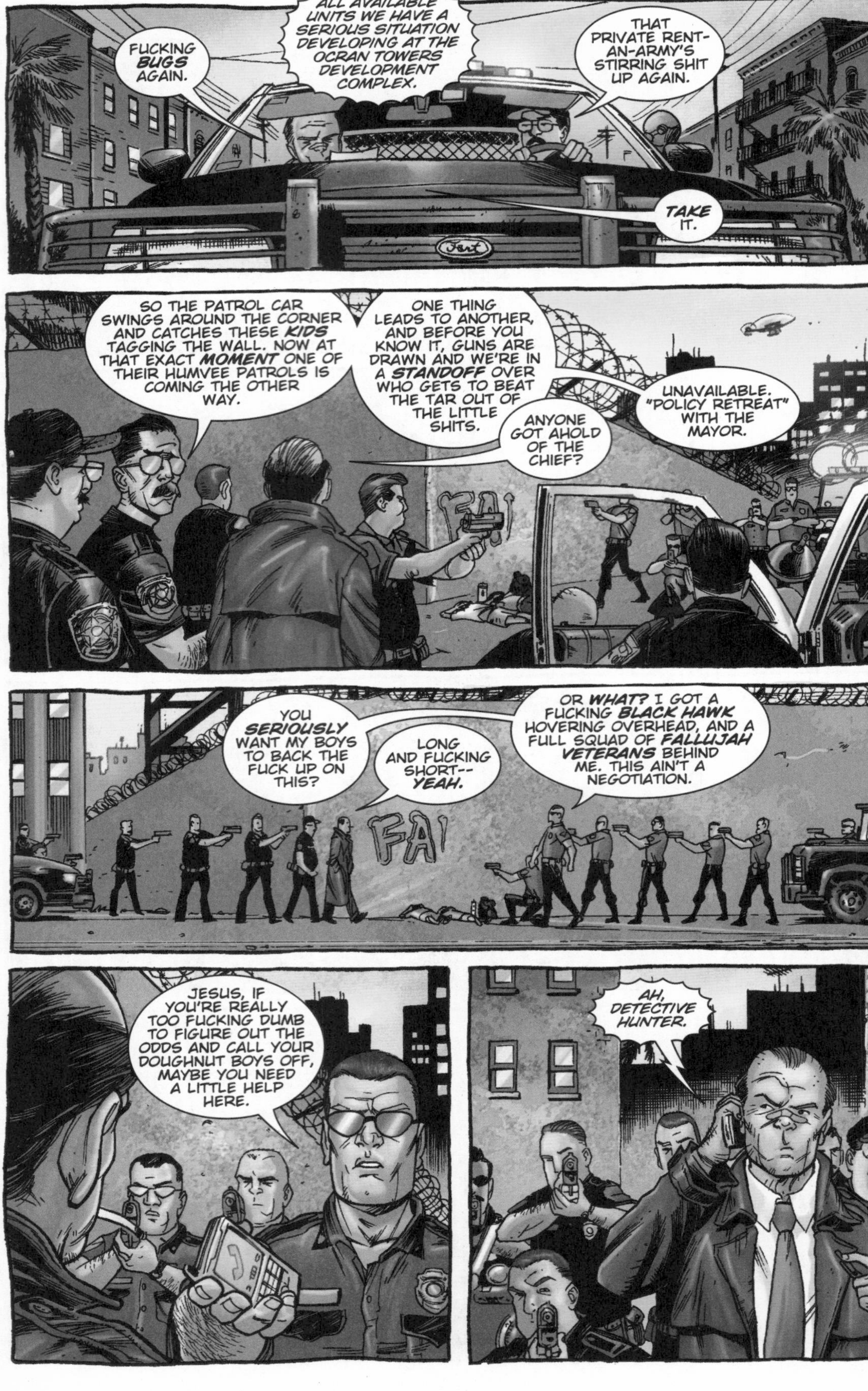
FUCKING BUGS AGAIN.
ALL AVAILABLE UNITS WE HAVE A SERIOUS SITUATION DEVELOPING AT THE OCRAN TOWERS DEVELOPMENT COMPLEX.
THAT PRIVATE RENT-AN-ARMY'S STIRRING SHIT UP AGAIN.
TAKE IT.
SO THE PATROL CAR SWINGS AROUND THE CORNER AND CATCHES THESE KIDS TAGGING THE WALL. NOW AT THAT EXACT MOMENT ONE OF THEIR HUMVEE PATROLS IS COMING THE OTHER WAY.
ONE THING LEADS TO ANOTHER, AND BEFORE YOU KNOW IT, GUNS ARE DRAWN AND WE'RE IN A STANDOFF OVER WHO GETS TO BEAT THE TAR OUT OF THE LITTLE SHITS.
ANYONE GOT AHOLD OF THE CHIEF?
UNAVAILABLE. "POLICY RETREAT" WITH THE MAYOR.
YOU SERIOUSLY WANT MY BOYS TO BACK THE FUCK UP ON THIS?
LONG AND FUCKING SHORT-- YEAH.
OR WHAT? I GOT A FUCKING BLACK HAWK HOVERING OVERHEAD, AND A FULL SQUAD OF FALLUJAH VETERANS BEHIND ME. THIS AIN'T A NEGOTIATION.
JESUS, IF YOU'RE REALLY TOO FUCKING DUMB TO FIGURE OUT THE ODDS AND CALL YOUR DOUGHNUT BOYS OFF, MAYBE YOU NEED A LITTLE HELP HERE.
AH, DETECTIVE HUNTER.

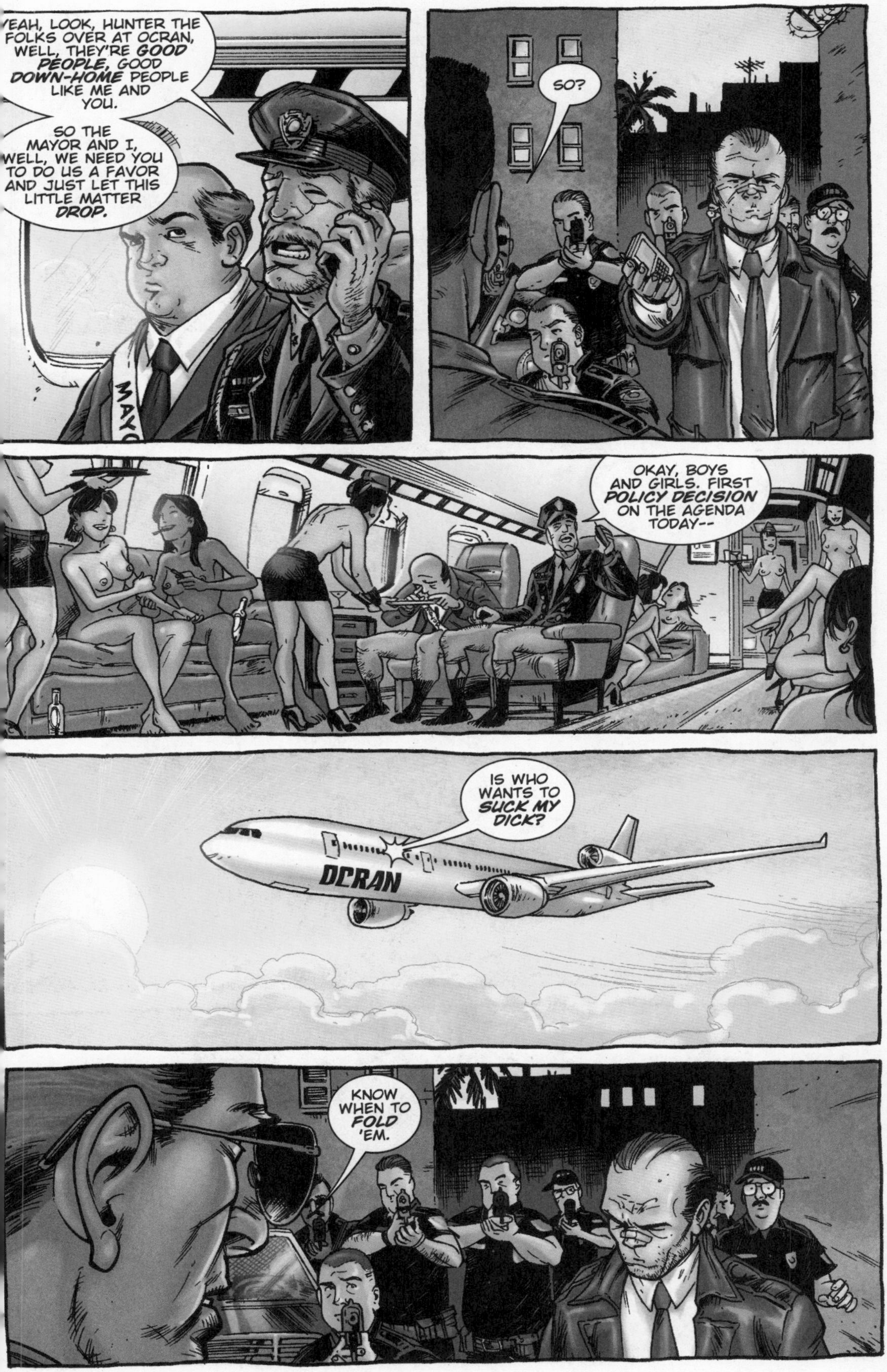
YEAH, LOOK, HUNTER THE FOLKS OVER AT OCRAN, WELL, THEY'RE GOOD PEOPLE, GOOD DOWN-HOME PEOPLE LIKE ME AND YOU.
SO THE MAYOR AND I, WELL, WE NEED YOU TO DO US A FAVOR AND JUST LET THIS LITTLE MATTER DROP.
SO?
OKAY, BOYS AND GIRLS. FIRST POLICY DECISION ON THE AGENDA TODAY--
IS WHO WANTS TO SUCK MY DICK?
OCRAN
KNOW WHEN TO FOLD 'EM.

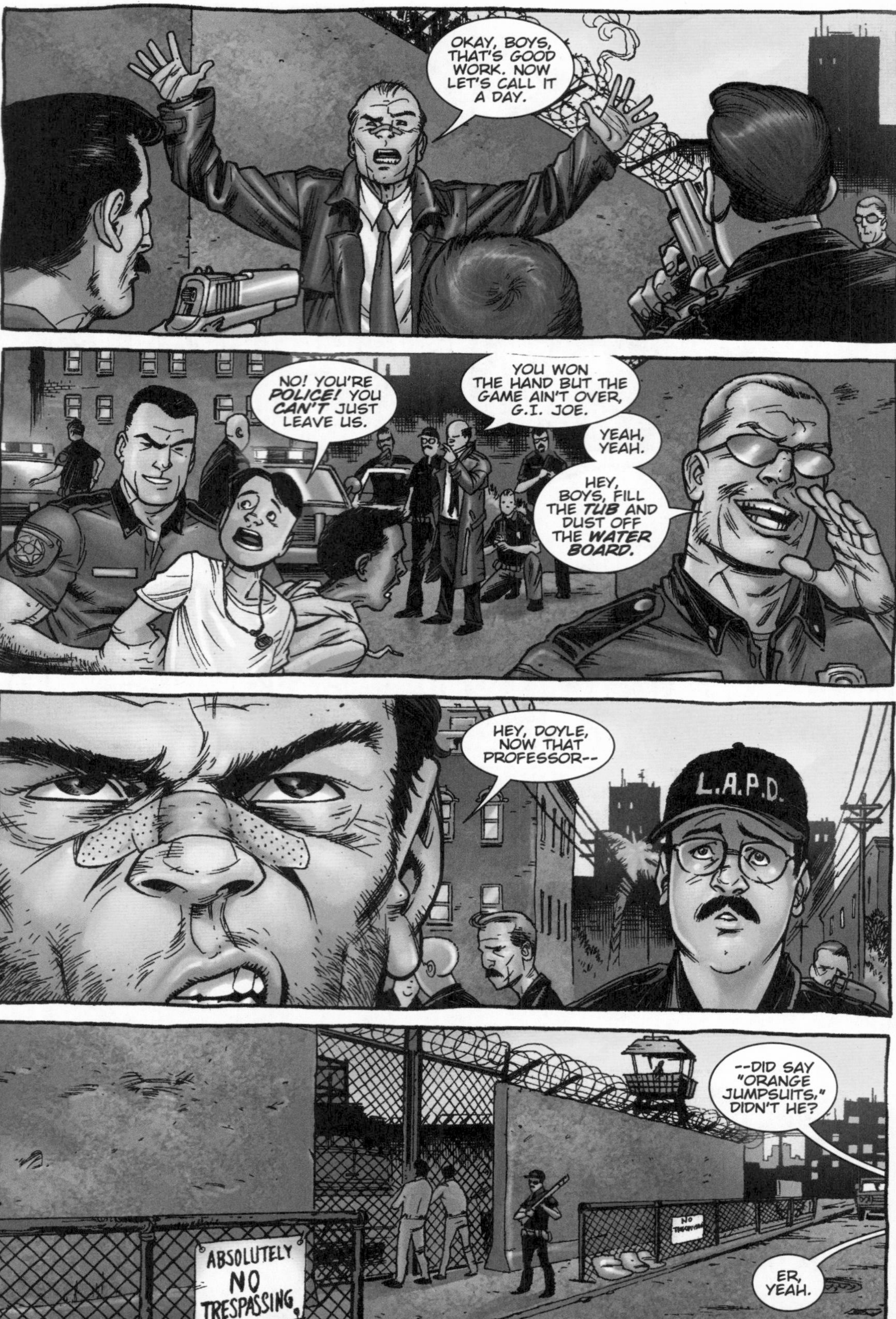
OKAY, BOYS, THAT'S GOOD WORK. NOW LET'S CALL IT A DAY.
NO! YOU'RE *POLICE!* YOU *CAN'T* JUST LEAVE US.
YOU WON THE HAND BUT THE GAME AIN'T OVER, G.I. JOE.
YEAH, YEAH.
HEY, BOYS, FILL THE *TUB* AND DUST OFF THE *WATER BOARD.*
HEY, DOYLE, NOW THAT PROFESSOR--
L.A.P.D.
--DID SAY "ORANGE JUMPSUITS," DIDN'T HE?
ER, YEAH.
ABSOLUTELY NO TRESPASSING

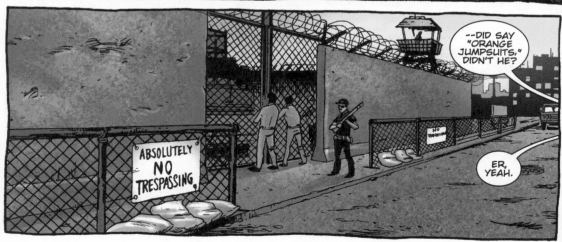

TONIGHT, *ASTRONOMY BUFFS* ARE PREPARING FOR A RARE *LUNAR ECLIPSE* OF SATURN.

TURN THE FUCKING RADIO OFF, I'M TRYING TO FUCKING *THINK* HERE.

SO WE GOT *BUGS*, EGYPTIAN KEYS AND GUYS IN ORANGE FUCKING JUMPSUITS AT THE MUSEUM.

WE GOT A *MERCENARY ARMY* PROTECTING AN EMPTY FUCKING BUILDING SITE, WHERE THEM JUMPSUIT FREAKS CROP UP AGAIN.

AND SOMEONE'S BOTHERED TO GO TO THE ADMITTEDLY SMALL EFFORT OF *BUYING* THE MAYOR AND THE POLICE CHIEF.

ER, DETECTIVE HUNTER.

SHUT UP, I'M *THINKING*.

SO WHAT THE FUCK ARE THEY KEEPING BEHIND THAT *WALL?*

WHAT THE HELL ARE YOU DOING?

WHAT HAPPENED TO THE FUCKING *SKY?*

YOU THINK IT'S THE *BUGS* FROM THE *MUSEUM?*

YEAH, AND I KNOW WHERE THEY'RE FUCKING *HEADING.* LET'S ROLL.

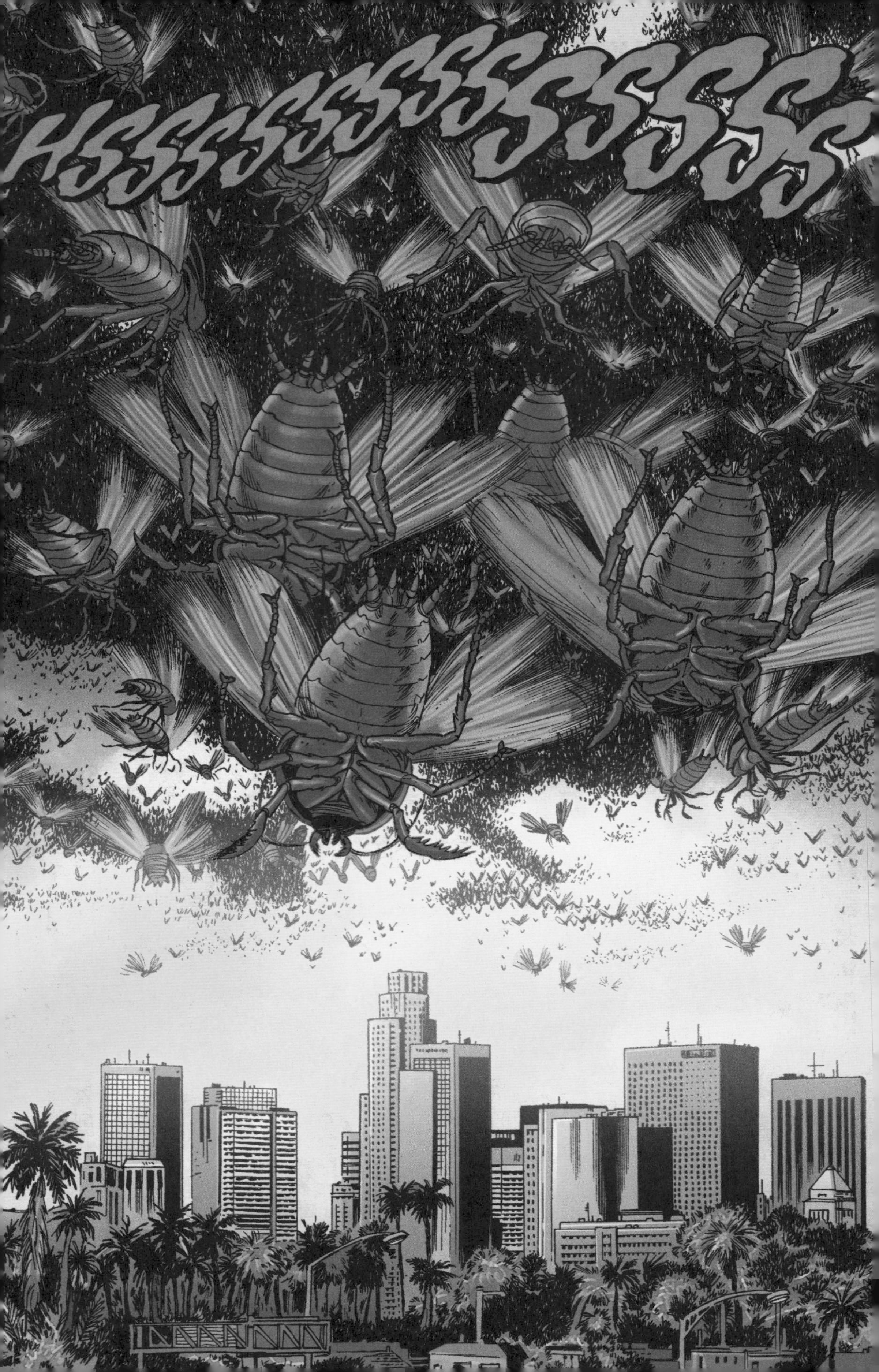
HSSSSSSSSSSSSSS

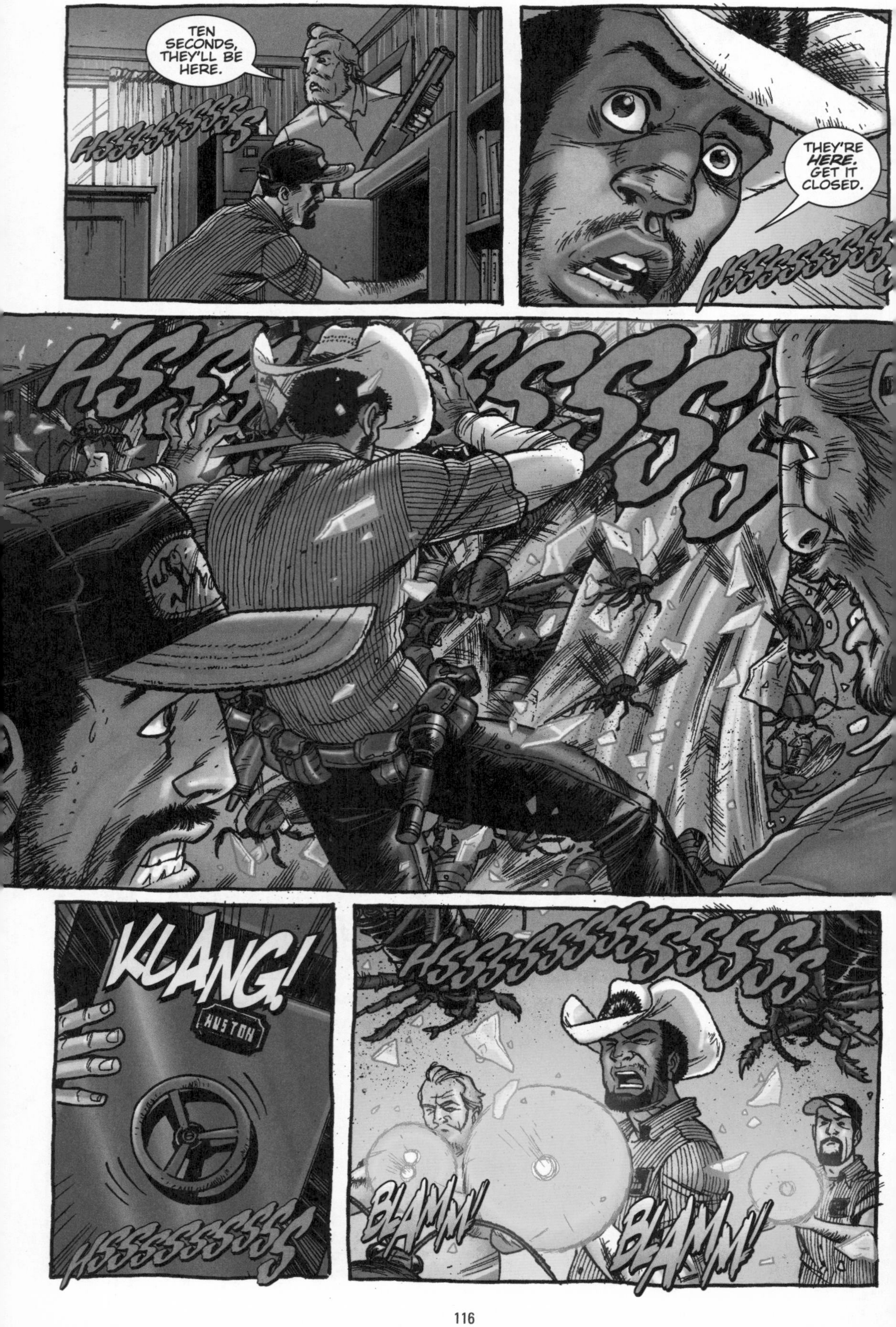
TEN SECONDS, THEY'LL BE HERE.
HSSSSSSSSS
THEY'RE HERE. GET IT CLOSED.
HSSSSSSSSSS
KLANG!
HUSTON
HSSSSSSSSSS
HSSSSSSSSSSSSSSS
BLAMM!
BLAMM!

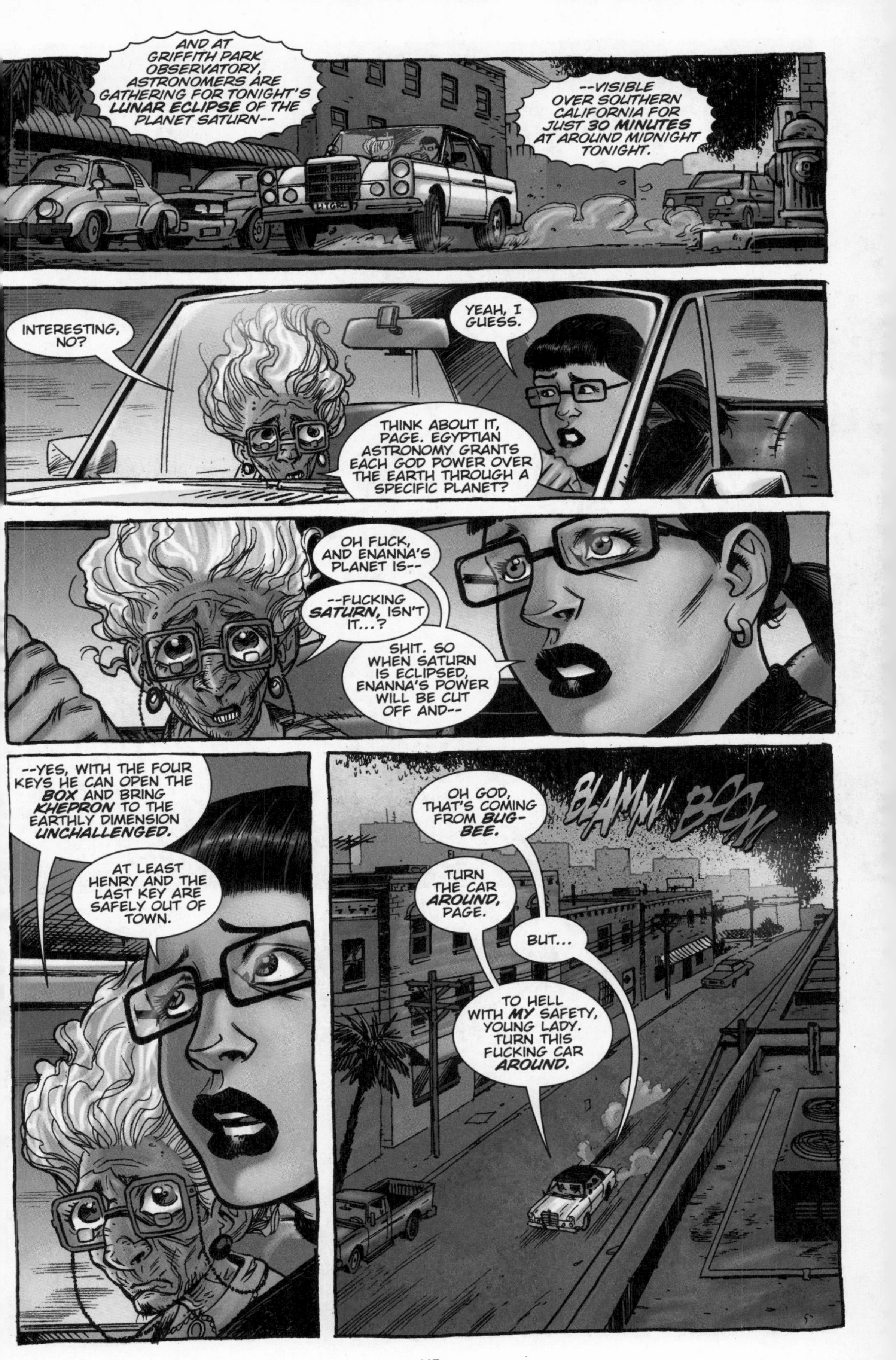
AND AT GRIFFITH PARK OBSERVATORY, ASTRONOMERS ARE GATHERING FOR TONIGHT'S LUNAR ECLIPSE OF THE PLANET SATURN--
--VISIBLE OVER SOUTHERN CALIFORNIA FOR JUST 30 MINUTES AT AROUND MIDNIGHT TONIGHT.
INTERESTING, NO?
YEAH, I GUESS.
THINK ABOUT IT, PAGE. EGYPTIAN ASTRONOMY GRANTS EACH GOD POWER OVER THE EARTH THROUGH A SPECIFIC PLANET?
OH FUCK, AND ENANNA'S PLANET IS--
--FUCKING SATURN, ISN'T IT...?
SHIT. SO WHEN SATURN IS ECLIPSED, ENANNA'S POWER WILL BE CUT OFF AND--
--YES, WITH THE FOUR KEYS HE CAN OPEN THE BOX AND BRING KHEPRON TO THE EARTHLY DIMENSION UNCHALLENGED.
AT LEAST HENRY AND THE LAST KEY ARE SAFELY OUT OF TOWN.
BLAMM! BOOM
OH GOD, THAT'S COMING FROM BUG-BEE.
TURN THE CAR AROUND, PAGE.
BUT...
TO HELL WITH MY SAFETY, YOUNG LADY. TURN THIS FUCKING CAR AROUND.

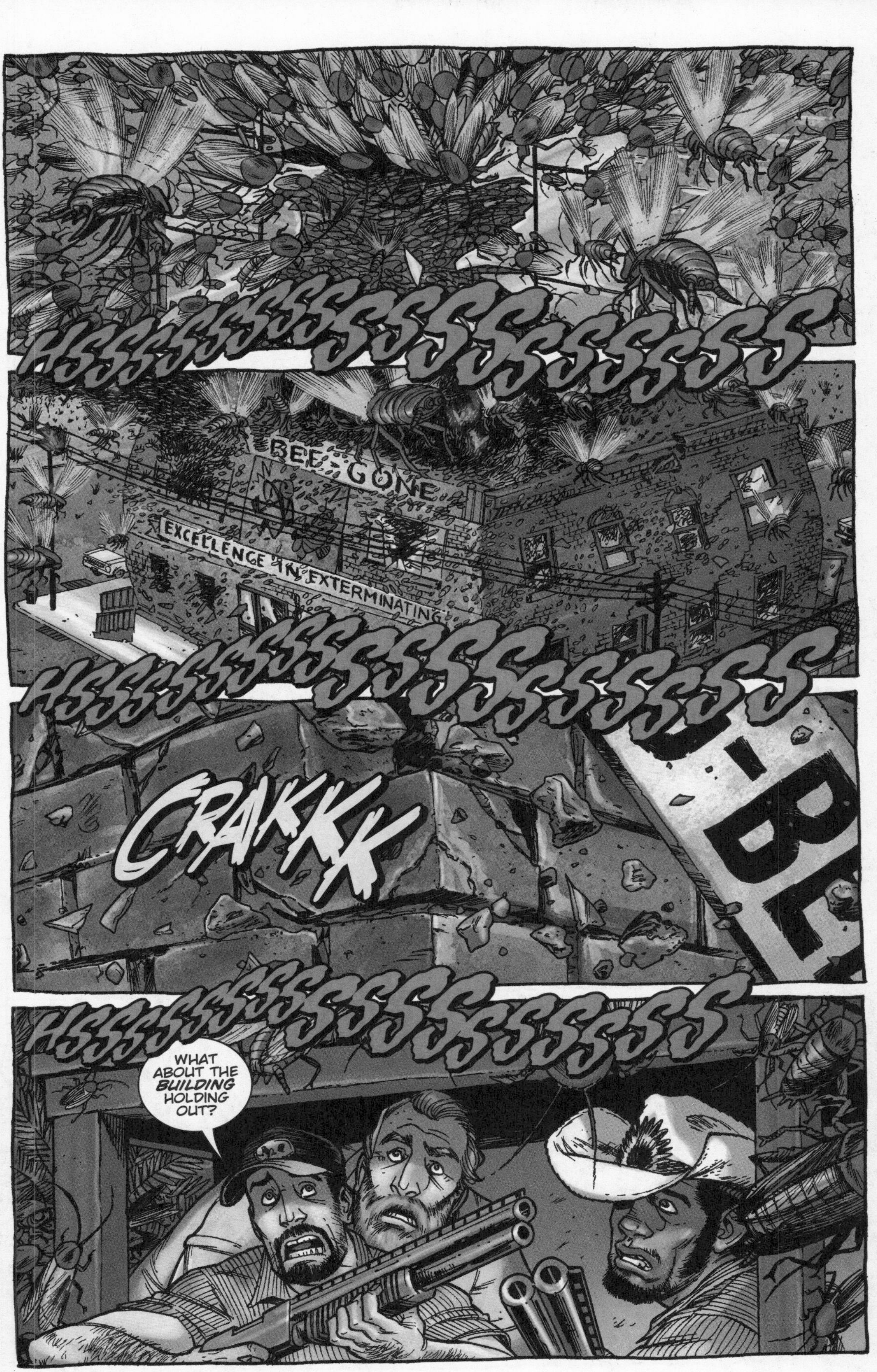
HSSSSSSSSSSSSSSSSSSSS
BEE-GONE
EXCELLENCE IN EXTERMINATING
HSSSSSSSSSSSSSSSSSSSS
CRAKKK
HSSSSSSSSSSSSSSSSSSSS
WHAT ABOUT THE *BUILDING* HOLDING OUT?

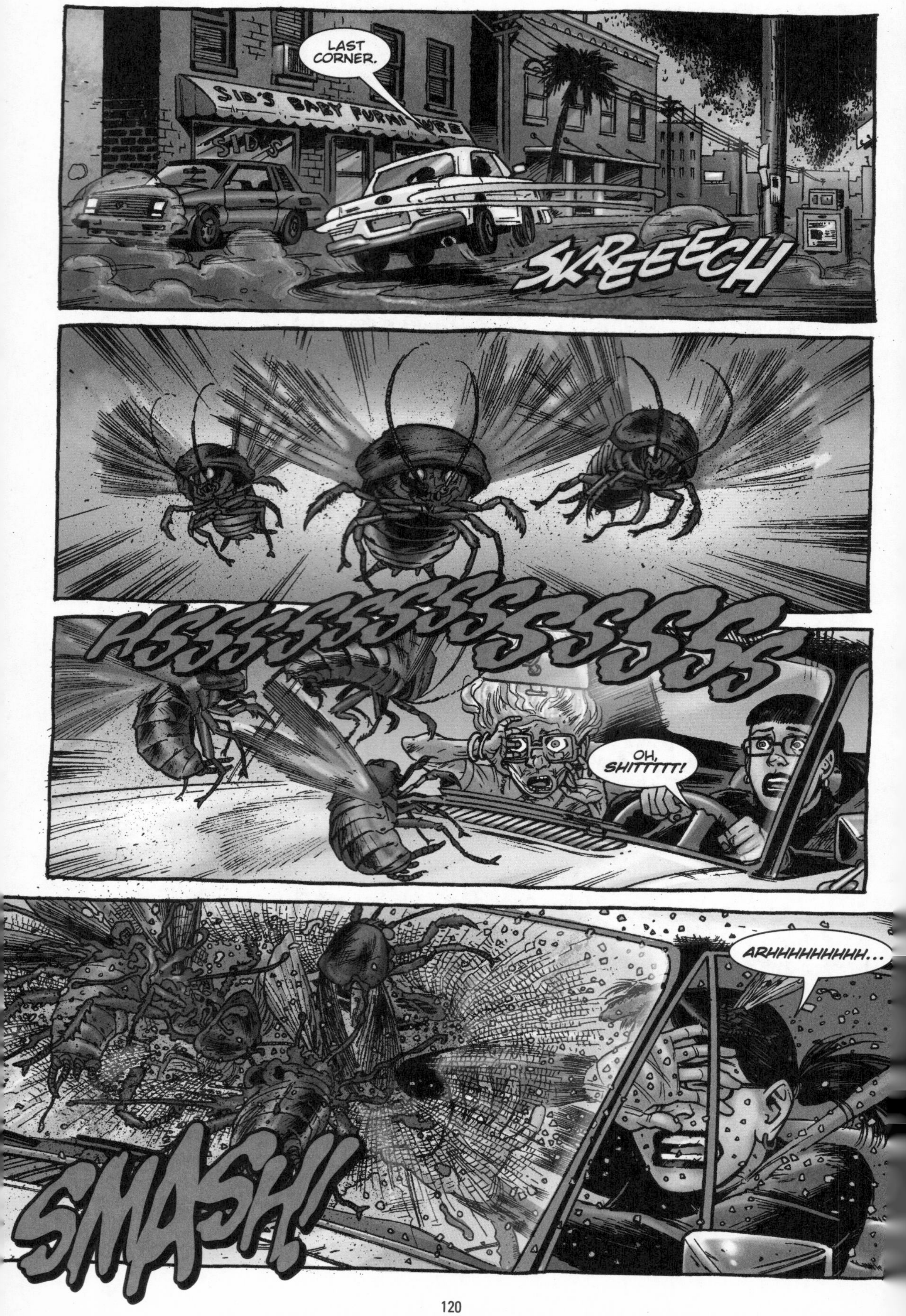
LAST CORNER.
SID'S
SKREEECH
HSSSSSSSSSSSS
OH, SHITTTTTT!
ARHHHHHHHHH...
SMASH!

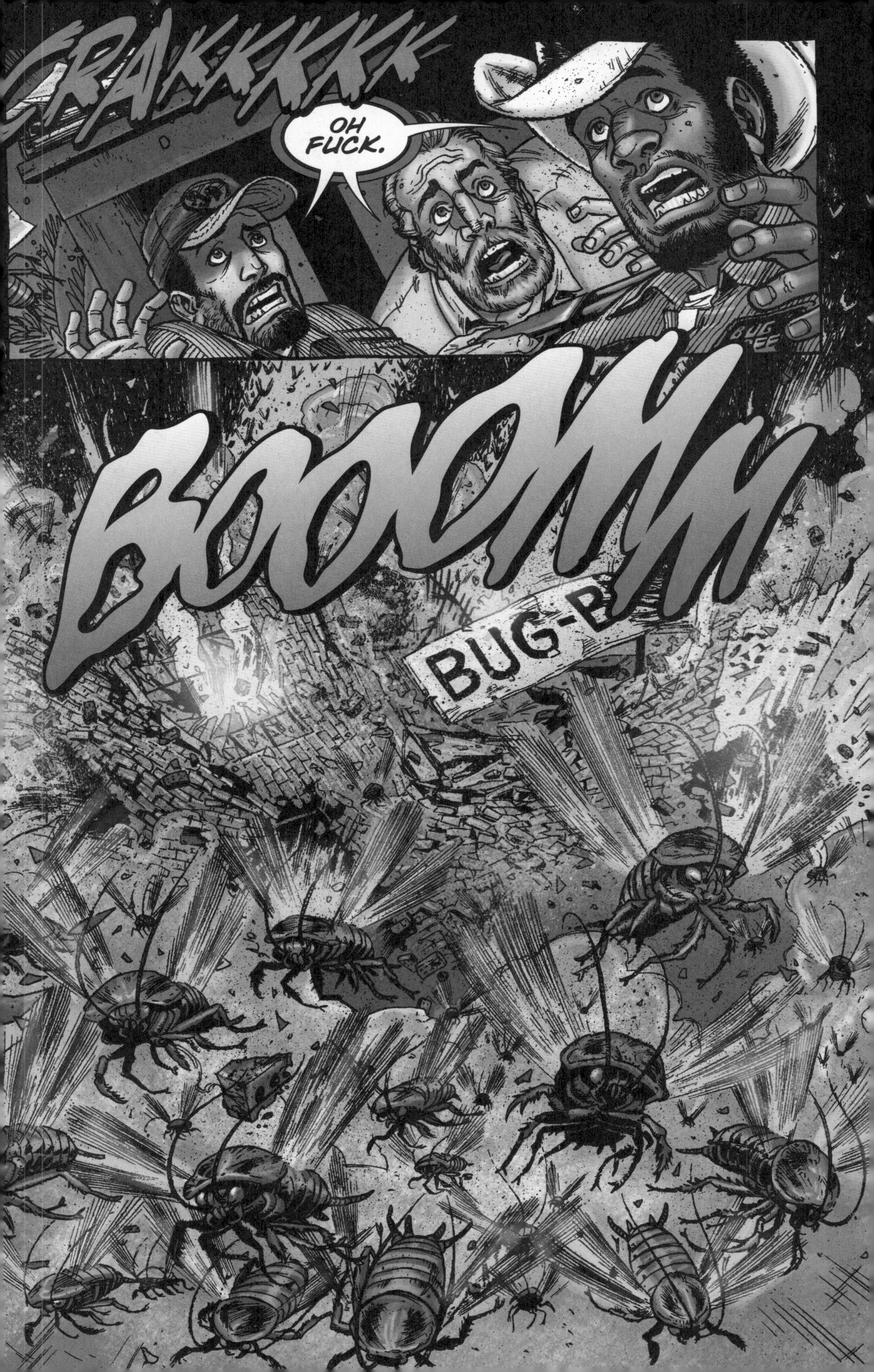
CRAKKKKKK
OH FUCK.
BOOOMM
BUG-B

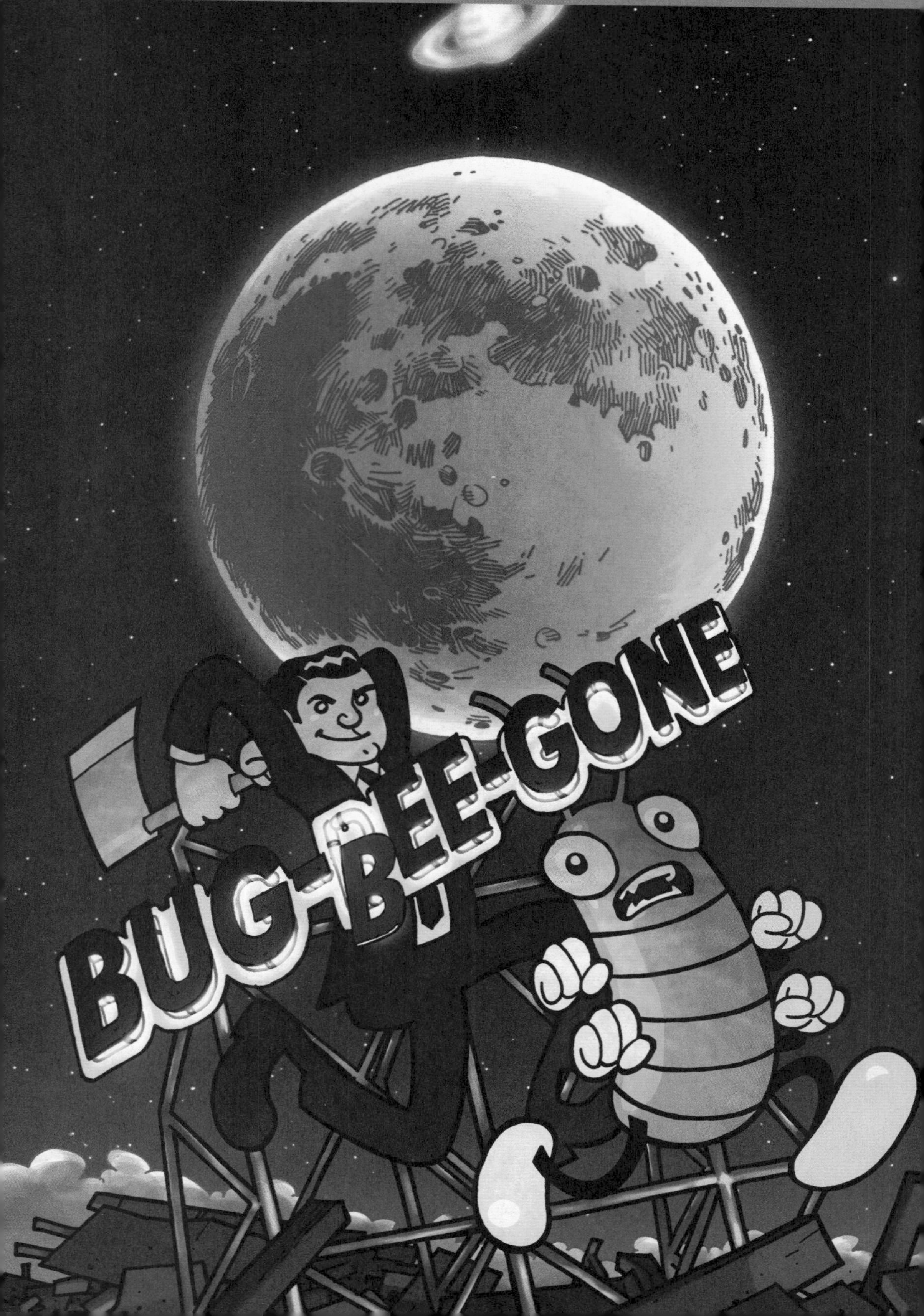
BUG-BEE-GONE

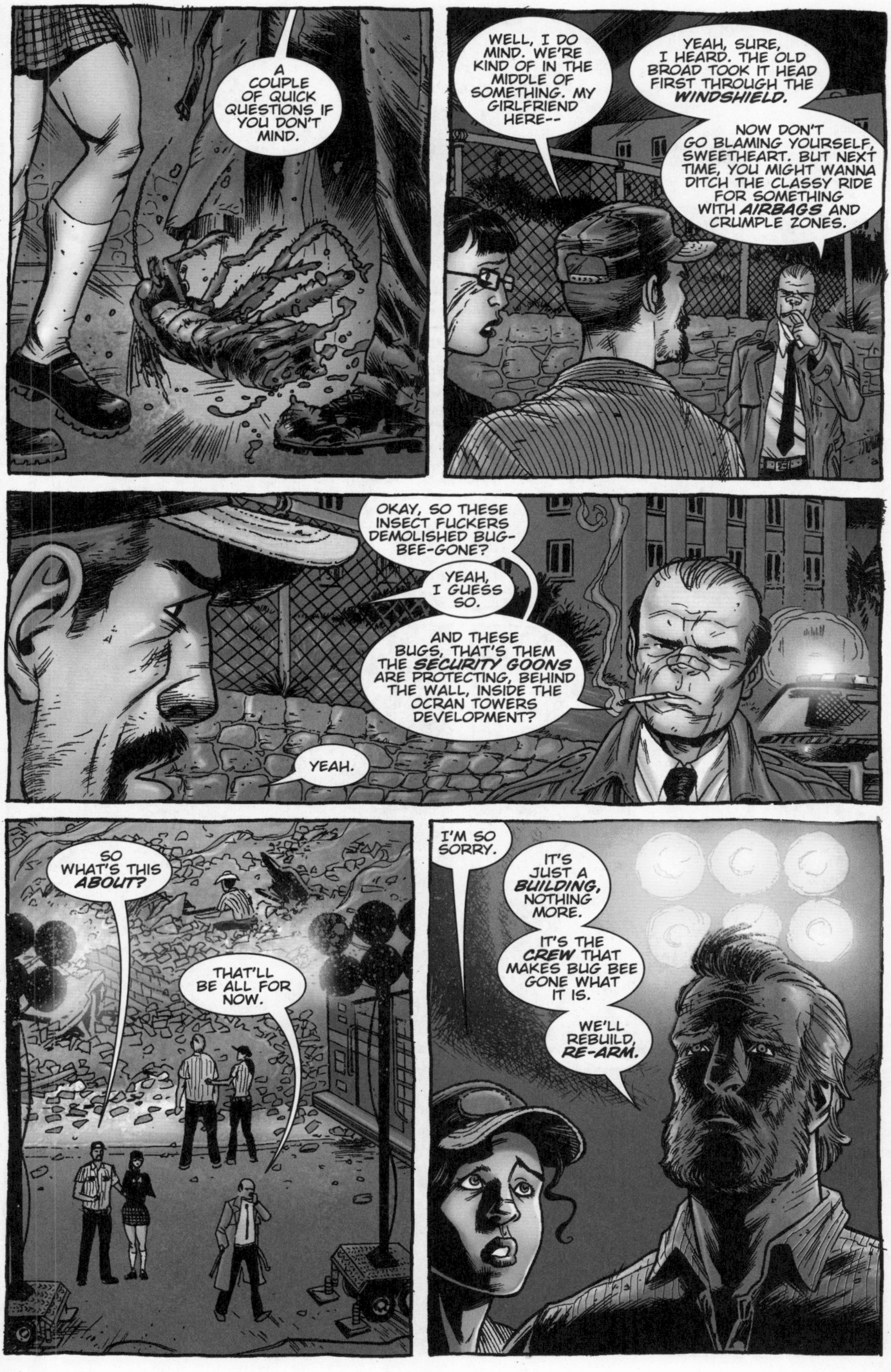

A COUPLE OF QUICK QUESTIONS IF YOU DON'T MIND.
WELL, I DO MIND. WE'RE KIND OF IN THE MIDDLE OF SOMETHING. MY GIRLFRIEND HERE--
YEAH, SURE, I HEARD. THE OLD BROAD TOOK IT HEAD FIRST THROUGH THE WINDSHIELD.
NOW DON'T GO BLAMING YOURSELF, SWEETHEART. BUT NEXT TIME, YOU MIGHT WANNA DITCH THE CLASSY RIDE FOR SOMETHING WITH AIRBAGS AND CRUMPLE ZONES.
OKAY, SO THESE INSECT FUCKERS DEMOLISHED BUG-BEE-GONE?
YEAH, I GUESS SO.
AND THESE BUGS, THAT'S THEM THE SECURITY GOONS ARE PROTECTING, BEHIND THE WALL, INSIDE THE OCRAN TOWERS DEVELOPMENT?
YEAH.
SO WHAT'S THIS ABOUT?
THAT'LL BE ALL FOR NOW.
I'M SO SORRY.
IT'S JUST A BUILDING, NOTHING MORE.
IT'S THE CREW THAT MAKES BUG BEE GONE WHAT IT IS.
WE'LL REBUILD, RE-ARM.

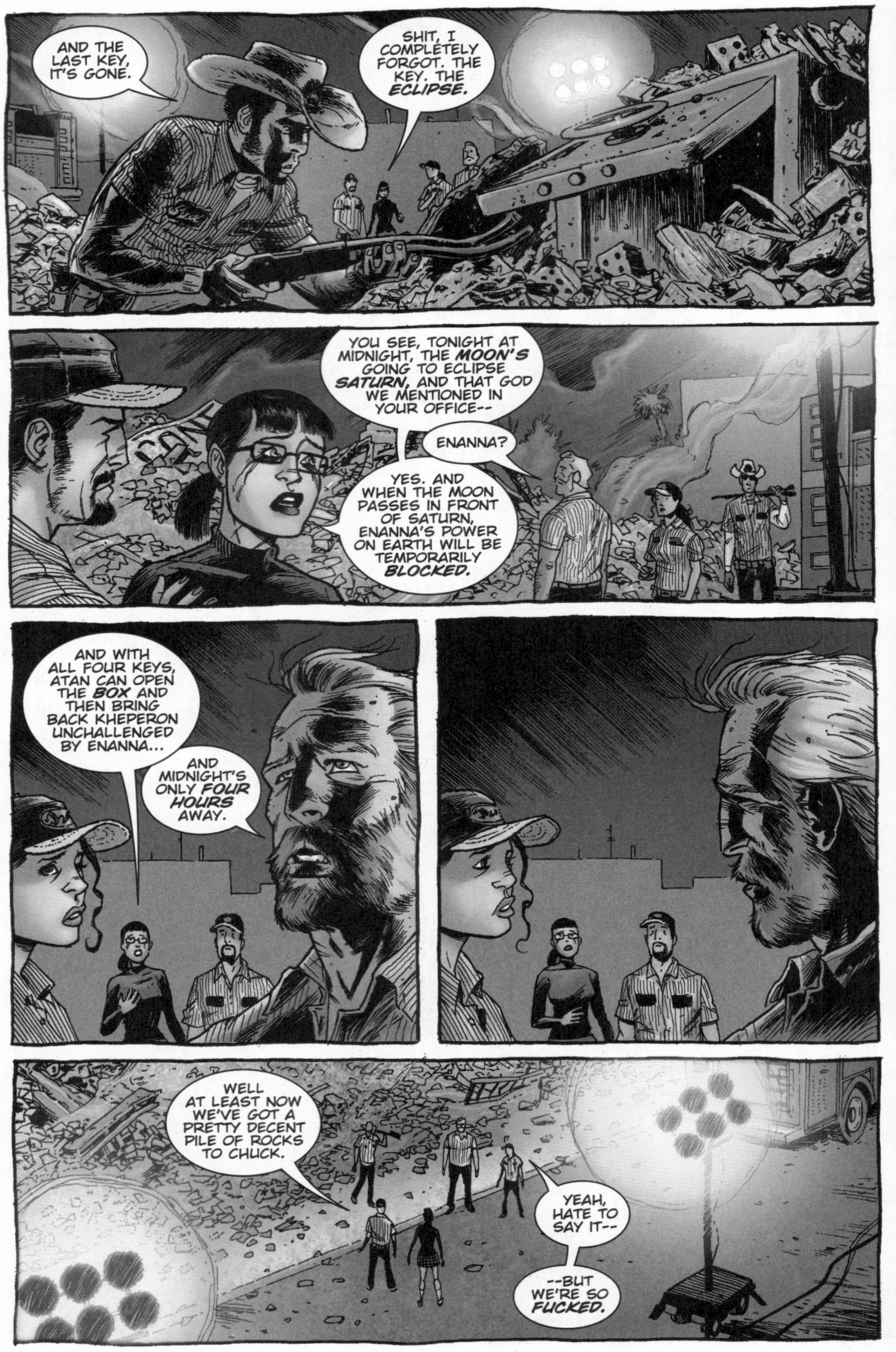
AND THE LAST KEY, IT'S GONE.
SHIT, I COMPLETELY FORGOT. THE KEY. THE ECLIPSE.
YOU SEE, TONIGHT AT MIDNIGHT, THE MOON'S GOING TO ECLIPSE SATURN, AND THAT GOD WE MENTIONED IN YOUR OFFICE--
ENANNA?
YES. AND WHEN THE MOON PASSES IN FRONT OF SATURN, ENANNA'S POWER ON EARTH WILL BE TEMPORARILY BLOCKED.
AND WITH ALL FOUR KEYS, ATAN CAN OPEN THE BOX AND THEN BRING BACK KHEPERON UNCHALLENGED BY ENANNA...
AND MIDNIGHT'S ONLY FOUR HOURS AWAY.
WELL AT LEAST NOW WE'VE GOT A PRETTY DECENT PILE OF ROCKS TO CHUCK.
YEAH, HATE TO SAY IT--
--BUT WE'RE SO FUCKED.

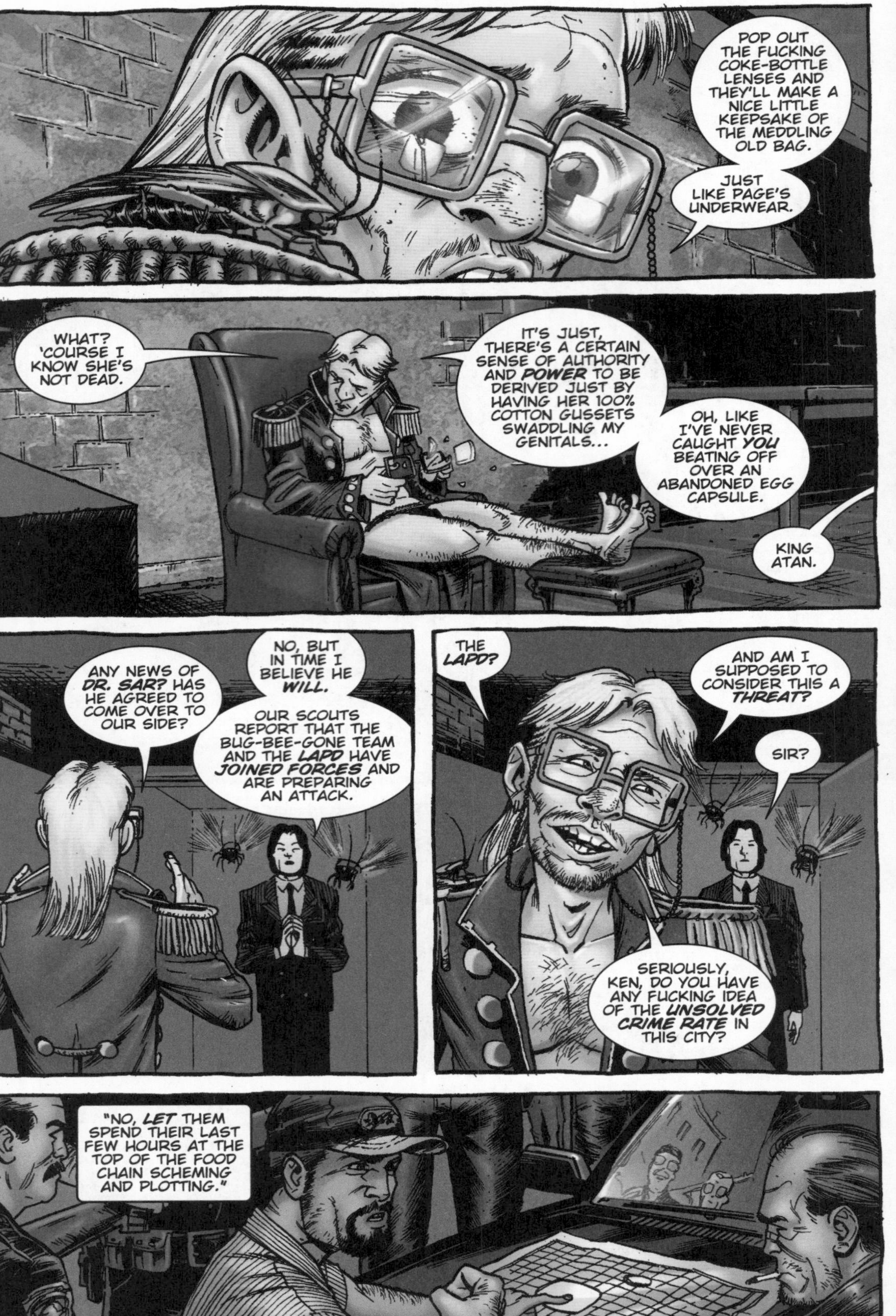
POP OUT THE FUCKING COKE-BOTTLE LENSES AND THEY'LL MAKE A NICE LITTLE KEEPSAKE OF THE MEDDLING OLD BAG.
JUST LIKE PAGE'S UNDERWEAR.
WHAT? 'COURSE I KNOW SHE'S NOT DEAD.
IT'S JUST, THERE'S A CERTAIN SENSE OF AUTHORITY AND POWER TO BE DERIVED JUST BY HAVING HER 100% COTTON GUSSETS SWADDLING MY GENITALS...
OH, LIKE I'VE NEVER CAUGHT YOU BEATING OFF OVER AN ABANDONED EGG CAPSULE.
KING ATAN.
ANY NEWS OF DR. SAR? HAS HE AGREED TO COME OVER TO OUR SIDE?
NO, BUT IN TIME I BELIEVE HE WILL.
OUR SCOUTS REPORT THAT THE BUG-BEE-GONE TEAM AND THE LAPD HAVE JOINED FORCES AND ARE PREPARING AN ATTACK.
THE LAPD?
AND AM I SUPPOSED TO CONSIDER THIS A THREAT?
SIR?
SERIOUSLY, KEN, DO YOU HAVE ANY FUCKING IDEA OF THE UNSOLVED CRIME RATE IN THIS CITY?
"NO, LET THEM SPEND THEIR LAST FEW HOURS AT THE TOP OF THE FOOD CHAIN SCHEMING AND PLOTTING."

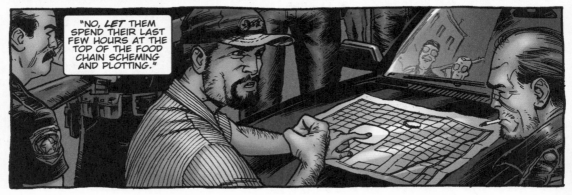

PAGE, I'VE BEEN THINKING ABOUT, YOU KNOW, WHEN ALL THIS IS *OVER*...

YEAH, GO ON.

WELL, I WAS *WONDERING* IF YOU WANTED TO--ER...

WANTED TO *WHAT*, EXACTLY, HENRY?

ER, YOU KNOW, MAKE "US" OFFICIAL, SORT OF.

DID YOU ACTUALLY JUST ASK ME TO *MARRY* YOU, HENRY JAMES?

HON HON

YEAH, I GUESS. I MEAN IF THAT'S WHAT YOU *WANT*.

FUCKWIT, GET YOUR ASS IN THE *CAR*.

WELL, I NEVER REALLY THOUGHT OF MYSELF AS THE MARRYING *KIND*.

OH.

HENRY, CAN WE TALK ABOUT THIS *LATER*?

LET ME *GUESS*. YOU ASKED HER TO MARRY YOU?

FUCK OFF, HUNTER.

NO, WHEN MY BALLS ARE IN THE VISE I CAN GET A LITTLE ROMANTIC TOO.

PROPOSED TO MY WIFE ON THE EVE OF THE WATTS RIOTS OF 1968.

THEN IN THE '92 RIOTS I MADE UP MY MIND TO FINALLY DIVORCE THE BITCH.

YOU BOTH UNDERSTAND THE IMPORTANCE OF GETTING *INSIDE* THE GUARD SHACK--

--AND GETTING THAT *GATE* OPEN.

WE CAN'T AFFORD TO GET BOGGED DOWN ON THE WRONG SIDE OF THE GATE. THAT'D LEAVE HENRY AND STRETCH WAY TOO *EXPOSED* IN THERE.

DON'T WORRY ABOUT US, NILS. KOKO AND ME HAVE GOT THIS PART ALL *COVERED*.

YOU SHOULD WORRY MORE ABOUT WHAT THESE SICK *COP* BITCHES ARE COOKING UP FOR THE HUMVEE PATROL.

'CAUSE I TELL YA, THIS IS ONE CHOLOLITO WHO'S GONNA THINK *TWICE* ABOUT EVER CROSSING THE LAPD.

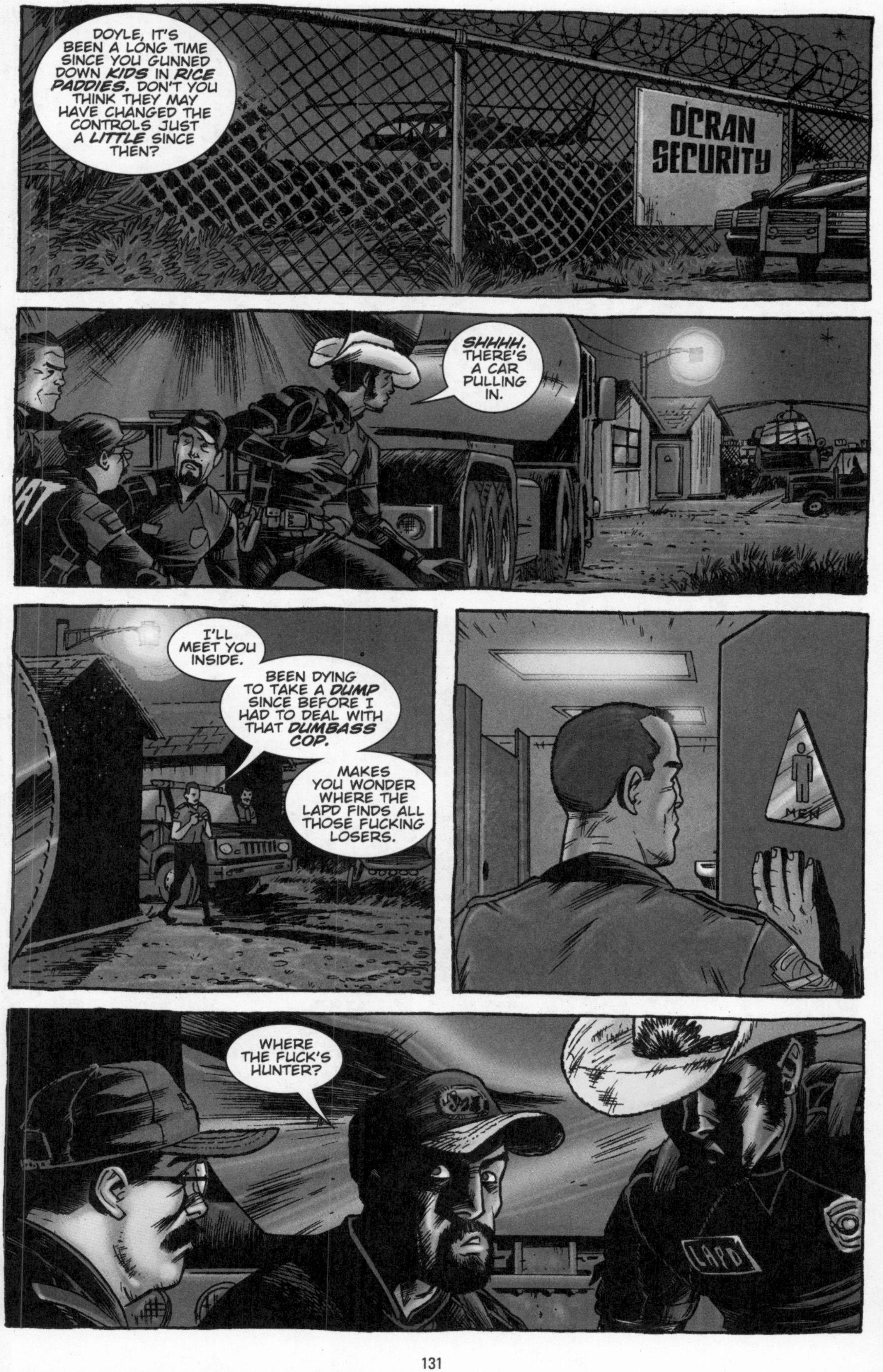
DOYLE, IT'S BEEN A LONG TIME SINCE YOU GUNNED DOWN KIDS IN RICE PADDIES. DON'T YOU THINK THEY MAY HAVE CHANGED THE CONTROLS JUST A LITTLE SINCE THEN?
OCRAN SECURITY
SHHHH. THERE'S A CAR PULLING IN.
I'LL MEET YOU INSIDE.
BEEN DYING TO TAKE A DUMP SINCE BEFORE I HAD TO DEAL WITH THAT DUMBASS COP.
MAKES YOU WONDER WHERE THE LAPD FINDS ALL THOSE FUCKING LOSERS.
MEN
WHERE THE FUCK'S HUNTER?
LAPD

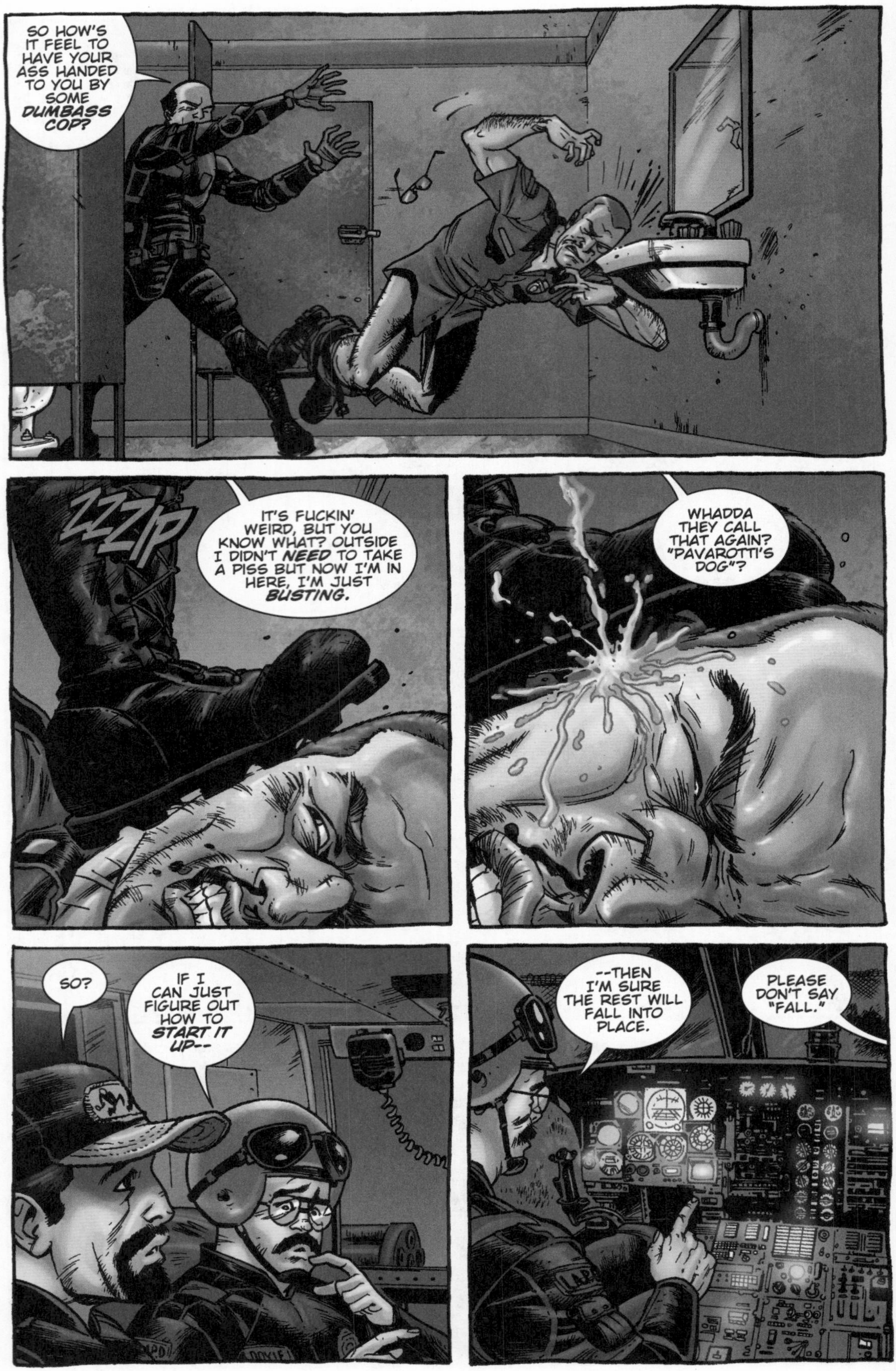
SO HOW'S IT FEEL TO HAVE YOUR ASS HANDED TO YOU BY SOME DUMBASS COP?
ZZZIP
IT'S FUCKIN' WEIRD, BUT YOU KNOW WHAT? OUTSIDE I DIDN'T NEED TO TAKE A PISS BUT NOW I'M IN HERE, I'M JUST BUSTING.
WHADDA THEY CALL THAT AGAIN? "PAVAROTTI'S DOG"?
SO?
IF I CAN JUST FIGURE OUT HOW TO START IT UP--
--THEN I'M SURE THE REST WILL FALL INTO PLACE.
PLEASE DON'T SAY "FALL."

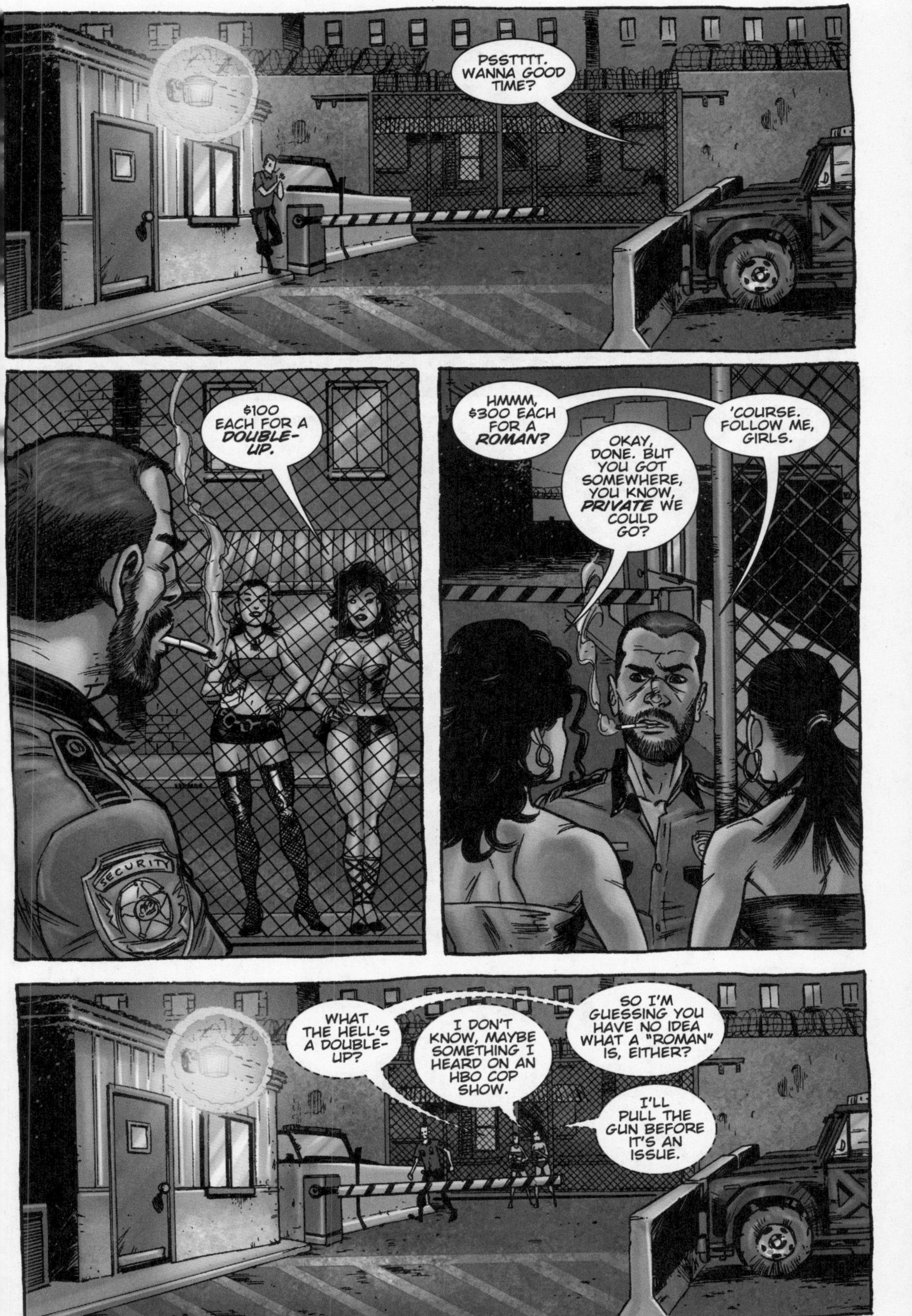
PSSTTTT. WANNA GOOD TIME?
$100 EACH FOR A DOUBLE-UP.
HMMM, $300 EACH FOR A ROMAN?
OKAY, DONE. BUT YOU GOT SOMEWHERE, YOU KNOW, PRIVATE WE COULD GO?
'COURSE. FOLLOW ME, GIRLS.
SECURITY
WHAT THE HELL'S A DOUBLE-UP?
I DON'T KNOW, MAYBE SOMETHING I HEARD ON AN HBO COP SHOW.
SO I'M GUESSING YOU HAVE NO IDEA WHAT A "ROMAN" IS, EITHER?
I'LL PULL THE GUN BEFORE IT'S AN ISSUE.

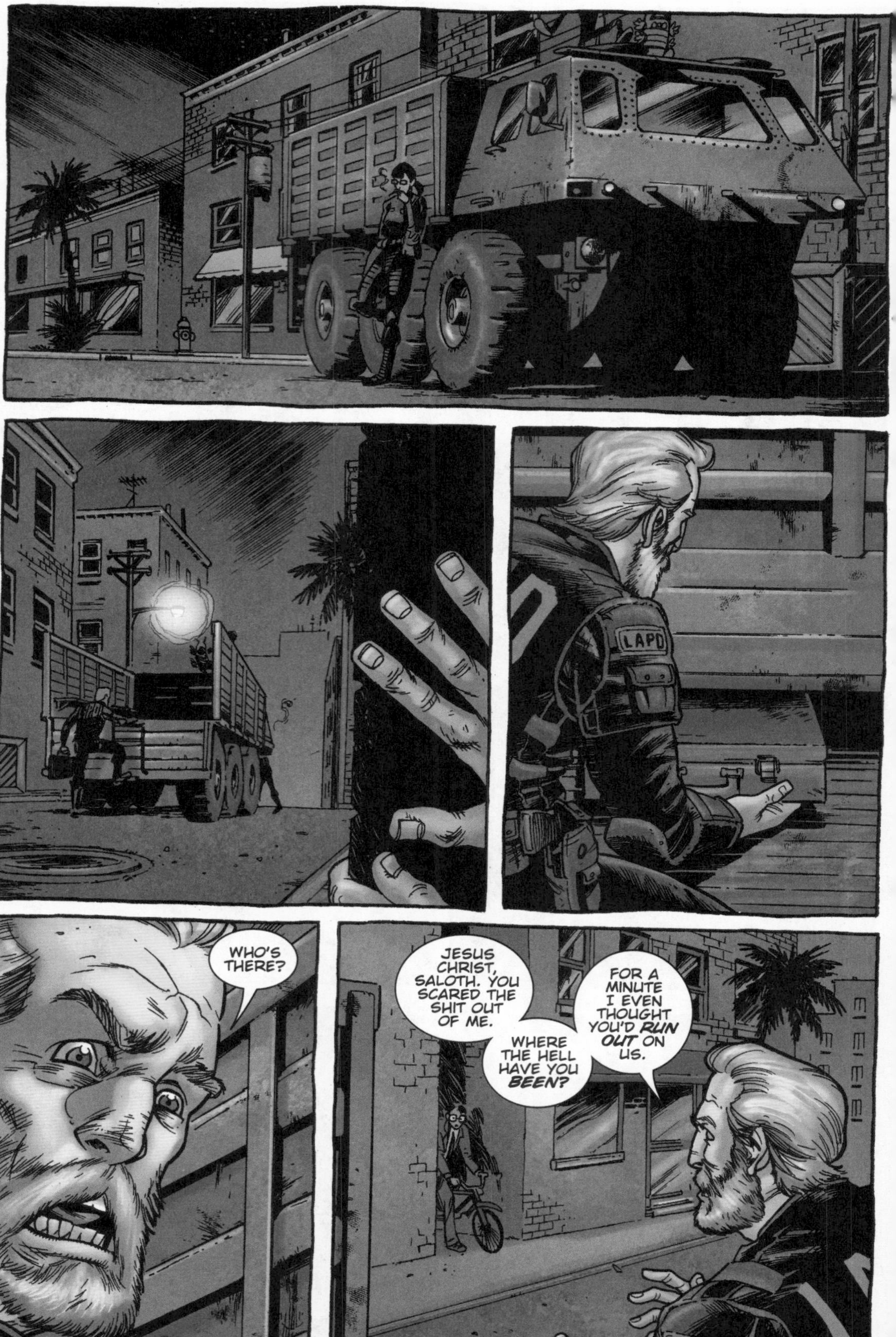
L.A.P.D
WHO'S THERE?
JESUS CHRIST, SALOTH. YOU SCARED THE SHIT OUT OF ME.
WHERE THE HELL HAVE YOU *BEEN*?
FOR A MINUTE I EVEN THOUGHT YOU'D *RUN OUT* ON US.
L.A.P.D

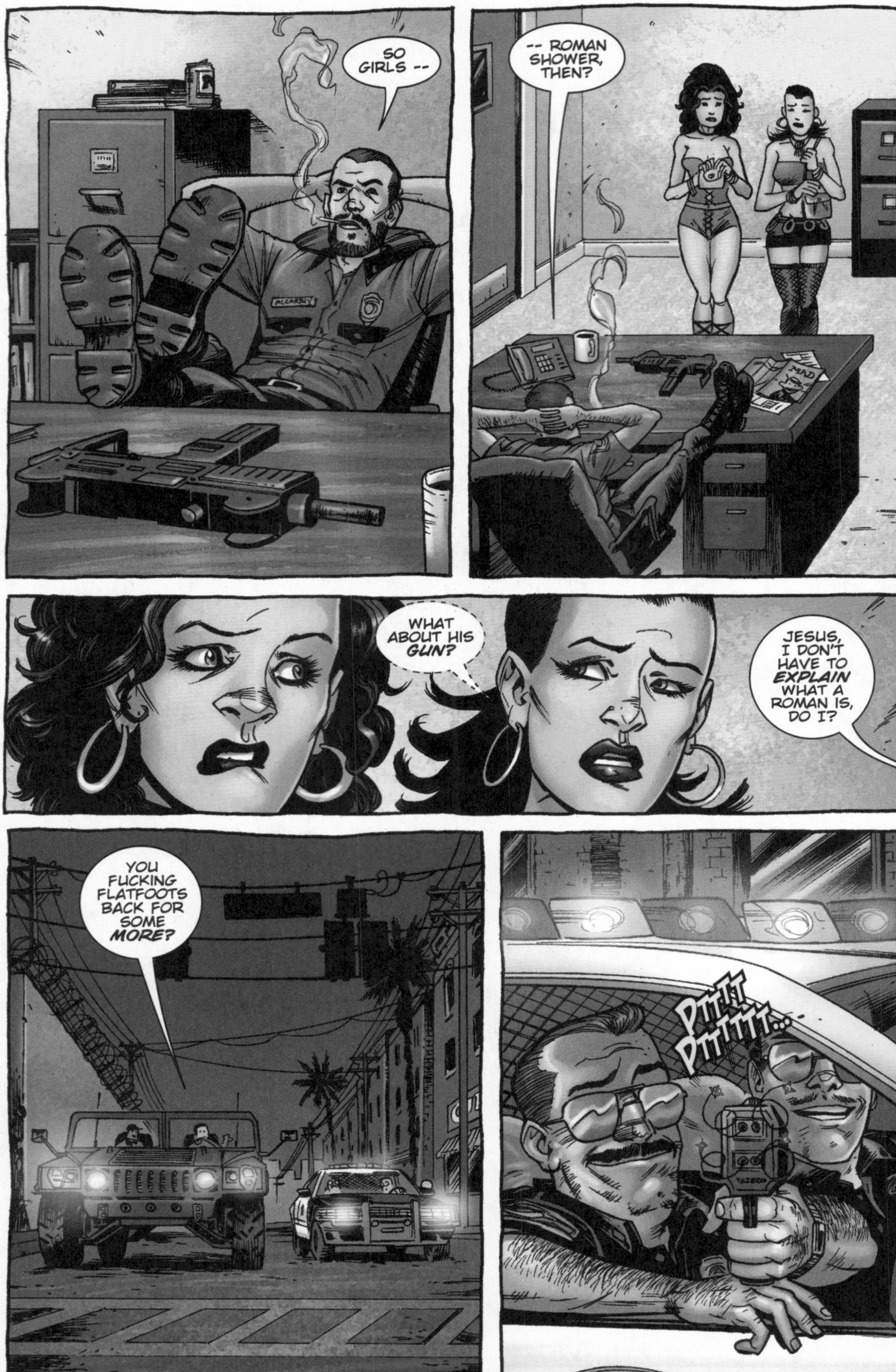
SO GIRLS --
-- ROMAN SHOWER, THEN?
MAD
WHAT ABOUT HIS GUN?
JESUS, I DON'T HAVE TO EXPLAIN WHAT A ROMAN IS, DO I?
YOU FUCKING FLATFOOTS BACK FOR SOME MORE?
PTTTT PTTTTTT...

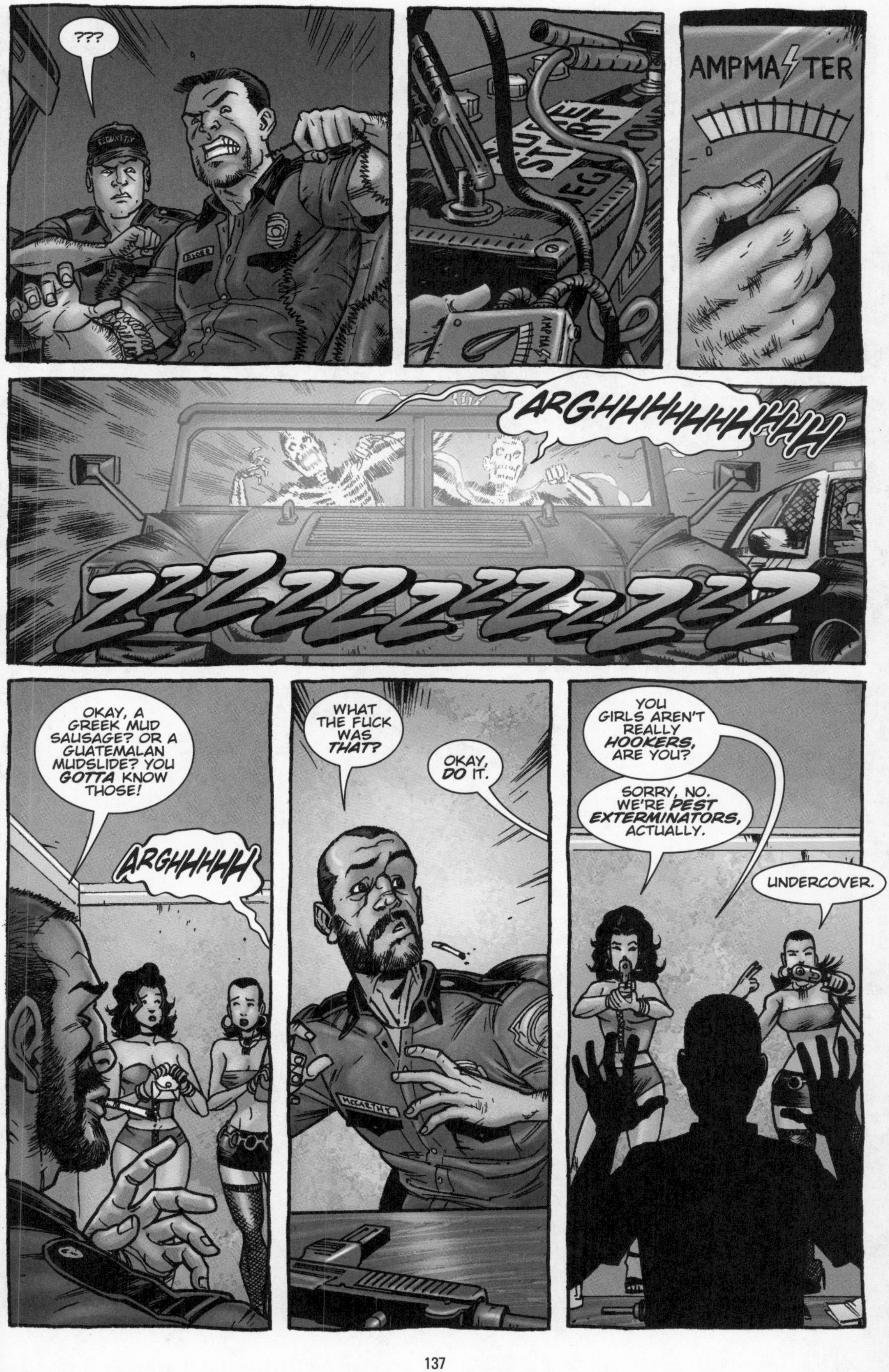
???
AMPMASTER
ARGHHHHHHHHHHH
ZZZZZZZZZZZZZZZ
OKAY, A GREEK MUD SAUSAGE? OR A GUATEMALAN MUDSLIDE? YOU GOTTA KNOW THOSE!
ARGHHHHH
WHAT THE FUCK WAS THAT?
OKAY, DO IT.
YOU GIRLS AREN'T REALLY HOOKERS, ARE YOU?
SORRY, NO. WE'RE PEST EXTERMINATORS, ACTUALLY.
UNDERCOVER.

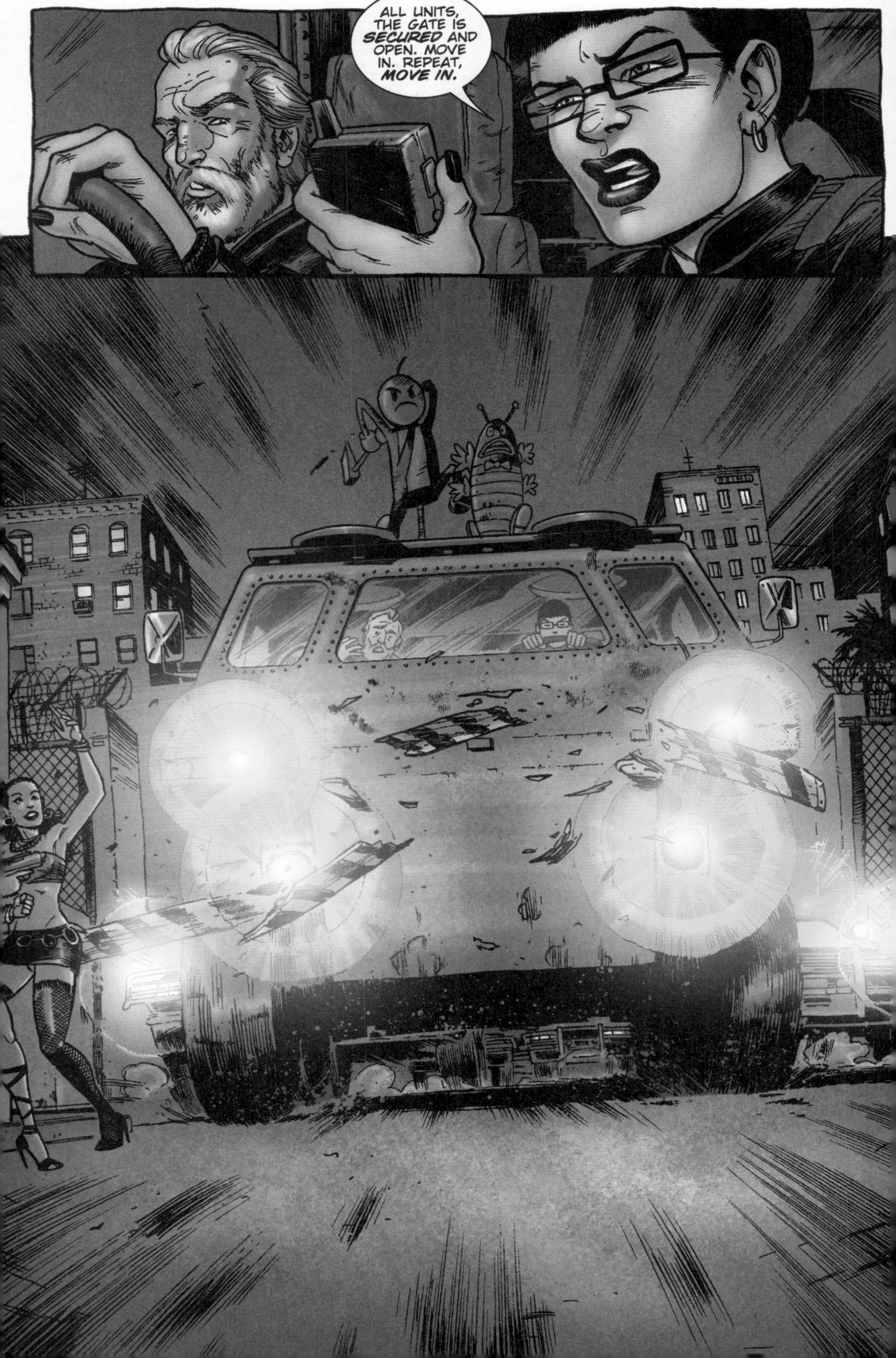
ALL UNITS, THE GATE IS *SECURED* AND OPEN. MOVE IN. REPEAT, *MOVE IN.*

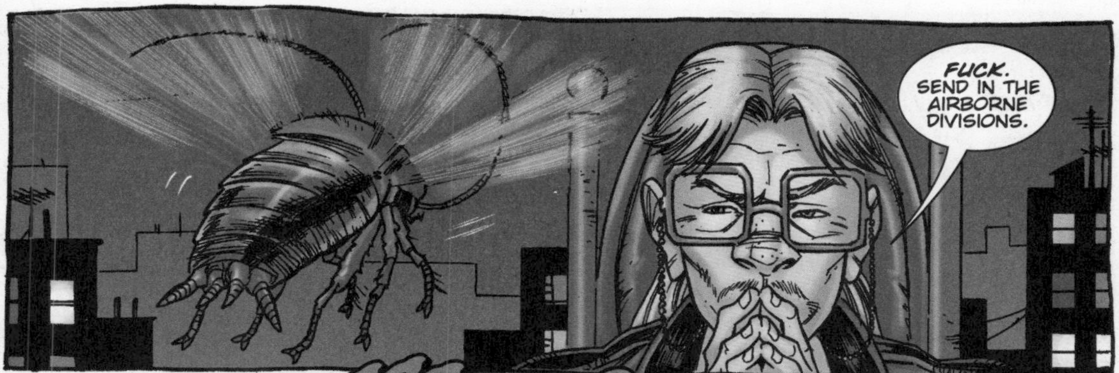
FUCK. SEND IN THE AIRBORNE DIVISIONS.

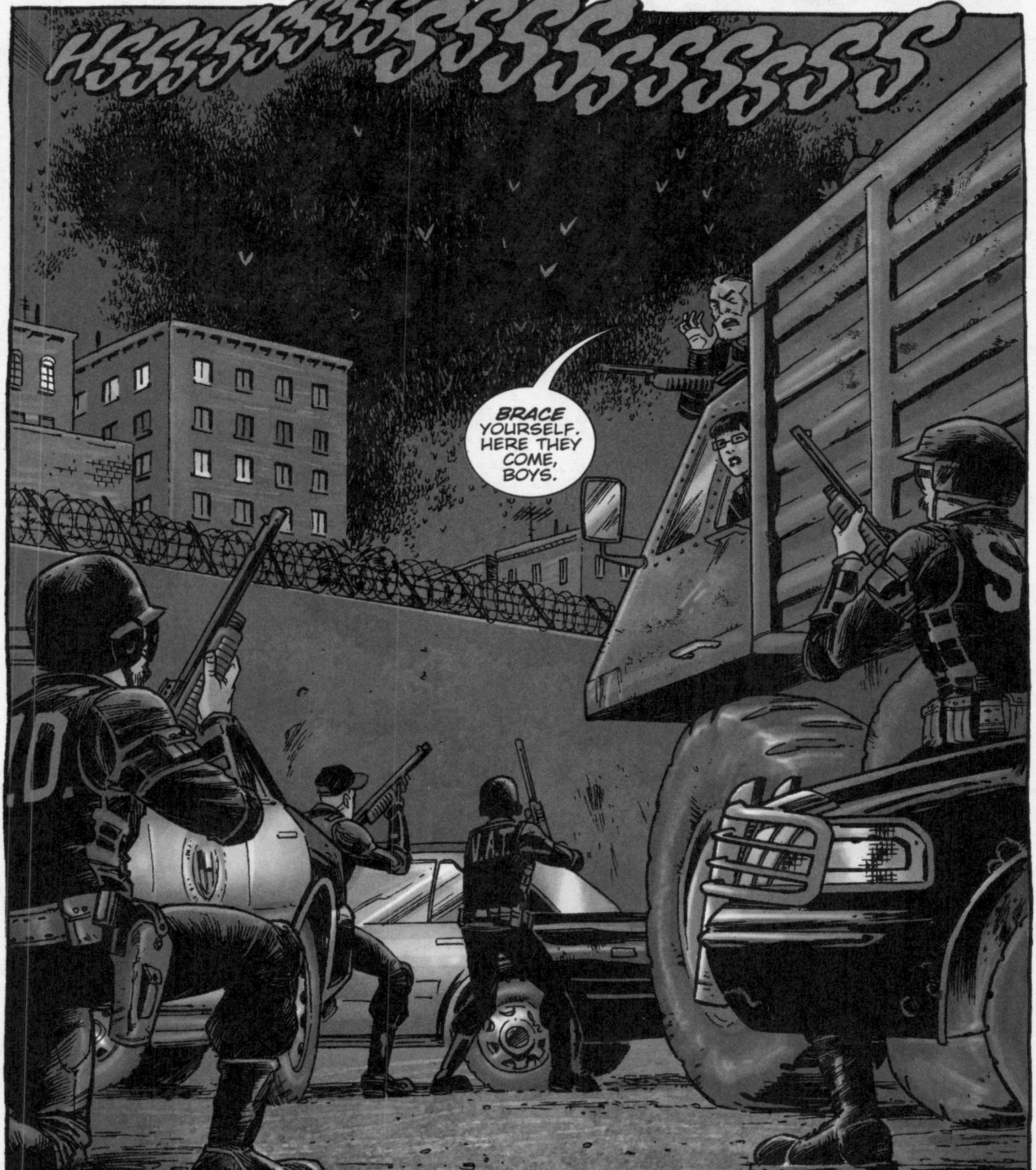
HSSSSSSSSSSSSSSSSSSSS
BRACE YOURSELF. HERE THEY COME, BOYS.

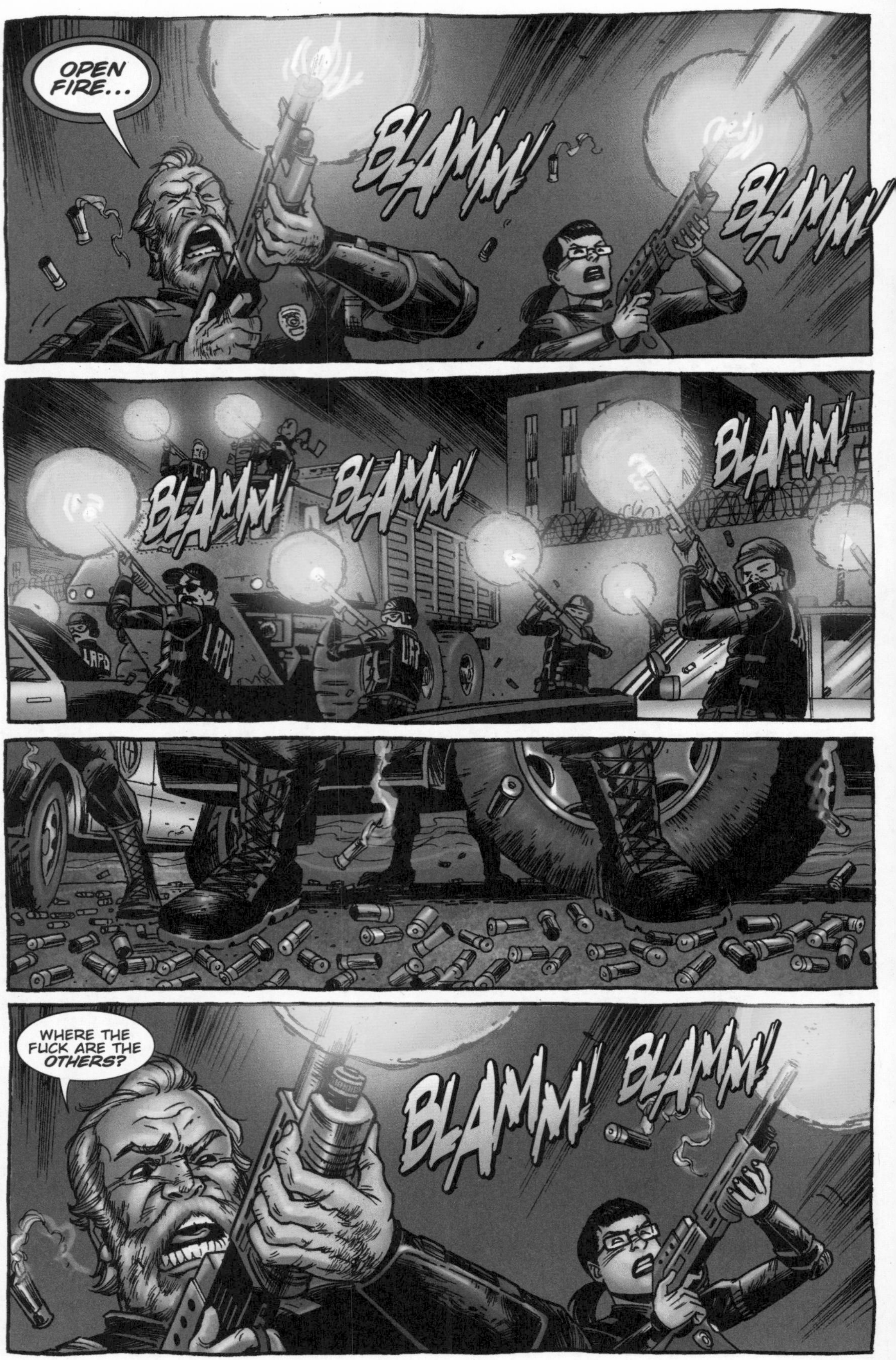
OPEN FIRE...
BLAMM!
BLAMM!
BLAMM!
BLAMM!
BLAMM!
WHERE THE FUCK ARE THE OTHERS?
BLAMM!
BLAMM!

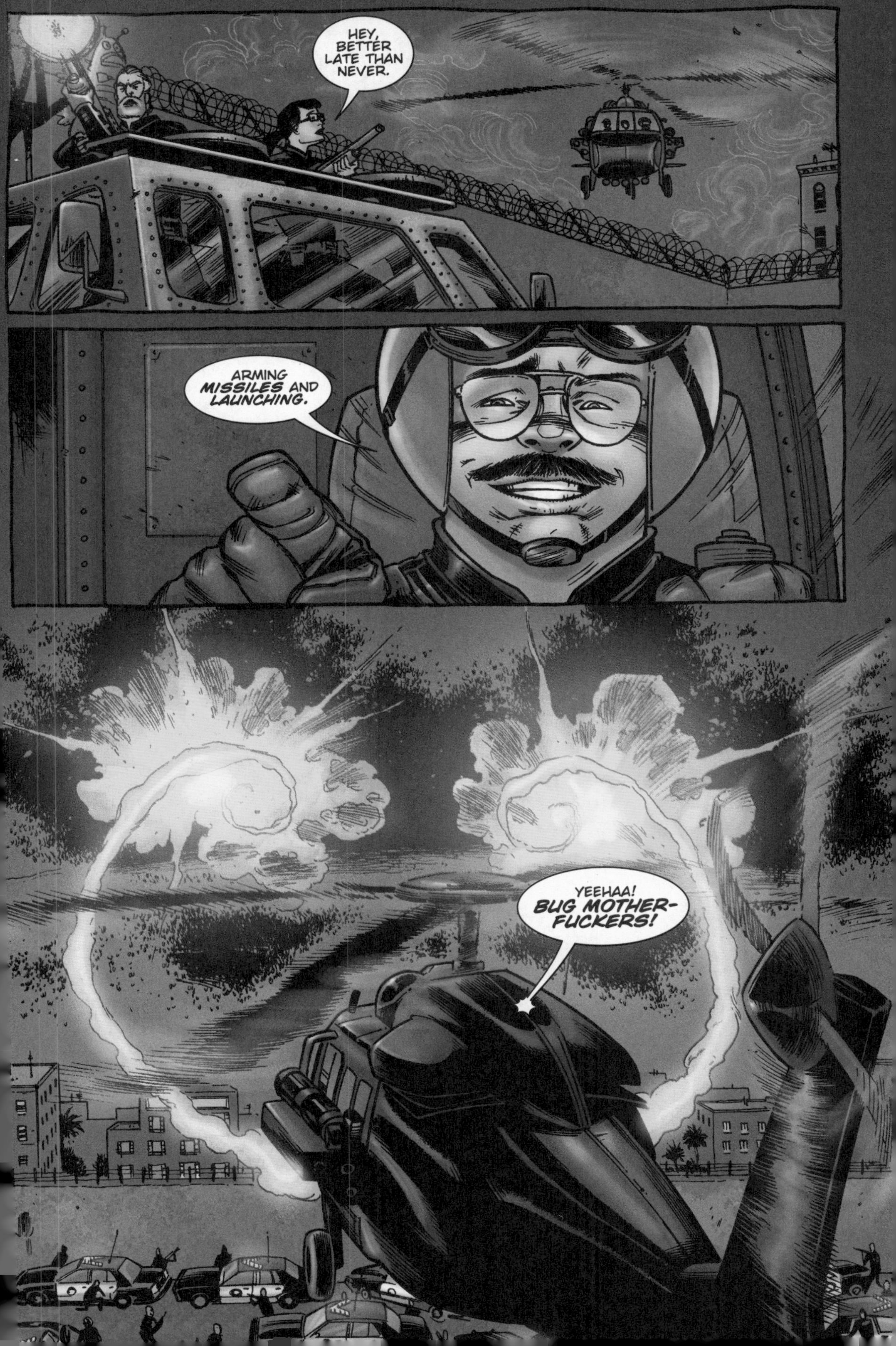
HEY, BETTER LATE THAN NEVER.
ARMING MISSILES AND LAUNCHING.
YEEHAA! BUG MOTHER-FUCKERS!

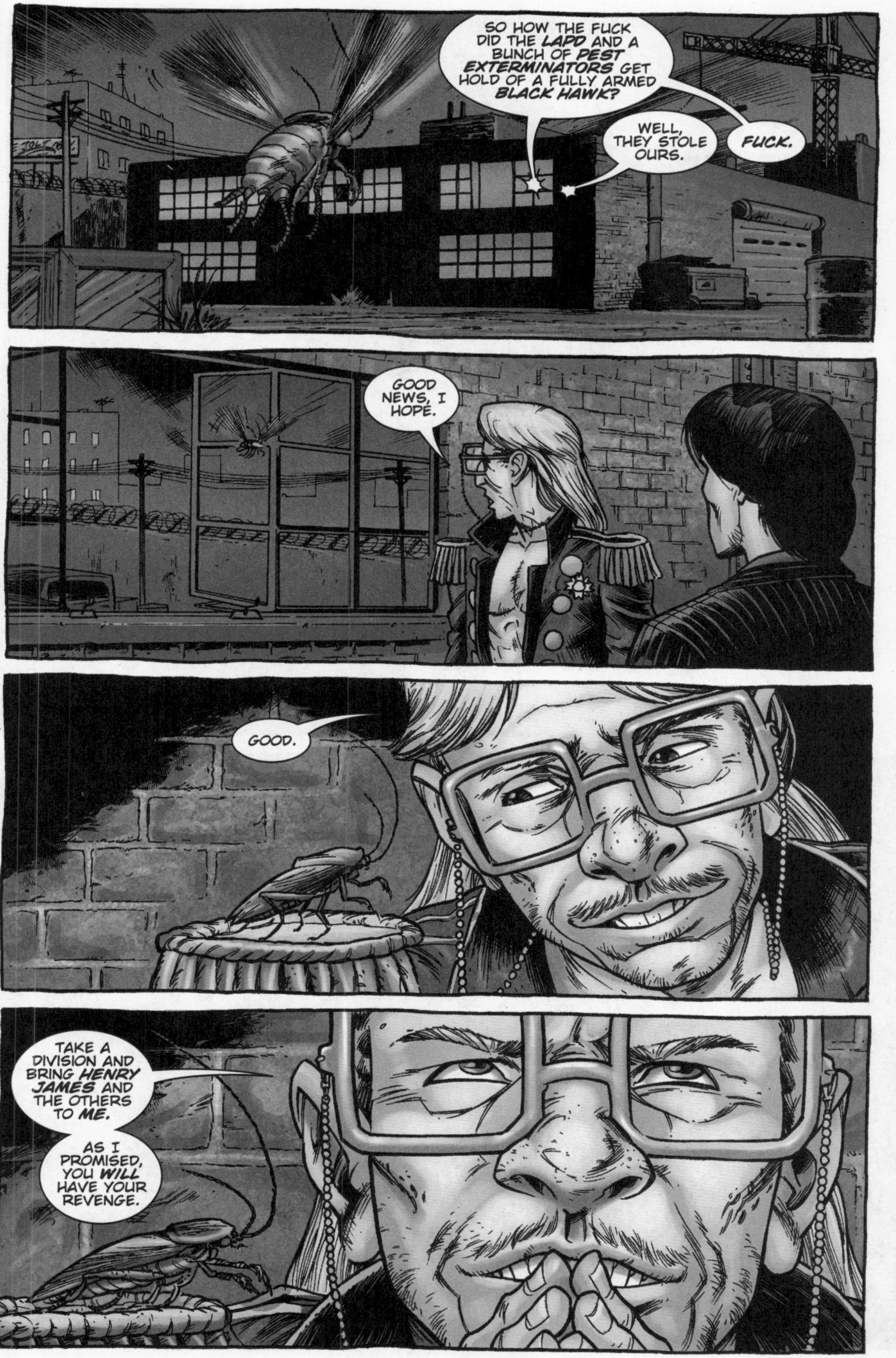
SO HOW THE FUCK DID THE LAPD AND A BUNCH OF PEST EXTERMINATORS GET HOLD OF A FULLY ARMED BLACK HAWK?
WELL, THEY STOLE OURS.
FUCK.
GOOD NEWS, I HOPE.
GOOD.
TAKE A DIVISION AND BRING HENRY JAMES AND THE OTHERS TO ME.
AS I PROMISED, YOU WILL HAVE YOUR REVENGE.

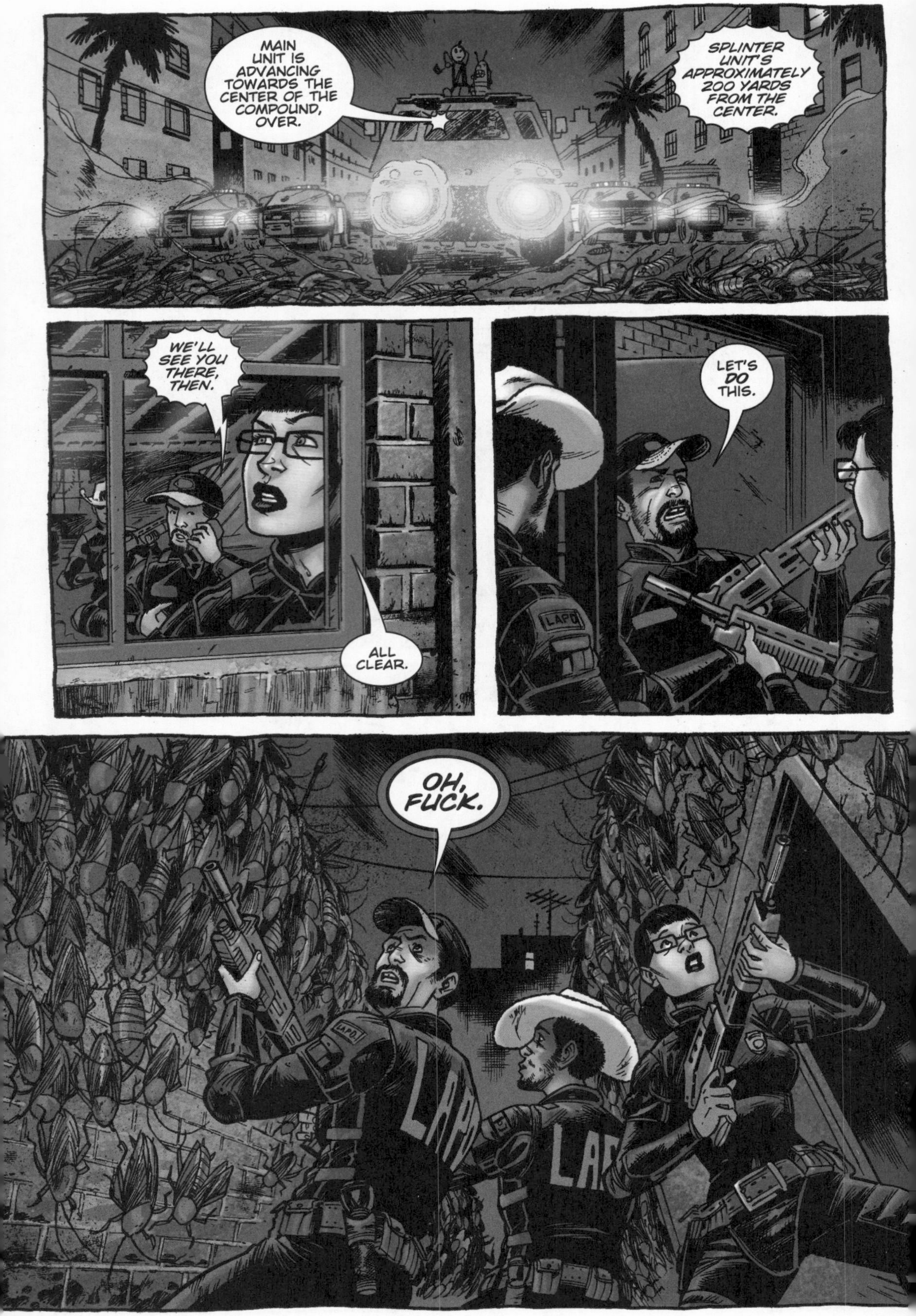

MAIN UNIT IS ADVANCING TOWARDS THE CENTER OF THE COMPOUND, OVER.
SPLINTER UNIT'S APPROXIMATELY 200 YARDS FROM THE CENTER.
WE'LL SEE YOU THERE, THEN.
ALL CLEAR.
LET'S DO THIS.
LAPD
OH, FUCK.
LAPD
LAP
LA

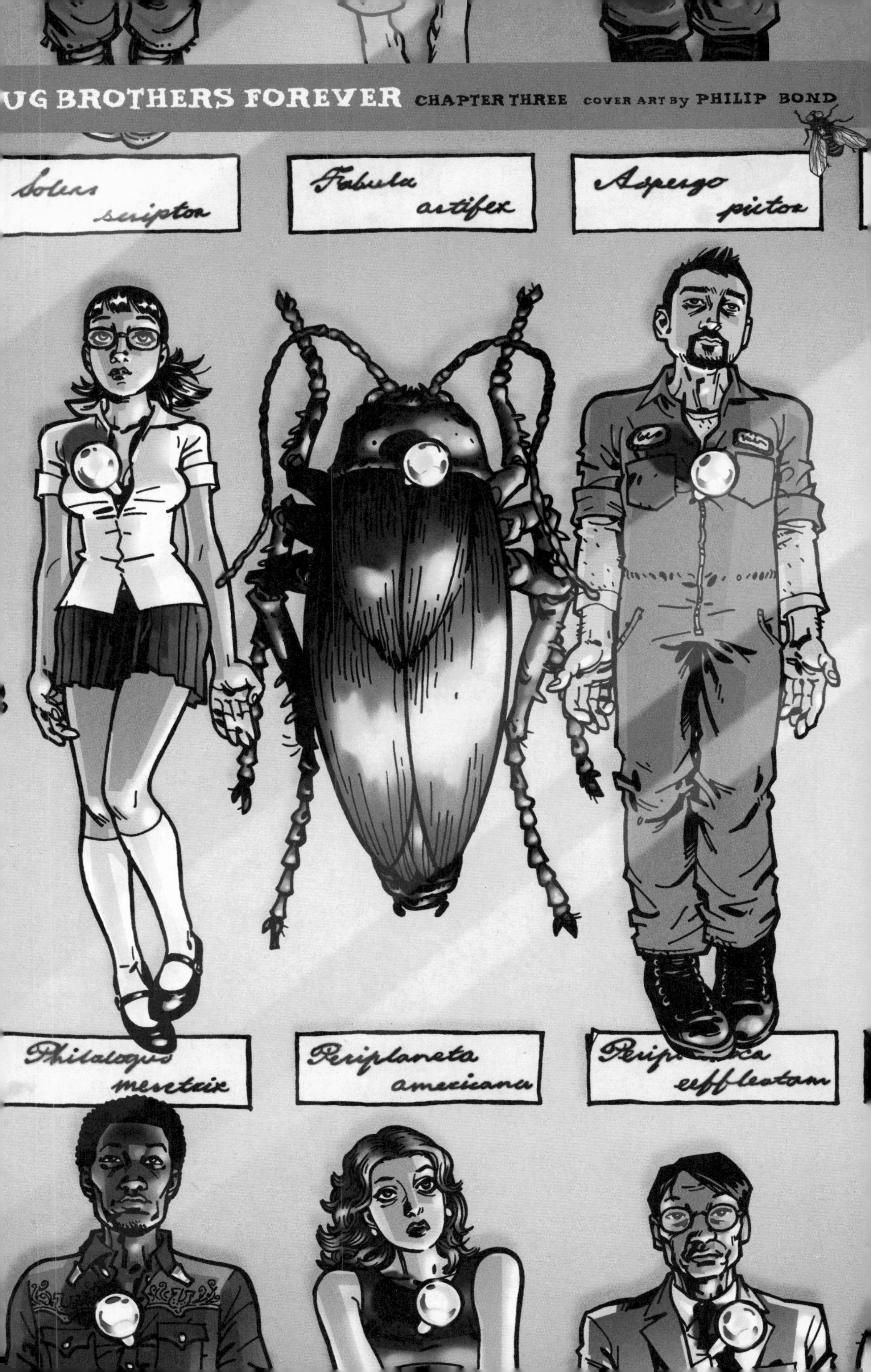
UG BROTHERS FOREVER CHAPTER THREE COVER ART BY PHILIP BOND
Fabula artifex
Periplaneta americana

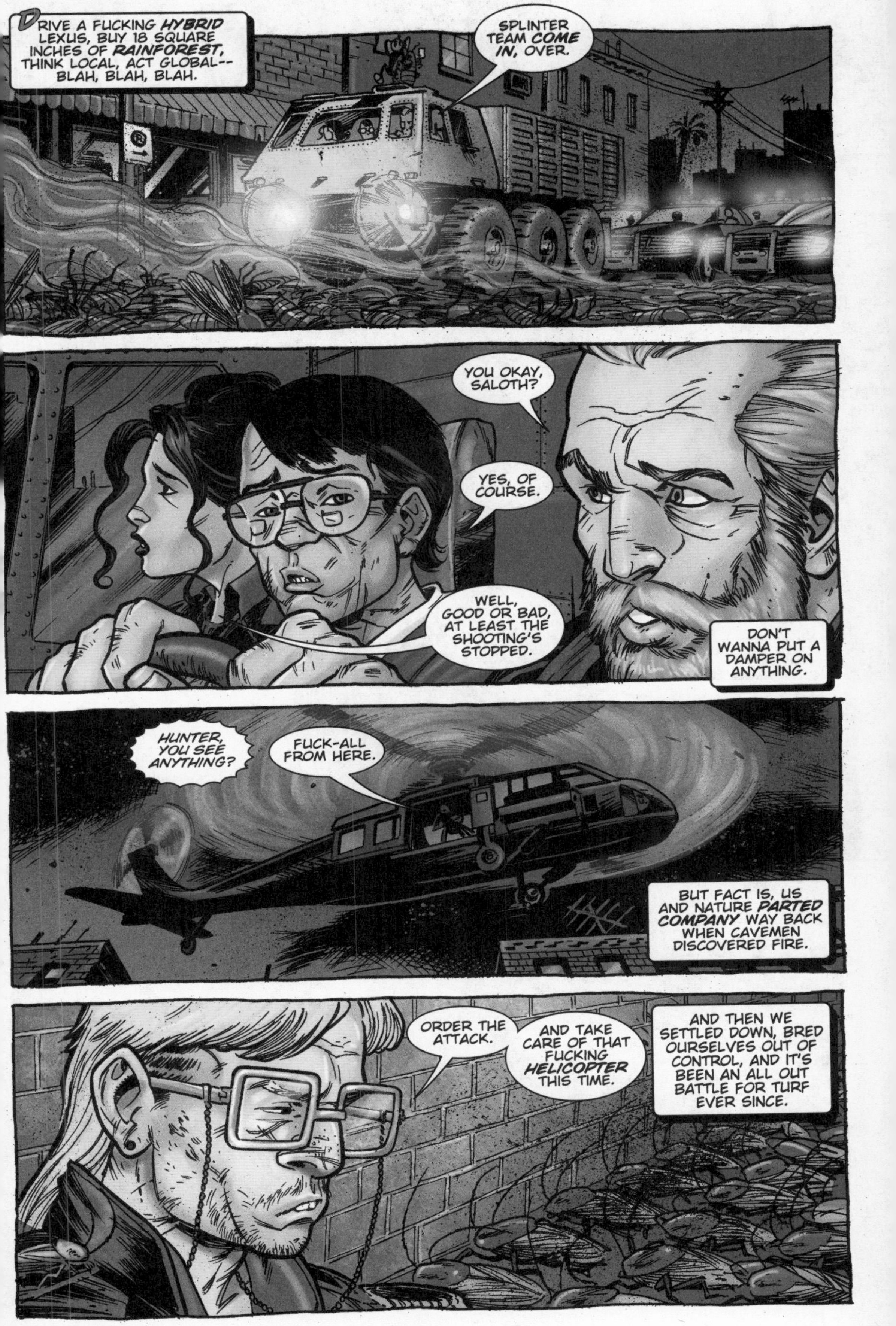
DRIVE A FUCKING HYBRID LEXUS, BUY 18 SQUARE INCHES OF RAINFOREST, THINK LOCAL, ACT GLOBAL-- BLAH, BLAH, BLAH.
SPLINTER TEAM COME IN, OVER.
YOU OKAY, SALOTH?
YES, OF COURSE.
WELL, GOOD OR BAD, AT LEAST THE SHOOTING'S STOPPED.
DON'T WANNA PUT A DAMPER ON ANYTHING.
HUNTER, YOU SEE ANYTHING?
FUCK-ALL FROM HERE.
BUT FACT IS, US AND NATURE PARTED COMPANY WAY BACK WHEN CAVEMEN DISCOVERED FIRE.
ORDER THE ATTACK.
AND TAKE CARE OF THAT FUCKING HELICOPTER THIS TIME.
AND THEN WE SETTLED DOWN, BRED OURSELVES OUT OF CONTROL, AND IT'S BEEN AN ALL OUT BATTLE FOR TURF EVER SINCE.

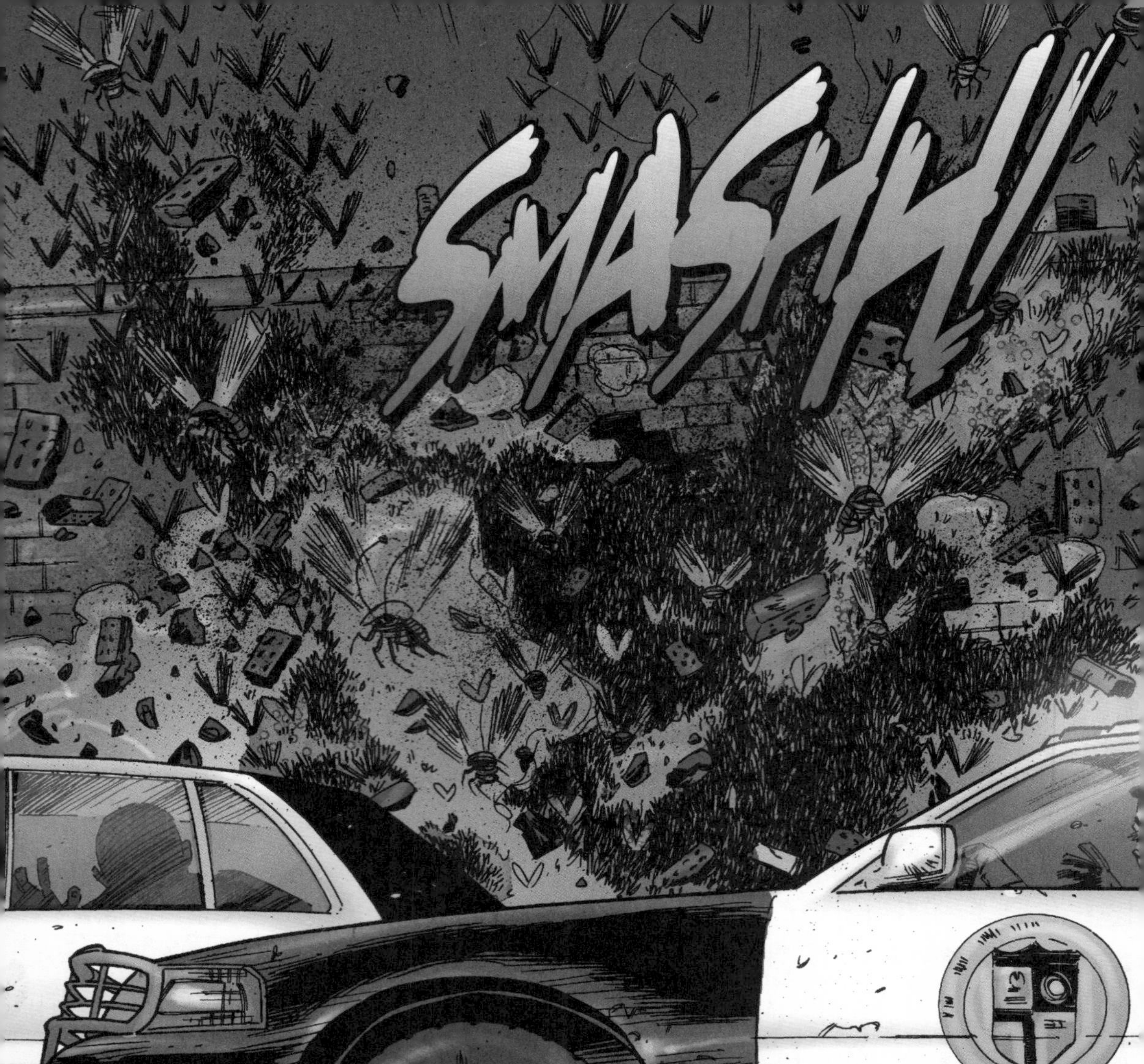
SMASH!

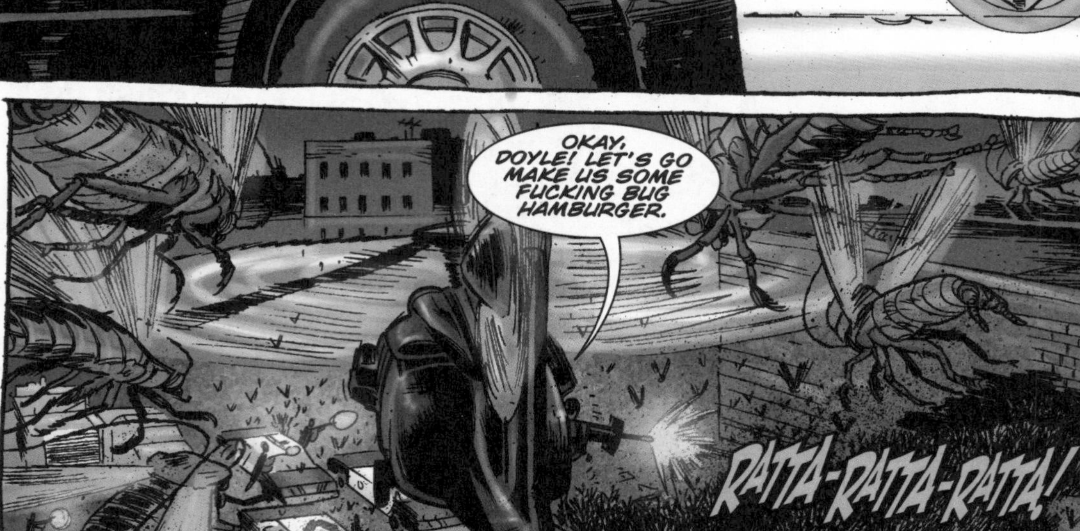
OKAY, DOYLE! LET'S GO MAKE US SOME FUCKING BUG HAMBURGER.
RATTA-RATTA-RATTA!

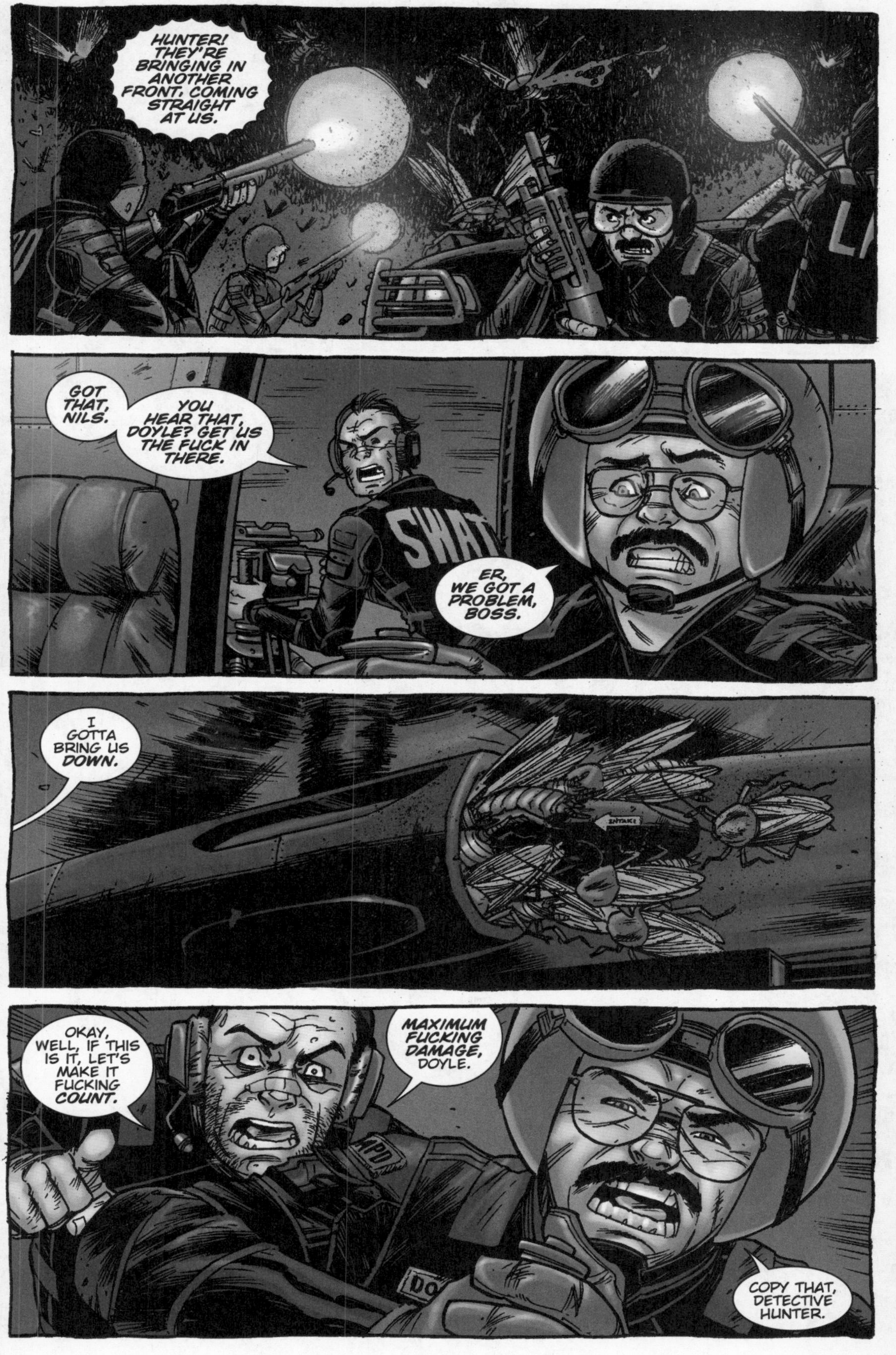
HUNTER! THEY'RE BRINGING IN ANOTHER FRONT, COMING STRAIGHT AT US.
GOT THAT, NILS.
YOU HEAR THAT, DOYLE? GET US THE FUCK IN THERE.
SWAT
ER, WE GOT A PROBLEM, BOSS.
I GOTTA BRING US DOWN.
OKAY, WELL, IF THIS IS IT, LET'S MAKE IT FUCKING COUNT.
MAXIMUM FUCKING DAMAGE, DOYLE.
COPY THAT, DETECTIVE HUNTER.

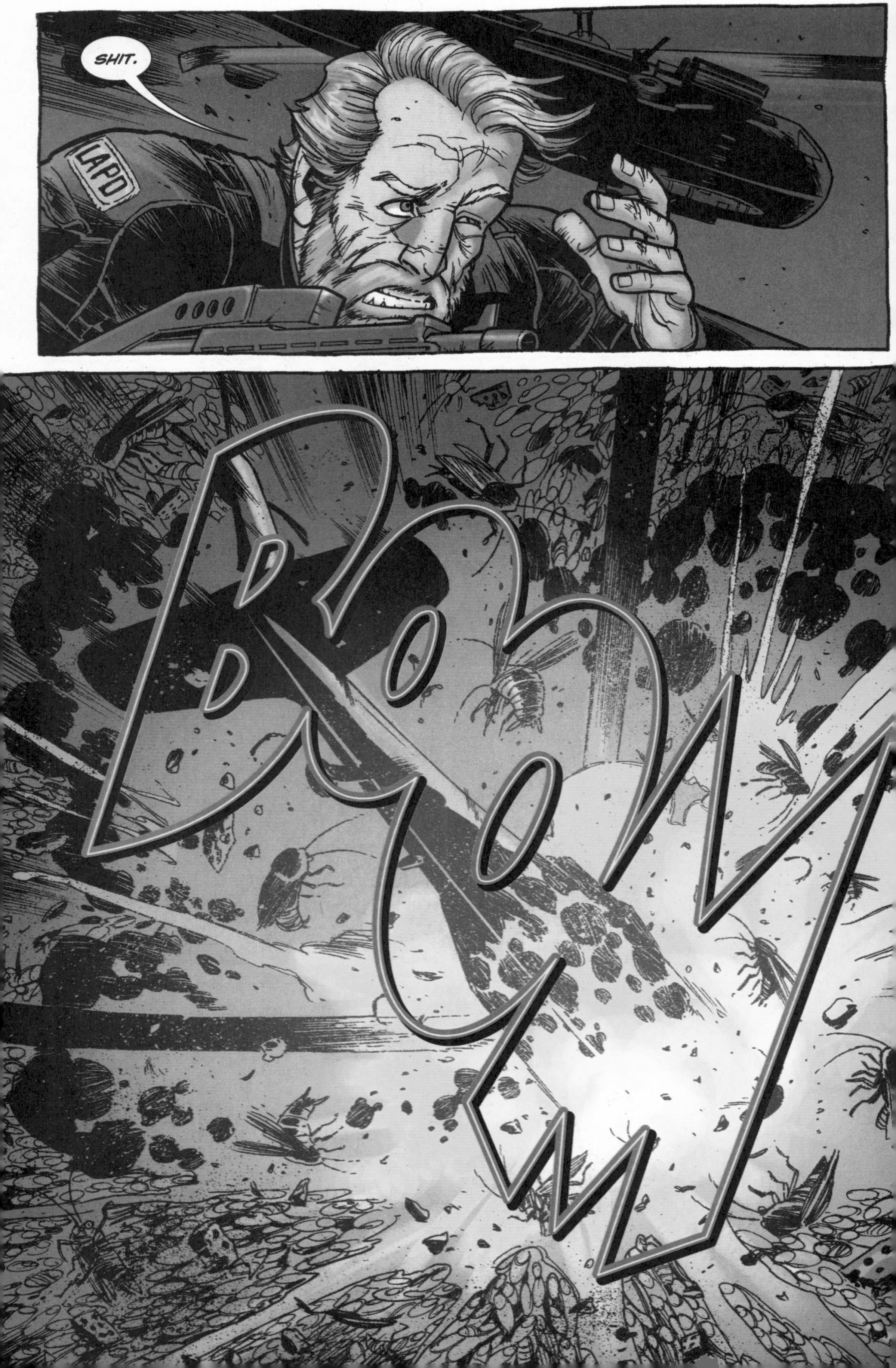
SHIT.
LAPD

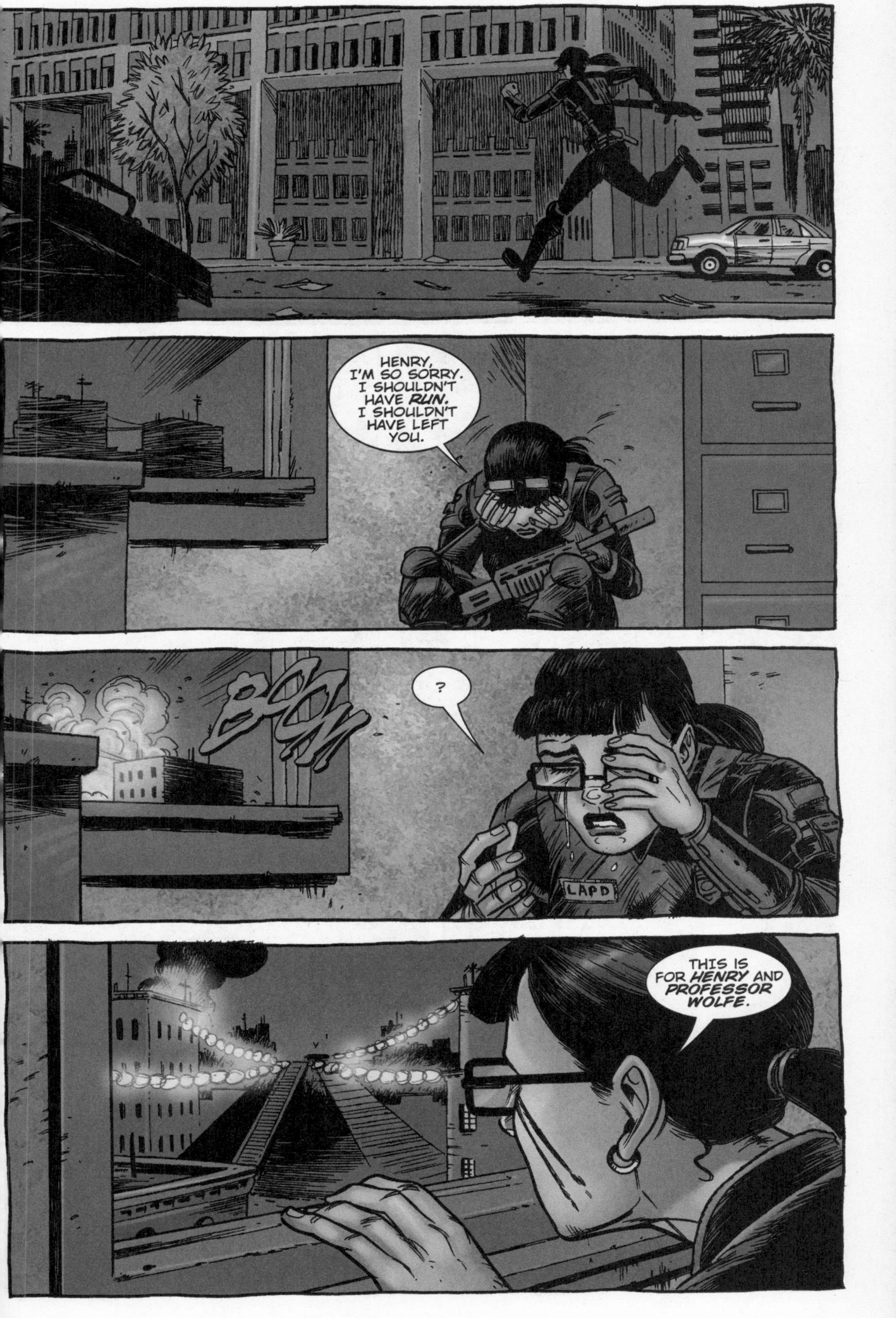
HENRY, I'M SO SORRY. I SHOULDN'T HAVE RUN. I SHOULDN'T HAVE LEFT YOU.
BOOM
?
LAPD
THIS IS FOR HENRY AND PROFESSOR WOLFE.

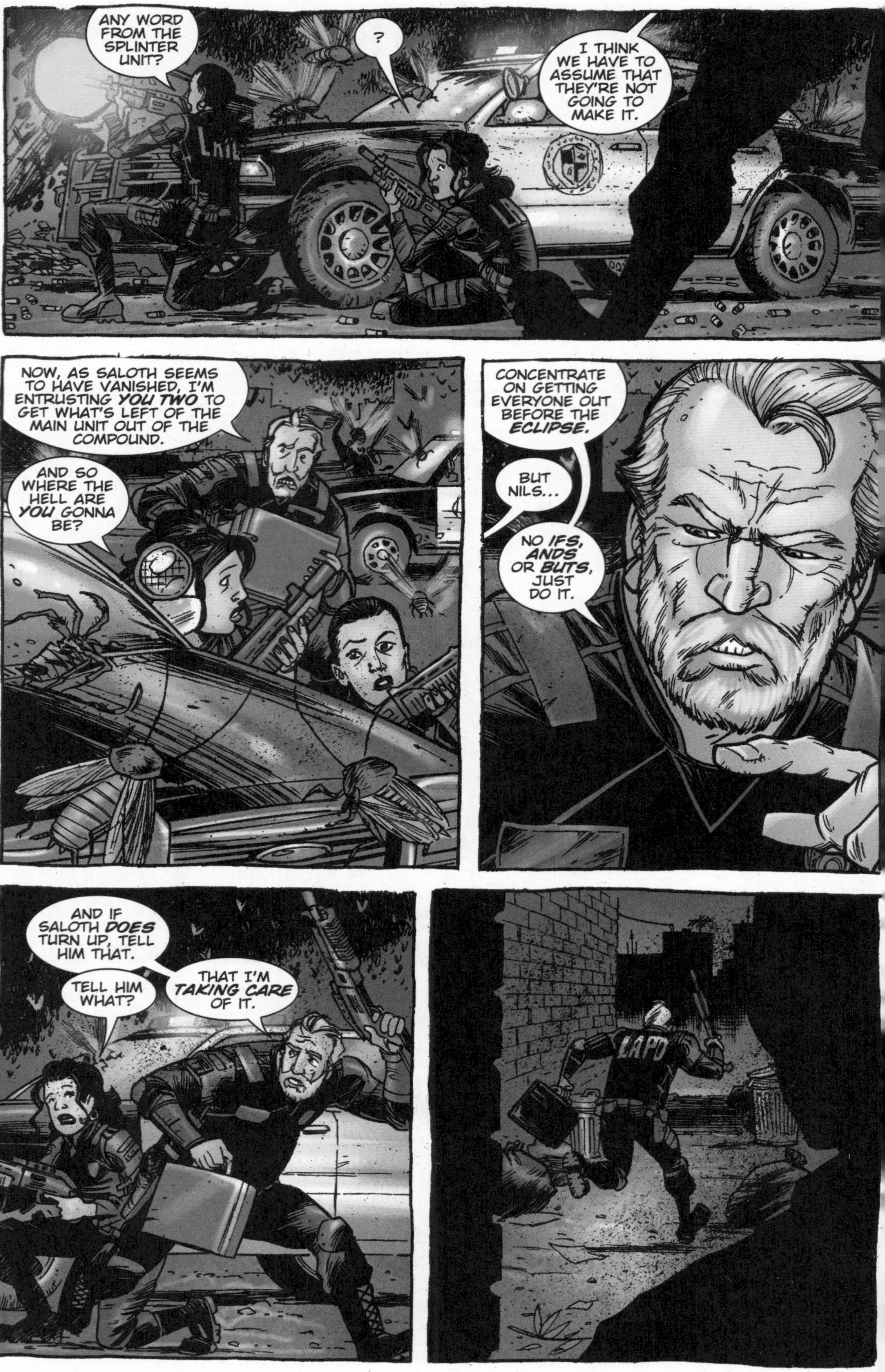
ANY WORD FROM THE SPLINTER UNIT?
?
I THINK WE HAVE TO ASSUME THAT THEY'RE NOT GOING TO MAKE IT.
NOW, AS SALOTH SEEMS TO HAVE VANISHED, I'M ENTRUSTING YOU TWO TO GET WHAT'S LEFT OF THE MAIN UNIT OUT OF THE COMPOUND.
AND SO WHERE THE HELL ARE YOU GONNA BE?
CONCENTRATE ON GETTING EVERYONE OUT BEFORE THE ECLIPSE.
BUT NILS...
NO IFS, ANDS OR BUTS, JUST DO IT.
AND IF SALOTH DOES TURN UP, TELL HIM THAT.
TELL HIM WHAT?
THAT I'M TAKING CARE OF IT.
LAPD

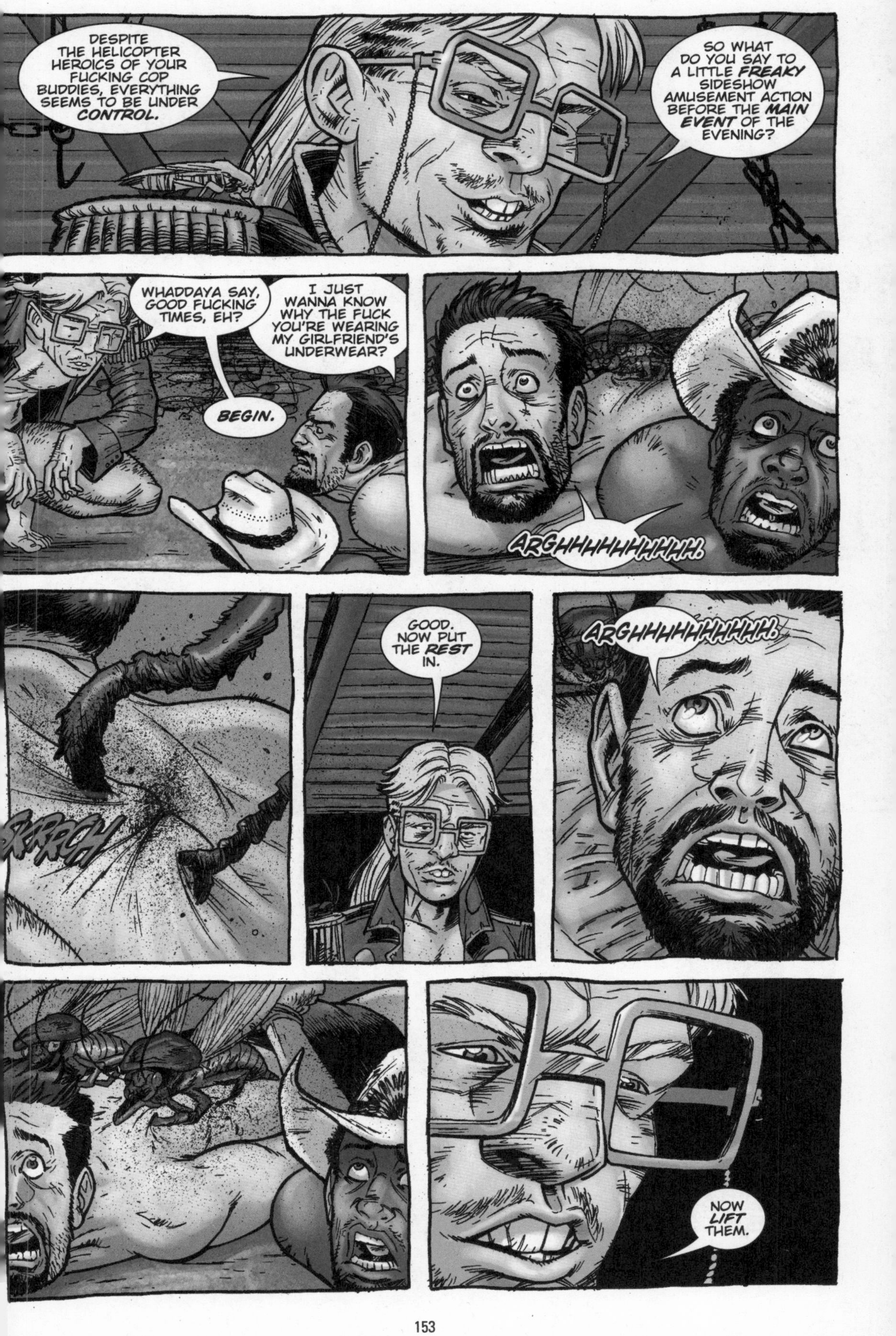
DESPITE THE HELICOPTER HEROICS OF YOUR FUCKING COP BUDDIES, EVERYTHING SEEMS TO BE UNDER CONTROL.
SO WHAT DO YOU SAY TO A LITTLE FREAKY SIDESHOW AMUSEMENT ACTION BEFORE THE MAIN EVENT OF THE EVENING?
WHADDAYA SAY, GOOD FUCKING TIMES, EH?
I JUST WANNA KNOW WHY THE FUCK YOU'RE WEARING MY GIRLFRIEND'S UNDERWEAR?
BEGIN.
ARGHHHHHHHHHHH.
SKRRCH
GOOD. NOW PUT THE REST IN.
ARGHHHHHHHHHHH.
NOW LIFT THEM.

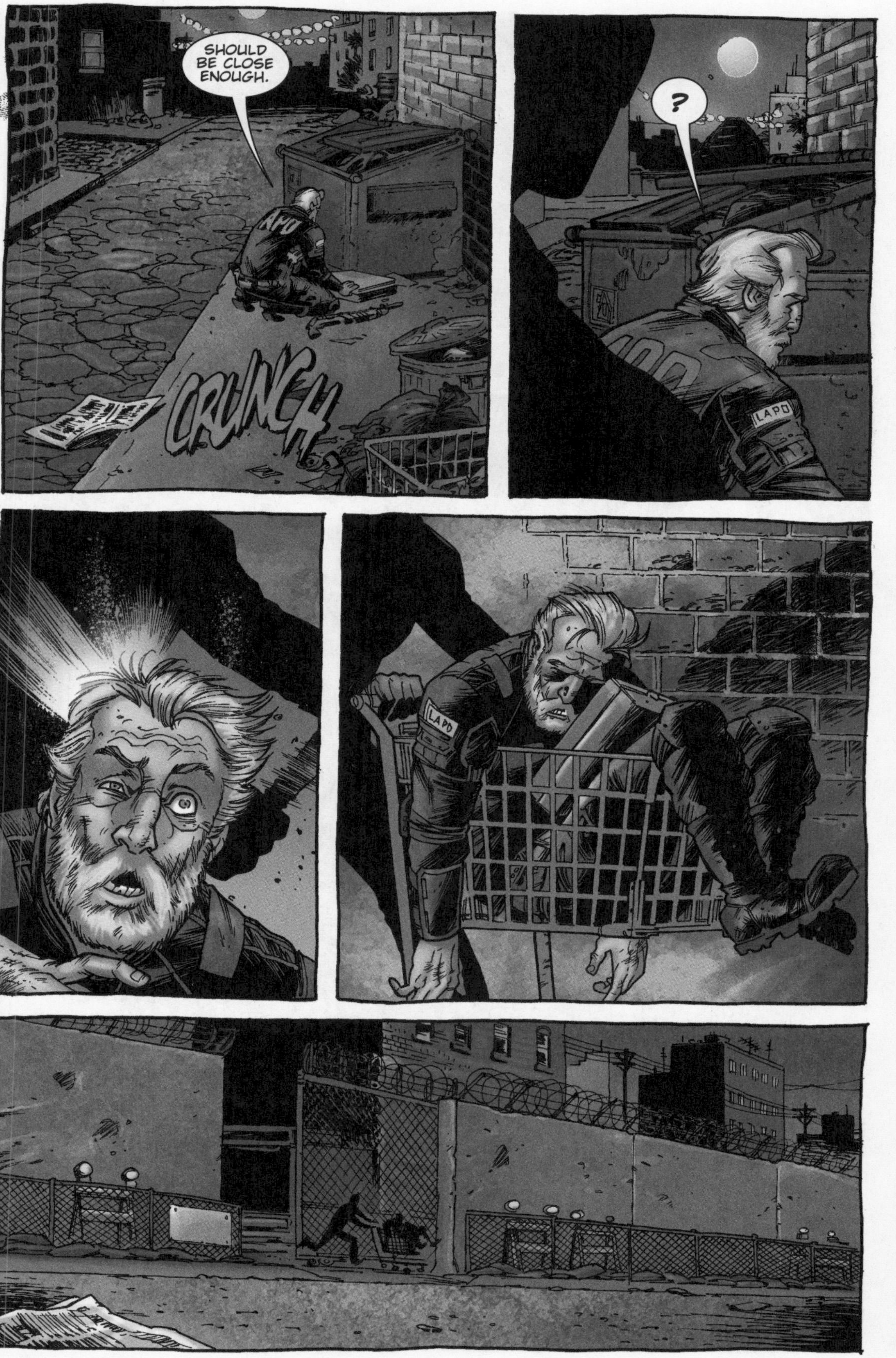
SHOULD BE CLOSE ENOUGH.
CRUNCH
?
LAPD
LAPD

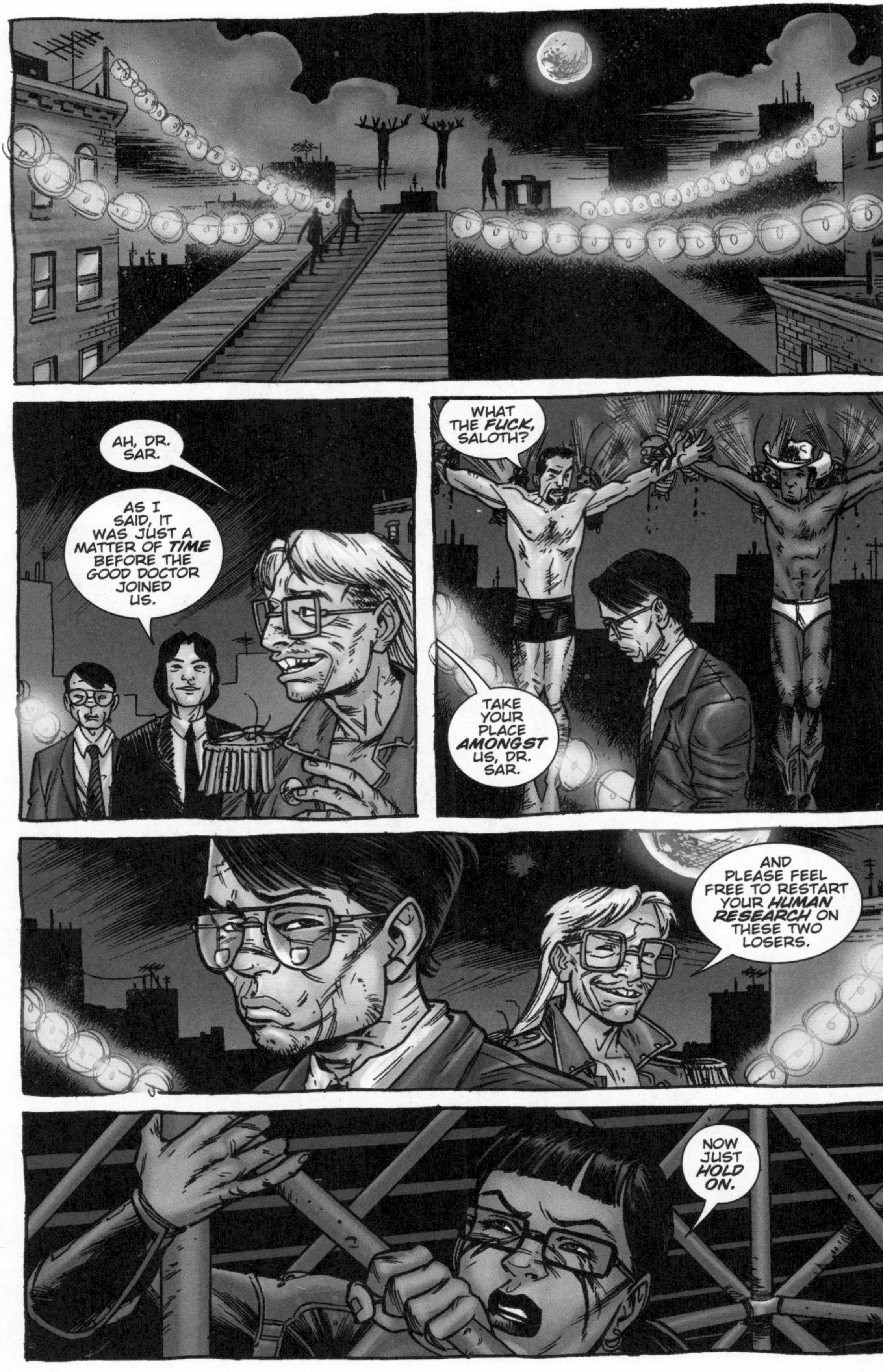
AH, DR. SAR.
AS I SAID, IT WAS JUST A MATTER OF *TIME* BEFORE THE GOOD DOCTOR JOINED US.
WHAT THE *FUCK*, SALOTH?
TAKE YOUR PLACE *AMONGST* US, DR. SAR.
AND PLEASE FEEL FREE TO RESTART YOUR *HUMAN RESEARCH* ON THESE TWO LOSERS.
NOW JUST *HOLD ON.*

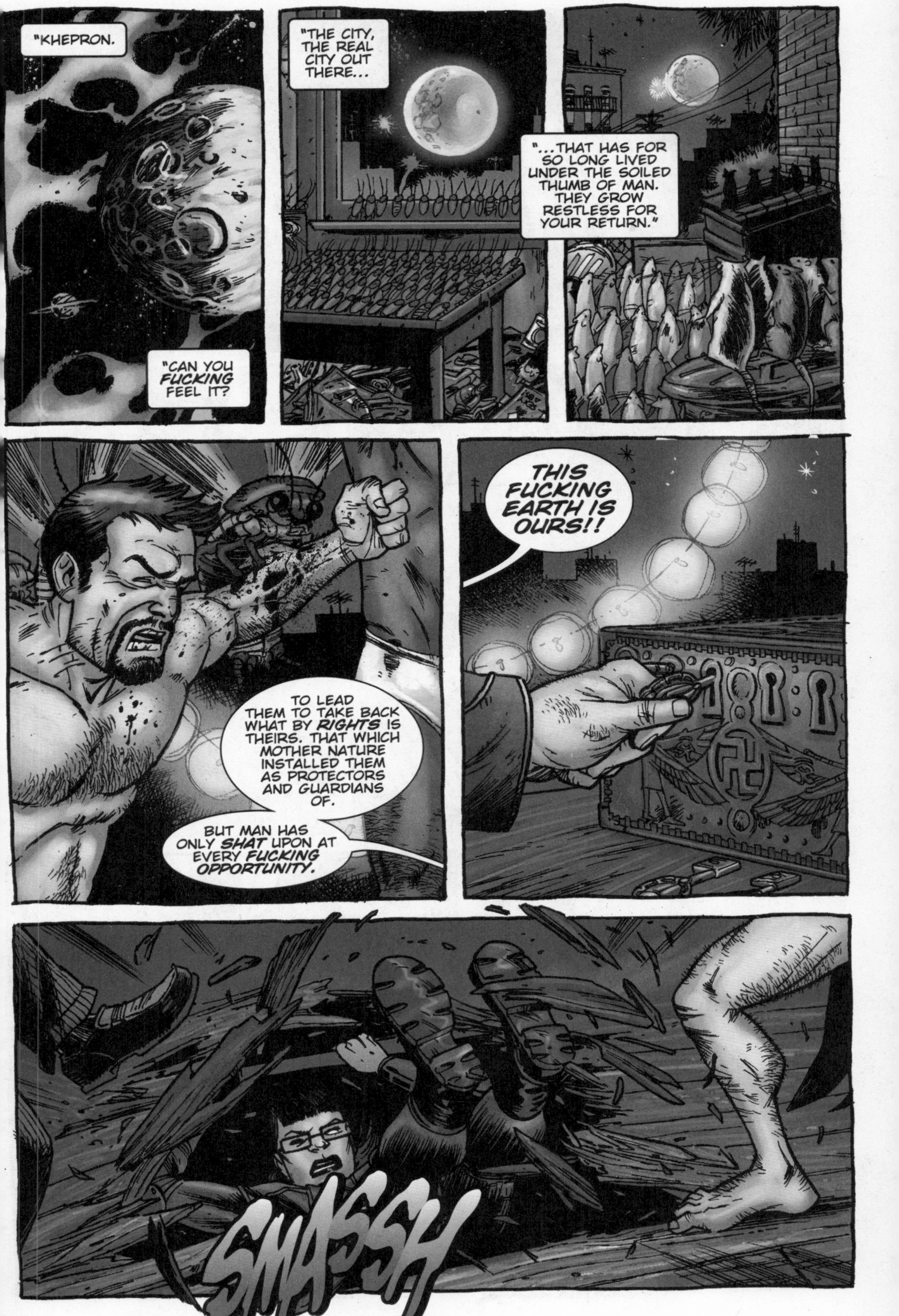
"KHEPRON.
"CAN YOU *FUCKING* FEEL IT?
"THE CITY, THE REAL CITY OUT THERE...
"...THAT HAS FOR SO LONG LIVED UNDER THE SOILED THUMB OF MAN. THEY GROW RESTLESS FOR YOUR RETURN."
TO LEAD THEM TO TAKE BACK WHAT BY *RIGHTS* IS THEIRS. THAT WHICH MOTHER NATURE INSTALLED THEM AS PROTECTORS AND GUARDIANS OF.
BUT MAN HAS ONLY *SHAT* UPON AT EVERY *FUCKING OPPORTUNITY*.
THIS FUCKING EARTH IS OURS!!
SMASSH

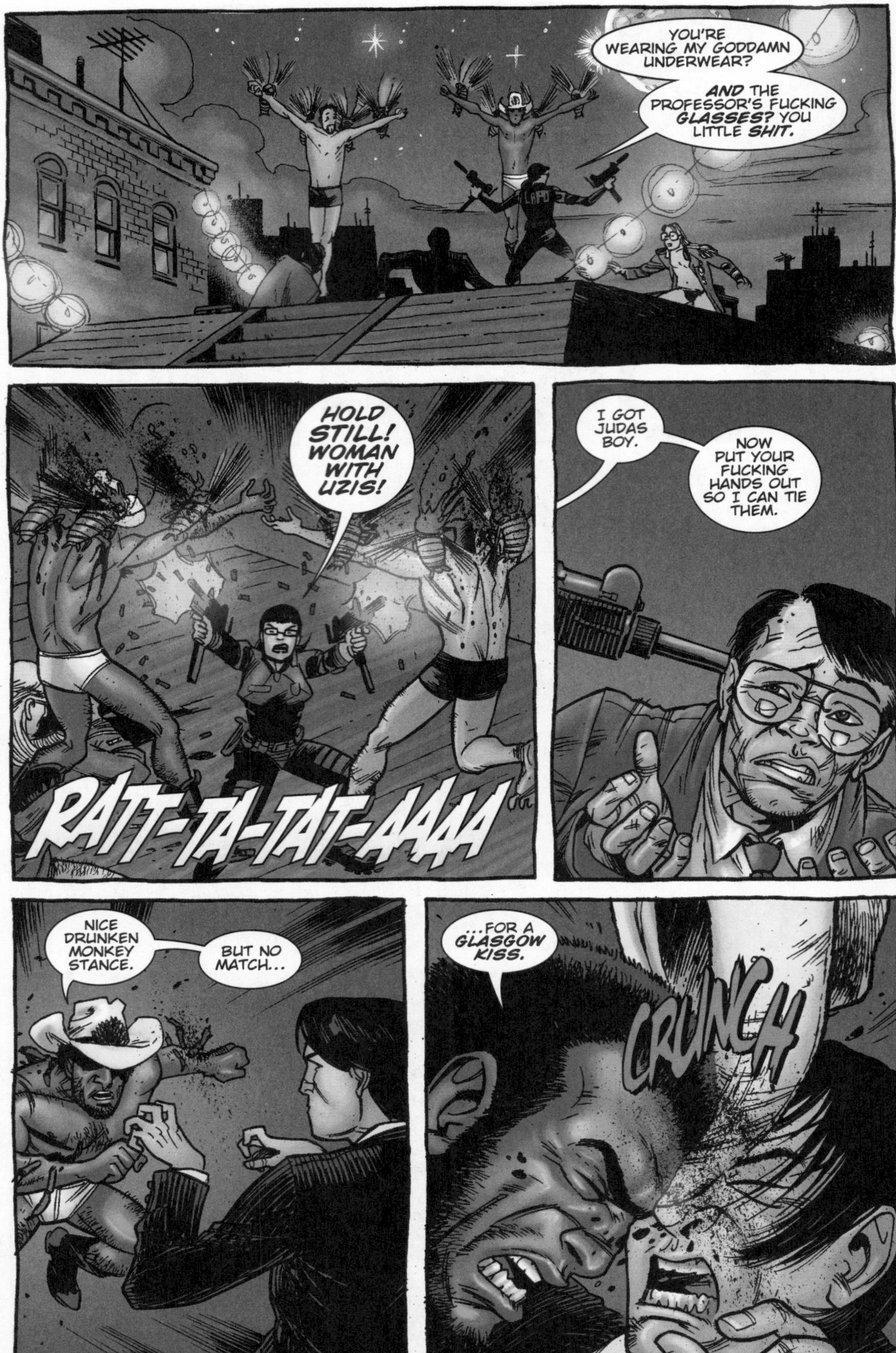
YOU'RE WEARING MY GODDAMN UNDERWEAR?
AND THE PROFESSOR'S FUCKING GLASSES? YOU LITTLE SHIT.
HOLD STILL! WOMAN WITH UZIS!
RATT-TA-TAT-AAAA
I GOT JUDAS BOY.
NOW PUT YOUR FUCKING HANDS OUT SO I CAN TIE THEM.
NICE DRUNKEN MONKEY STANCE.
BUT NO MATCH...
...FOR A GLASGOW KISS.
CRUNCH

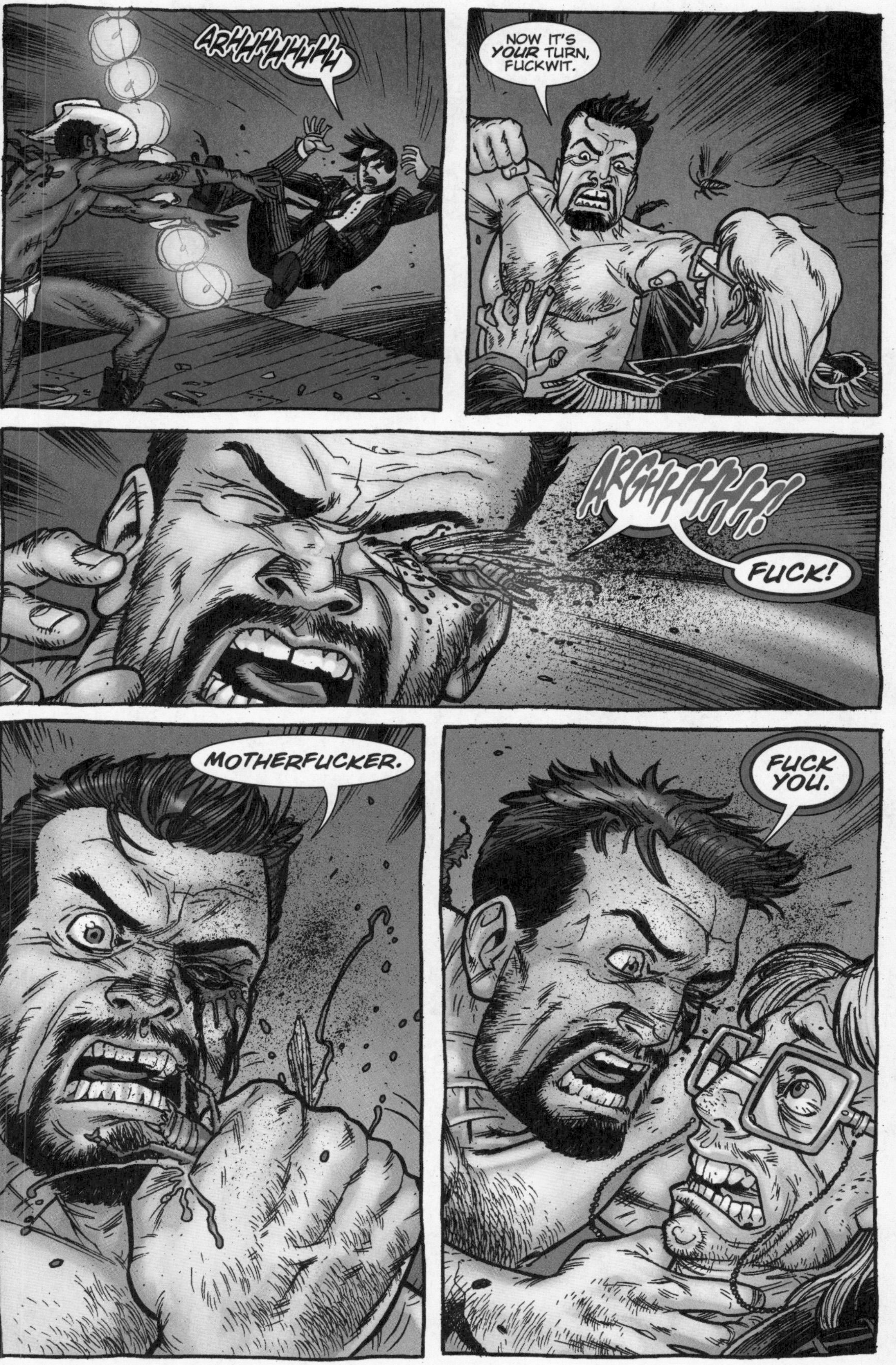
ARHHHHHHHH
NOW IT'S YOUR TURN, FUCKWIT.
ARGHHHHHH!
FUCK!
MOTHERFUCKER.
FUCK YOU.

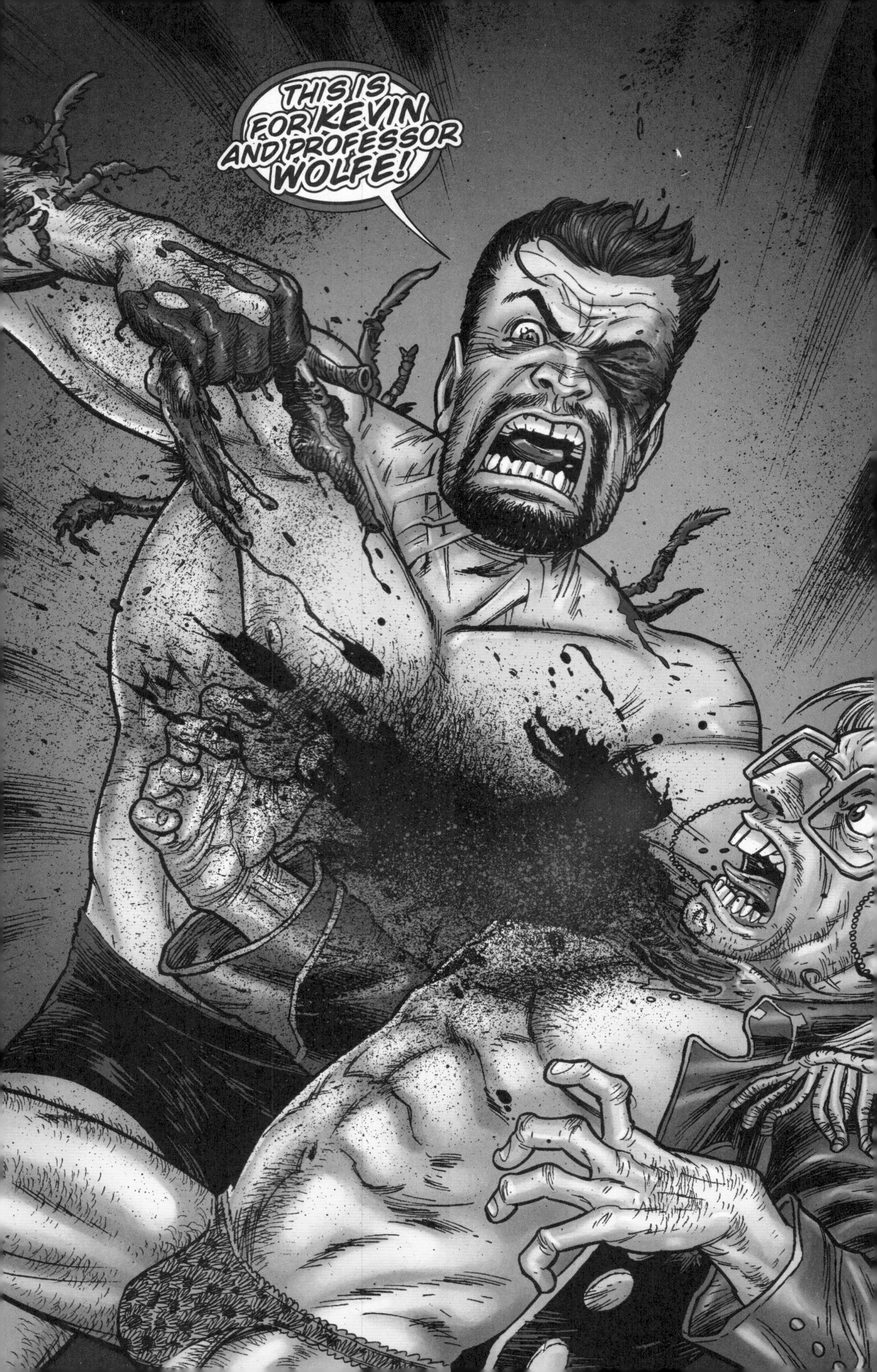
THIS IS FOR KEVIN AND PROFESSOR WOLFE!

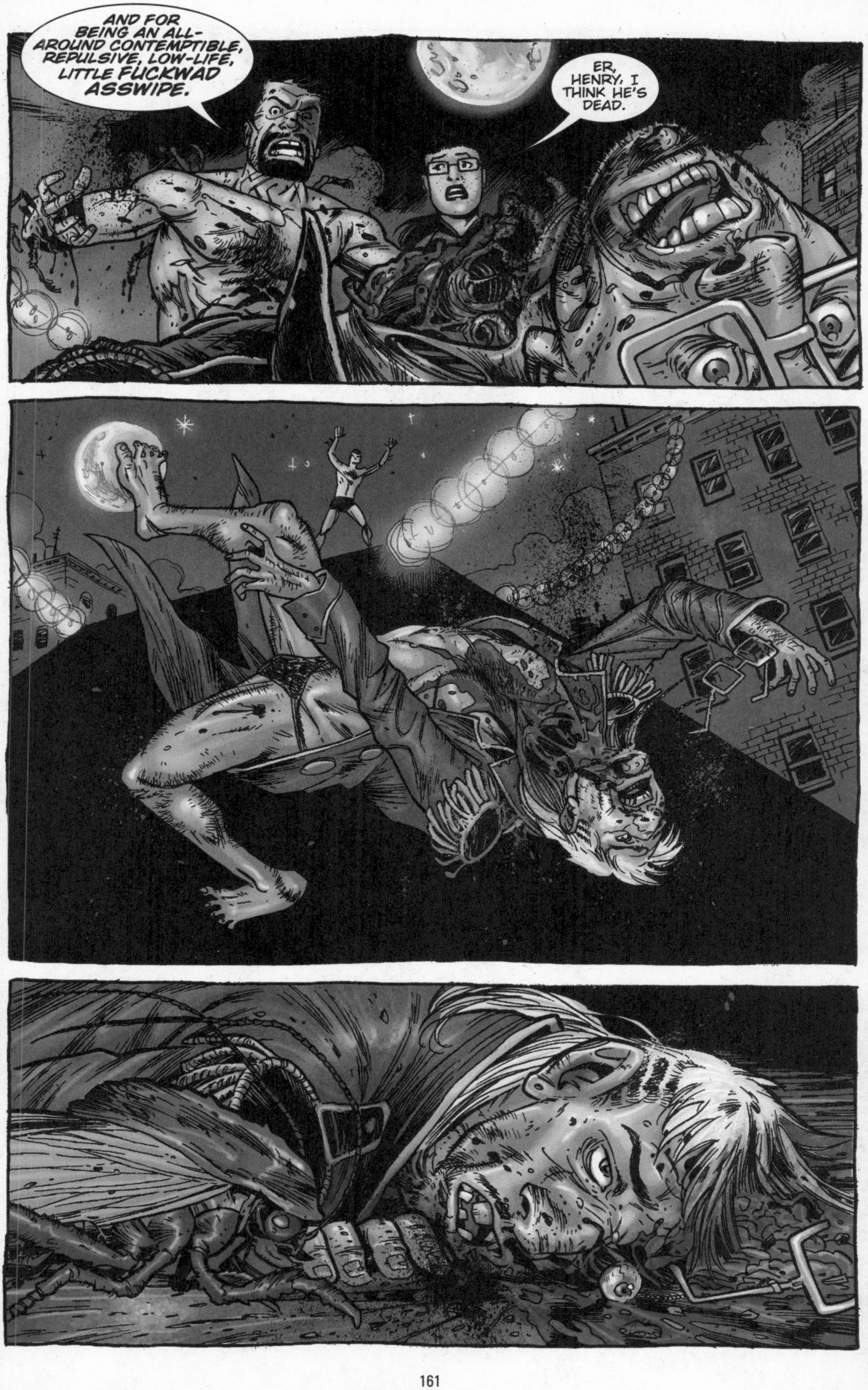
AND FOR BEING AN ALL-AROUND CONTEMPTIBLE, REPULSIVE, LOW-LIFE, LITTLE FUCKWAD ASSWIPE.
ER, HENRY, I THINK HE'S DEAD.

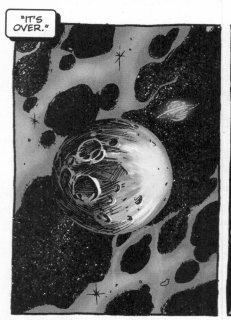

"IT'S OVER."

AND I'M GONNA DO WHAT I SHOULD HAVE DONE RIGHT AT THE START OF ALL THIS.

TURN THIS THING INTO FUCKING *MATCHWOOD* AND SCATTER IT IN SANTA MONICA BAY.

KHEPRON'S HOMECOMING MAY BE SCRATCHED, BUT REMEMBER, IT *AIN'T OVER.*

NOT WHILE *EVERY SINGLE ONE* OF THOSE MAYAN FUCKERS BELOW US HAS THE DESTRUCTION OF THE HUMAN SPECIES HARD WIRED INTO THEIR DNA.

HENRY, THERE'S A STORM DRAIN COVER UNDER THE PYRAMID. WE COULD *MAKE IT.*

I'M TALKING ABOUT RUNNING TO FIGHT ANOTHER DAY, HENRY.

NO, STRETCH IS RIGHT. WE *CAN'T* JUST RUN.

THE SUITCASE.

WHAT THE FUCK?

IT'S BIG ENOUGH TO TAKE OUT A TEN CITY-BLOCK RADIUS.

NILS' BACKUP PLAN?

YES. YOU THREE CAN STILL MAKE IT.

AND YOU?

LONG AGO I ABANDONED MY HUMANITY FOR SCIENTIFIC VANITY. THIS IS MY CHANCE AT REDEMPTION.

ARE YOU *SURE?*

VERY.

UNTIE ME, AND LET ME FINISH THIS.

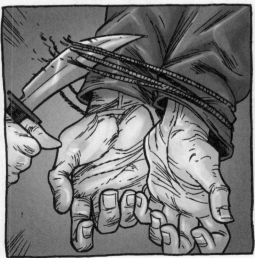

AND YOU SHOULD PROBABLY KEEP A HOLD OF THIS.

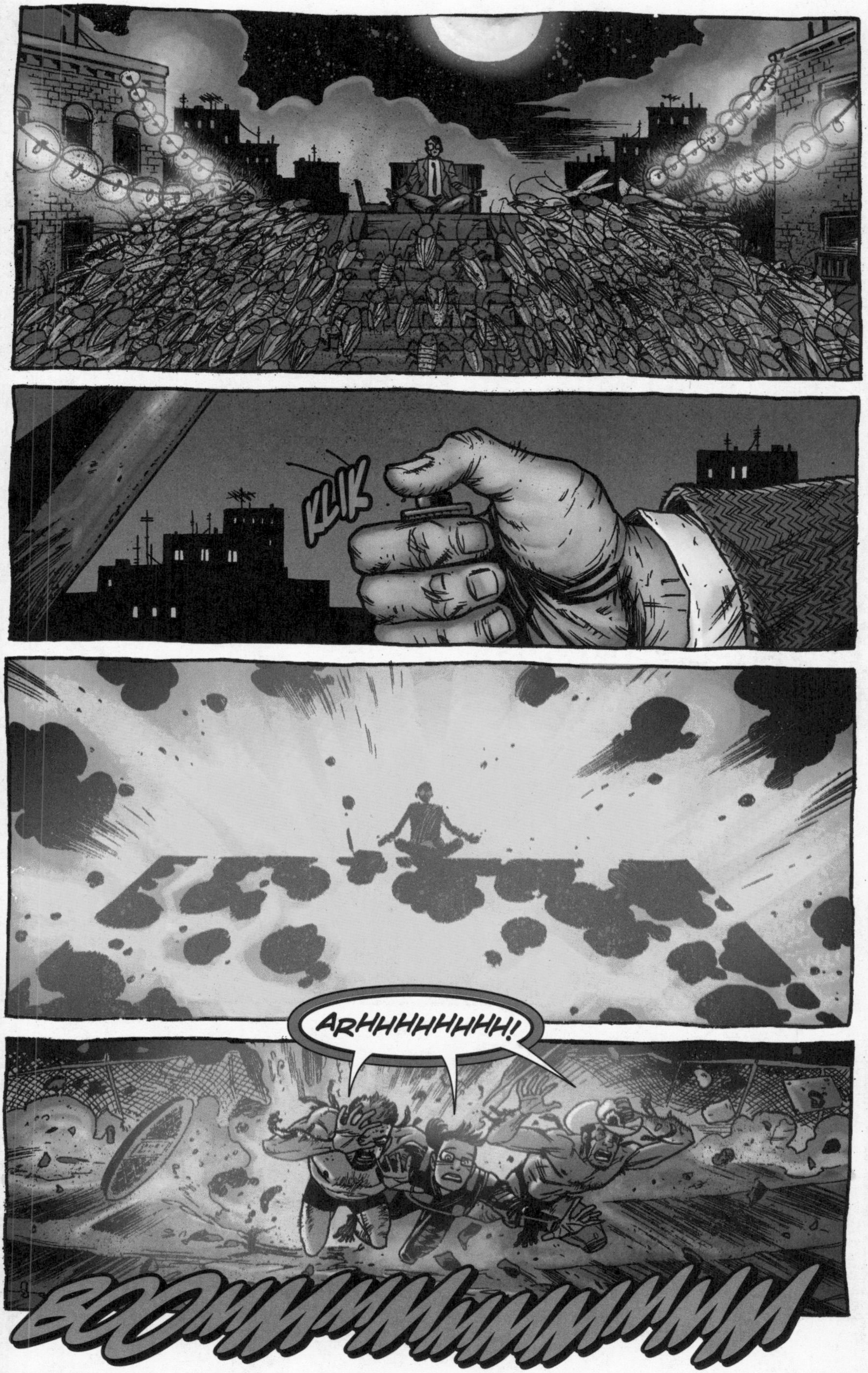
KLIK
ARHHHHHHHH!
BOOMMMMMMMMMMMM

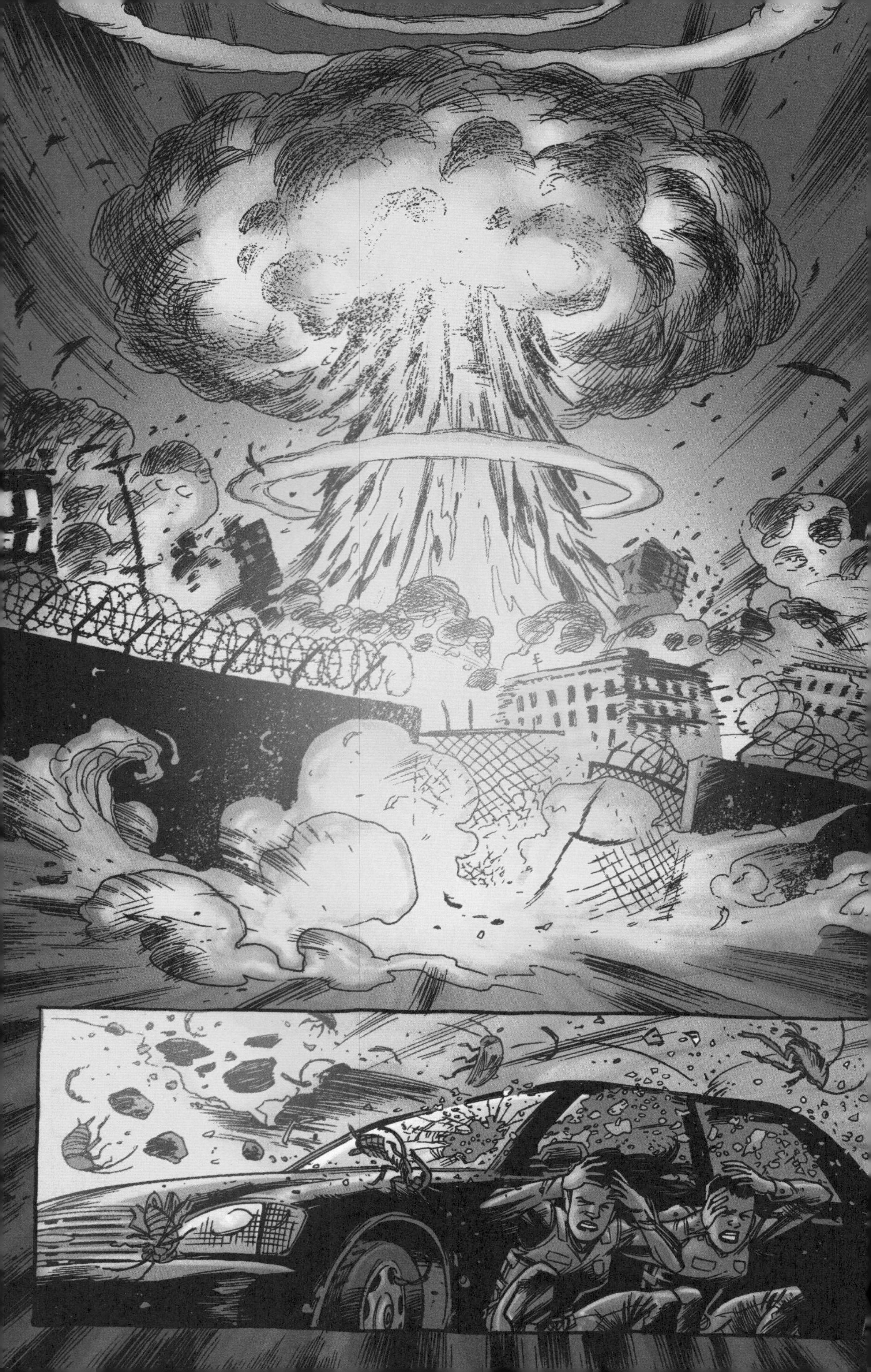

ONE YEAR LATER.

GOOD MORNING, *BUG-BEE-GONE*. HERE TO DEAL WITH ALL YOUR PEST CONTROL NEEDS.

OUR NEW FRIENDS OVER AT THE LAPD HANDLED THE AFTERMATH.

WITHIN AN HOUR, THE SMALL *NUCLEAR EXPLOSION* THAT HAD WIPED OUT THE MAYAN COMPOUND WAS PINNED ON WHATEVER RADICAL GROUP WAS TOP OF THE LIST THAT DAY AT THE STATE DEPARTMENT.

AND YEAH, I LOST AN *EYE*. BUT I GAINED A *WIFE*.

PAGE GAVE UP THE LIT-PORN GIG AND IS NOW TRYING TO BALANCE HER PH.D. IN EGYPTOLOGY WITH A SIDE CAREER IN *PEST CONTROL*.

AND, ALL IN ALL, THINGS PRETTY MUCH RETURNED TO NORMAL.

ALTHOUGH, THE NUCLEAR FALLOUT *HAS* CAUSED US A FEW PROBLEMS.

BLAMM

A *BREEDING* PAIR. YOU CALLED US JUST IN TIME.